# FAMILY
# CONSTELLATION

Drawings—Miné Okubo

# Theory and Practice of a Psychological
# GAME

# FAMILY CONSTELLATION

**By Walter Toman, Ph.D.**
*Associate Professor of Psychology, Brandeis University*

SPRINGER PUBLISHING COMPANY, INC.
NEW YORK, N. Y.

# Preface

In this book the reader will find a theory based on ten years of clinical psychological work during which the family constellations of over 400 persons were studied. This includes the functions of each person's own sibling position, of his parents, and of his children (where possible also of his grandparents), as well as of losses within the family constellation. These elements have been integrated into a system comprising eight basic types of sibling position and sixty-four basic types of conflict possible between a person and his or her parents.

The eight basic sibling positions are presented in the form of extensive character portraits. They depict, above all, the enduring relationships to people—men, women and children—and the impact of incidental losses of those people, but they also outline attitudes toward authority, property, work, politics, religion, and philosophy. These portraits are composites of trends and features taken from a number of people. Hence not every detail or concrete example applies in every single case. The details and examples will help, though, to reveal the core of the portrait that has been found to be consistent in all cases of a given sibling position.

Something similar holds for the sixty-four types of conflict between people and their parents. However, only the basic aspects of these conflicts have been delineated; details have merely been sketched or have been omitted for the sake of clarity. Interpolation in cases of intermediary sibling position is also concisely presented. Interpretations of family constellations of specific clinical cases are demonstrated in several examples: these may be called the exercises. Chapters on symbolic notation and quantitative treatment of major aspects of family constellation round out the book.

It is likely that the reader will discover some of his friends, relatives, family members, and even himself in this book. Some of the psychological problems and puzzles in his relationships with them may appear in a new light. Before long he may find himself thinking in terms of family constellations; with their help he may figure out persons, relationships, and conflicts, and wonder why he never thought of this before. But that is not so, he *has* thought of it, but he has done so tacitly, implicitly, and without much order. This book merely spells things out.

Professional people among the readers (educators, ministers, physicians, psychologists, psychiatrists, social workers, personnel managers) will not be deceived by the casual guise of this book. They will readily discover the body underneath. For, in a way, Freud, Adler, and Jung have been co-originators of the theory presented here. Freud has brought systematic attention to a person's relationship to his parents and has contributed conceptual vigor to the age-old quest for man's motivation. Adler was helpful with his early emphasis on character structure and (at least some) sibling positions. Jung has spotted the problem of pre-existent conflict between parents and their children, although his solution—using concepts such as animus, anima, and actual parent—leaves a little to be desired, not so much in principle as in practice. At any rate, after a while of reading and comparing, professional people working in areas related to psychology will probably find this book useful, at least until most of it has sunk in.

WALTER TOMAN

Waltham, Massachusetts
September, 1961

# Contents

PART IV:  EXAMPLES OF THE GAME

PART V:  SOME THEORETICAL CONSIDERATIONS

# PART I

# The Game in Brief

## CHAPTER 1

## The Nature of the Game

We all like our games, whether they be tennis, gossip, golf, hunting, betting on horses or stocks, winning votes, customers, quizzes, laughs, attention, or what not. Some of them are more physical than others, although even domino or rummy is physical of sorts. The pieces have to be put in place, and cards have to be dealt, their faces hid from the partners, and the like. Some games are more complex and elegant than others. Compare boxing to fencing, checkers to chess, or even a poor ball game to a good one. And some games are more serious than others. Playing the stock market has probably led more often to pervasive success or individual catastrophies than has a tennis game, a good tease, or a yo-yo contest.

Life as lived by people, however, is more complex than all of them. It is the game of a thousand games at once, played on all kinds of levels and with one, two, ten, hundreds, and even millions of partners all side by side. No single one of these games can be claimed to be a fair representative of a person's game of life, and most of them are not even adequate emissaries. Yet some of these games man is engaged in, or a certain sample of such games, may rank higher than other games or samples. To be played at all, some games simply require more of a person. The purely physical, simple, and irrelevant games will probably do less for us than the intelligent, complex, and articulate ones. The latter are more likely to approach a person's game of a thousand games, no matter how short they still fall of representation.

An intelligent, complex, and articulate game may very well

2

be a game with few and simple rules. As a matter of fact, it often is. Bridge, e.g., is composed of four sets of thirteen cards, each ranking in turn from thirteen to one in power. After shuffling and dealing, the four players try to make the most of the ranks and powers that they have in their hands. All the rest of the game as well as the entire science of bridge follow of necessity from these rules. Chess would be another such game, although chance is practically ruled out here. Whatever happens in chess is the doing of the players, whereas in bridge the players get any one of a practically infinite number of distributions of cards to play with.

Are there such intelligent, complex, and articulate games also in the game of a thousand games? And are they ever serious enough by themselves to stand a chance, even a slight one, of being fair representatives of the players' lives?

This is the question that I kept asking myself after finding too little satisfaction with many of the choices that psychiatry and clinical psychology have made in these respects. All psychological tests, including the projective tests, are games of that nature, i.e., supposedly samples of how the person in question is playing in real life, but not too many tests have lived up to their promises, or have done so only in a rather clumsy and, above all, quite limited way. Diagnostic schemes and interviewing patterns, oriented toward a person's affects and motives, may have been more successful, but often they are not very articulate in their rules and regulations. Particular players may hit the jackpot with a person in question, but often they do not know how they did it—a predicament that cannot make for a very good game. And if these schemes and patterns are articulate, their compositions often tend to derive from a hodgepodge of reasons or no reason at all.

Counselling of a certain kind, psychotherapy, and psychoanalysis are about the only "games" that stand a chance. They do seem to sample a person's real life. Yet, they do not do so because the rules are few, simple, or even outspoken; rather they sample a person's real life because the players take their time, and, as they go along, implicit rules develop together with a handful of explicit ones. The latter, however, are heuristic principles rather than rules, somewhat like Darwin's survival of the fittest. If the therapist can "leave out his own problems" from his patient's treatment—one of the basic rules—he is merely qualified to do the job. Psychological treatment is a never-ending test of this specification. And if the patient can really say everything that comes to his mind—another rule in psychoanalysis and some forms of psychotherapy—he is either completely gone or cured.

We may call psychological treatment a game of a hundred games and concede that, in its course, they boil down to a few elemental ones dealing, among other things, with people (in the patient's life and mind) who nurture and feed, with people who are also, or chiefly, powers, and with people who have differentiated into men and women. But even these elemental games are intermingled with each other and with circumstances of life and psychological treatment in such complicated manners that it takes years of special training and experience before somebody has learned how to direct these components even reasonably well, and many more years before he would be considered fit to teach other prospective "leaders" in these cumbersome, infinitely implicit and inarticulate ways.

Yet there exists a game simple enough in its ingredients and explicit enough in its rules to be quick to acquire, even from a book; and yet a game capable of complexities comparable to those of bridge, and approximating in sample form even the game of a thousand games. What is more, the ingredients and rules are all around us, waiting to be picked up. (As a matter of fact, it is strange that the present book was not written a few decades ago; but it was not.) What is still more, every human being is a participant in the game whether he likes it or not. Other games, such as golf, chess, gossip, politics, acting, banking, or dice, are at our discretion. We need not play any of them, if we do not want to. This is true even of the game of psychological treatment, at least in its professional form. Nobody has to undergo it, even if he should. But the ingredients and rules of the game I am suggesting are inevitably present in everybody's life. As a matter of fact, in this game the cards have already been dealt for a person by the time he wises up to it. There are limits within which he will have to play it, but he does have choices, and the most important decisions in this game are still his. Stranger still: the most important decisions in this game coincide with the most important decisions in his life, in his "game of a thousand games." The game I am suggesting could, therefore, be quite relevant. Its mastery, even if accomplished only to a moderate degree, could make a difference in a person's entire life. It may not only be a fair sample of that life but even an integral part of it.

The game is about the *individual person*, what he is like in some of his most basic aspects, what he does in some of the most crucial matters, and what he wishes to do. The principal ingredients are people—those *who have been living with him* the longest, most intimately, and most regularly—and all incidental *losses of such people* wherever they have occurred. First of all, the game concerns a person's parents and siblings, but then also the parents' parents and siblings. (Needless to say that their numbers may vary greatly.) The rules of the game derive from the rules of combination of only two characteristics of these people: their sexes and their age ranks.

Life, to be sure, is infinitely richer. But so is even a particular game of bridge. Its players are people in their own rights. They are more than the hands they are holding. They have different looks, plans, bank accounts, and different sentiments for each other. Not only that. Their set of cards is different from other sets of cards—different in material, design, color, etc.—and, even within each set, the cards are of different esthetic, emotional, or what have you, appeal. Yet it would hardly be a game of Bridge, if the cards were played by those appeals in addition to their defined powers—if the players' bank accounts or jewels would interfere with the game, say if a player would buy cards from other people's hands, or bribe a partner, or play the cards that would look most beautiful with those on the table.

All these aspects are accidental to bridge. And in the game to be introduced, all other characteristics of people, such as complexion, intelligence, economic background, schooling, etc., as well as all those millions of specific experiences that make an individual unique, are secondary. They will always matter, of course. In radical cases they will even bias the outcome of a particular game, but that need concern us as little as the fact that some bridge games end by the table being overthrown. Rather it is hoped that a person catching on to the game will have little difficulty, before long, handling the accidentals in their proper perspectives. They will be part of the fun.

This is the major idea of the "new" game: whatever people a person chooses for spouses, friends, partners, assistants, superiors, and the like, will be co-determined by the kinds of people a person has been living with the longest, most intimately, and most regularly, and by all incidental losses of such people. In short: new interpersonal relationships will be co-determined by old ones. More precisely and elaborately: *new (extra-familial, non-incestuous) interpersonal relationships will duplicate the earliest (intra-familial, incestuous) interpersonal relationships in degrees varying from complete duplication to none at all.* What is more: *the closer the new relationships come in kind to old ones, to those already entertained, other things being equal, the better will the person be prepared for the new ones, and the greater their likelihood to last and to be happy and successful* (Toman 1959 b, c, 1960 a, c).

This thesis can be derived from psychoanalytic theory, more cumbersomely from a general learning theory, and even from common sense. Some emphasis will, of course, have to be put on "other things being equal." As a matter of fact, critics may claim that this clause renders the thesis meaningless to begin with. Other things are never equal. The individual is beyond comparison. But things are not that bad. First, the very concept of an "individual" implies others to distinguish him from, and I would not know how this is possible without comparing and without resorting to general dimensions along which this can be done. Secondly, the thesis is claimed to apply only to a game. What this thesis and the entire game will do for life in general is up to the reader to decide, preferably, of course, after he has come to know the game.

At any rate, a person can be the first, second, third, and so on, child of altogether one, two, three, and so on, children, and the sexes may be distributed in many different ways. Varying only position and sex, as indicated before, will yield four different constella-

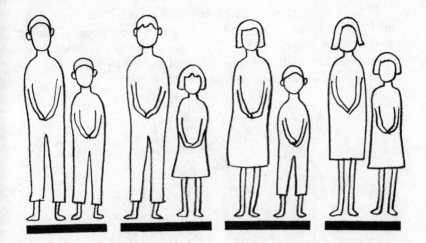

tions with only two children (male-male, male-female, female-male, female-female), eight different constellations with three, sixteen with four, or, in short, $2^n$ constellations, where n is the number of children in the family. Given the sex of the person in question, the number of different sibling configurations of which he can be a member will be equal to $n2^{n-1}$. The same holds for each of his parents. Hence their match will be one of $(n2^{n-1})^2$ constellations, if both of them have the same number of siblings, or one of $nm2^{n+m-2}$, if the numbers of their siblings differ. The same would also hold for any spouse, friend, partner, etc., with whom the person in question might establish relationships, and for the parents of all such persons. In other words, the number of different constellations of siblings and ancestry from which a given person may derive is legion, and any match he might enter with another person will multiply the possibilities by the number of different constellations from which that other person derives. Allowing for n to vary between 1 and 10 children, and observing only rank and sex, the number of possible configurations of ancestry of which a given match of two persons would be a sample outnumbers the population of the earth. Those concerned about the individual might want to take notice of that fact. Just as in Bridge, we will not run out of variety for a while.

If *both partners* of a dual relationship, say of *marriage*, have had but *one sibling each*, and if we ignore their parents' sibling configurations, their match will be one of sixteen possible types of matches. Let us briefly pursue all of them and get a *first impression of* what *the game* to come is all about.

Suppose the *older brother of a sister* marries the *younger sister of a brother*. They are getting in marriage precisely the (peer) relation that they had at home. He is used to a girl his junior, and she to a boy her senior. Hence there should be no conflicts over their seniority rights. And both of them are used to the other sex. Hence they should have no great sex conflicts either.

If the *older brother of a sister* chooses the *older sister of a brother*, they fall a little short of what they had been used to since their childhoods. Neither should have much trouble accepting the other sex, but each would try to be the older one for the spouse, and to transform him or her into a younger sibling. There will be rivalries over their seniority rights. Once they have children, however, preferably of both sexes, they may henceforth be happy with each other. At last they have got their younger siblings.

If the *older brother of a sister* marries the *older sister of a sister*, they too would tend to have conflicts over their seniority rights. Both were superior to their siblings in childhood. But the wife would also have some difficulty accepting the other sex. After all, they had been three girls in her family (mother, sister, and she herself) with only one male, father, to share. If they did not want to get into each other's hair, they had to learn how to like each other regardless of the man in the family. They had to become somewhat more homosexual. If they could not work out such a solution, the girl would tend to be only too anxious to get a man of her own; which, by the way, is not the best condition for taking such an important step.

If the *older brother of a sister* marries the *younger sister of a sister*, they would have no problem over seniority. The wife would be used to having a peer her senior, and her husband to having one his junior. Yet she is not quite so used to having a man.

Similar arguments could be raised for the *older brother of a brother* who marries the older sister of a brother or of a sister, or the younger sister of a brother or of a sister. In these cases, it is he who would tend to have trouble accepting the other sex. Among those four, the match most alien to what the partners had been used to in their childhoods would be the marriage of an *older brother of a brother* to the *older sister of a sister*. Both of them would be likely to have trouble accepting the other sex, and in addition they would tend to be in conflict over their seniority rights. As soon as they have children, however, they get their longed-for juniors, although there will be a tendency for the father to gang up with the boys against the girls, and for the mother to do analogously with her daughters.

Similar conditions would also prevail for the *younger brother of a sister* who marries the younger sister of a brother or of a sister, or the older sister of a brother or of a sister. Among these there is one combination that would come close to an optimal one again, namely the marriage between the *younger brother of a sister* and the *older sister of a brother*, although there will be a touch of a reverse authority relationship. The wife will tend to be somewhat dominant, and the husband dependent.

Finally, the *younger brother of a brother* may marry the older sister of a brother or of a sister, or the younger sister of a brother or of a sister. Other things being equal, the worst of these and, at the same time, the worst of all sixteen combinations would be the match between the *younger brother of a brother* and the *younger sister of a sister*. Both of them would find it difficult to accept the other sex, and they would be in conflict over their juniority rights. Both want older siblings. Therefore not even a child of their own would make a difference, as it does with the older brother of a brother who marries the older sister of a sister. In fact, they would probably not want a child in the first place. But if they get one— and one would be plenty—they will tend to force that child into the role of an older sibling at the earliest possible time. This, of course, means trouble for all involved.

Spouses, or partners in any kind of interpersonal relationship, do come not only from families with two children, but also from those with three, four or more children, and sometimes with only one child. It can be expected that, in cases of $n > 2$, the relationships sketched above would tend to hold at least for the oldest and youngest siblings, while those in between would usually learn in their childhood how to assume double and triple roles. Consequently they should be somewhat better prepared for all eventualities of matchmaking and other relationships than the oldest or youngest sibling are, although the latter may well be more exuberantly happy when they make the optimal choice of those open to them.

The *single child* has only his parents to draw on, so to speak. This does not mean that children from other sibling constellations do *not* draw on their parents. On the contrary, parents are the most important people in any child's life. They are strong cards in this whole game. Psychologically speaking, parents are able to change their children's age ranks and even their sexes. What will happen in families with two, three, four, or more children, however, is that children turn to each other for what they cannot get from their parents. The parents, if they are happy with each other, will tend psychologically to move into the background. It is easy for the children to come to terms with such parents. Hence, the

siblings will become relatively stronger determinants. Only parents
who are unhappy with each other may keep their children anxiously
focused on them, i.e., unable to find even fair satisfactions with
each other. They are the children who, in their own choices of
spouses, may try to break away from their parents' type of match
and seek the opposite. Yet almost as often as not they will end
up close to the match of their parents. They cannot quite manage
to escape them, in a way, because their parents are the only ones
they've got, irrespective of their conflicts. In large families this will
particularly apply to the older children. The younger ones may,
by "interpolating" their older siblings, spare themselves the full
impact of their parents' conflicts. The same general trend holds
for sibling configurations. People will be best used to, and prepared for, those types of relationships to other people that they've
had at home, although they might sometimes (i.e., in cases of
strong parental conflicts) try very hard to have, and even be, the
opposite of what they *are*.

Well, normally the *single child* is in that position even with

happy parents. Such a family could be called a mildly deficient one. The child has only his parents to turn to. He or she does not learn what children of larger families can learn from their parents: how to treat children. Therefore, singletons tend to look rather for a father or mother in a potential spouse than for a sibling and, more often than others, tend to be content without children of their own. They want to remain the children themselves. Under certain conditions, however, they may attempt to break out of it and have children of their own, occasionally even many children.

There are other complications. Sometimes an oldest brother appears like a youngest. He wants guidance from his spouse even though she is a youngest sibling herself. One of the reasons may be that his father had been the youngest in his, the father's family, and died, or left, early. Sometimes a girl acts very much like a boy, because her father had come from a family of boys only, expected at least some boys of his own, got only girls, and had to transform one of them into some kind of a son. Not infrequently four children split up into two couples. And sometimes a middle brother behaves like an oldest, because his older brother happened to be of low intelligence, and his older sister ran away from home when she was twelve and he only six. This left him and his two juniors.

Sometimes a greater than usual difference of chronological age between the partners may compensate for a rank conflict. Sometimes, the missing other sex, or missing siblings, may have been provided by cousins or good neighbors and friends. Conflicts over rank and sex may be mitigated by additional relationships established with in-laws and friends. Marriage is not a priori exclusive of all kinds of friendships that may carry over or be newly formed. The partners may assemble an extended family around them with their friends and thereby get, in number and in kind, what they had at home.

Things are not at all simple. But if they were, would it be a very good game?

There is one more and quite important complication that has already been mentioned: *losses*. People that have been living with a person the longest, most intimately, and most regularly, may drop out for good at any point of a person's life. They may die or leave permanently. Or they may turn insane. They may go to jail for ninety-nine years. These drop-outs for good are by no means the only kind of losses that a person may suffer. There are all kinds of temporary and partial losses. People may leave the person in question for days, months, or years. They may leave and continue to provide (many, some, or few) reminiscences and reminders, such as pictures, letters, telephone calls, presents, etc. People may turn into physical offenders, sexual seducers or become bed-ridden. Parents may turn traitors when they hand their child over to a hospital for surgery, to a dentist, a day-camp, and the like. Certain aspects of these people are being lost. What had been thought impossible, because it had never happened before, has become possible. If they did it once, they can do it again. They will never be quite the same.

Yet all these temporary and partial losses must be assumed small compared to final losses, whether through death or any of its psychological equivalents. As a matter of fact, final losses come to bear on a person in question even if it is only his parents who have suffered them. If the father had been an orphan since early childhood, the person in question, while learning how to be like his father, will inevitably adopt some features of being an orphan. And a girl whose mother had been left by her husband cannot help but identify to an extent with a forsaken woman, her mother. This is not surprising, since parents will also transmit their rank and sex conflicts when their children would have none of their own accord.

The effects of a final loss will ordinarily be the more severe, a) the less time has passed since the loss occurred; b) the earlier it has occurred in a person's life; c) the smaller the number of people that have lived with a person the longest, most intimately, and most regularly (in other words, the smaller his family); d) the greater the imbalance of sexes resulting from it; e) the longer the responsible survivors took to secure a full-fledged substitute; f) the greater the number of losses, and the severer the losses, that have occurred before.

The people that have been living with a person the longest, most intimately, and most regularly, constitute his family. Hence all patterns of sex, rank, and final losses prevailing among a person's siblings, parents, and ancestors are patterns of family configuration. The people mentioned, including all incidental losses of such people, constitute a person's *family constellation*. And this, precisely, is the name of the game to be introduced.

## CHAPTER 2

## Methodological Considerations

Before we go into the details of the game, a few more remarks are necessary. One concerns the chronological ages involved in senior-junior relationships. If siblings are six or more years apart, they show a tendency of growing up like single children. Often it will take an older girl a trifle longer to become aloof than it will an older boy. If siblings are four to six years apart, they would be siblings all right, psychologically speaking. The older one would even be cognizant of the newcomer's sex. Hence it will make a difference whether it is a boy or a girl. If siblings are two and three years apart, the older one will at first be unlikely to notice much, if anything, of the sex of his rival. He is merely a threat to his power, to his command of the parents. When after some time the older one can recognize the younger one's sex he will either find that things are not so bad after all (if the younger one is of the opposite sex) or that they are even worse than he had originally thought (if the younger one is of the same sex). If siblings are only about one year apart, the newcomer is not a rival as a power in general, but merely as an oral manipulator, as an eater and screamer. That, however, is an extremely vital threat. General power is versatile. Oral power is just about an all-or-none affair.

As we have seen, chronological age does make a considerable difference in a senior-junior relationship. One could argue that things become more uniform as siblings grow older. Even siblings seven years apart will have lived together for thirteen years by the time the older one has turned twenty. Hence they must have got

used to some kind of senior-junior relationship and recognition of the other sibling's sex. And siblings only one year apart will not forever remain the vital threat to each other that the older one perceived at the beginning. Broader power aspects and even the sex of the other person will be "recognized" to some extent.

On the other hand, the first years are, of necessity, the most formative years. If the members of the immediate family are the *only people* who matter or are really known, their impact on the individual in question must be considerably greater than if they had mattered and had been known *along with* many other people. And anything new the individual learns about the members of his immediate family is being grafted on earlier, more radical, and more pervasive, experiences of them.

This is to say that the older sibling will have established more of his own individuality and independence, the longer the younger sibling takes to come into psychological existence. The newcomer can do less harm to him, although the conscious experience of whatever threat there is will tend to increase with the age gap. But the smaller their age gap, the longer (at a given later age) will the older sibling have been exposed to the younger sibling. They will be better used to each other, at least in all those aspects that do not tap, or border on, the original conflict. And this will be mutual, since the older one will generally tend to set the tone for the younger one. The junior will learn from his senior how to interpret their relationship to each other. In short, the forces at work are somewhat complementary. Perhaps one could summarize it this way: the smaller the age gap between siblings, the more severe their conflicts with each other, but the greater also their inclination not to let go of each other in later life.

In addition there is a statistical reason permitting us to underplay the specificities of chronological age. Extreme age gaps are relatively rare among siblings. Few are separated from their nearest brothers and sisters by a year or less—excluding twins which are a special case altogether—and few by as many as seven, eight, or more years.

Another remark concerns the sexes. By his physiological make-up, a boy may be more or less of a male, and a girl more or less of a female. Of two siblings of the same sex, the one with the greater proclivity for transformation into the opposite sex will usually be chosen by his family members for such a purpose. But even with two siblings of opposite sex, physiology may make for a very masculine girl and a very feminine boy. Both of them would tend toward manifest homosexuality in later life. Sometimes a parent's unusual physiological make-up may affect the children psychologically, although the very fact that he or she has become a parent almost precludes the worst. In other words, male and female is no all-or-none proposition either. But again we can assume that the vast majority of persons will tend to act and feel like *their* sex.

Similar considerations would hold for losses. Death (or its equivalent) of a given member in a person's family constellation, at a given time, may still occur in many different forms—long foreseen or entirely unexpected, as a clean or a messy affair, wished for to various degrees by the person in question or by other members of the family, hence leaving severe or mild guilt in the

loser, or none at all. The loss may affect many people or merely
the person in question and perhaps his siblings. It may be a loss
to the nation, or an insignificant loss, etc.

All these considerations will also hold for friendships and
marriage, the relationships that a person may enter of his own
accord. What is more: with these, as well as with all relationships
in the original family, chronological age, physiological background,
and the circumstances of losses, and even different ethnic and
legal conventions, will come to play in a variety of forms when
the crude data are the same. They will vary *around* the crude
data, so to speak.

It should also be understood that it will make a difference whether
an oldest brother has had a father who was a youngest brother himself, or a middle brother, or an oldest, or whether he has had a mother
who was the oldest sister of nothing but girls, or nothing but boys, or
an only child. A middle sister of two brothers will, again, be a
different person depending on whether her parents were middle
siblings, too, or oldest, or youngest, whether rank and sex conflicts
prevailed among them or not, and whether losses decimated her
parents' families in their early lives, or later on, or not at all.
In other words, the parents' sibling configurations, losses, and the
characters of the grandparents are powerful dèterminants of people's own characters. And their grandparents' characters, in turn,
would be a function of their own sibling configurations, losses,
and of *their* parents' characters. Moreover, the characters of a
person and his parents and grandparents are also determined by
hereditary givens, appearances, resemblances to other family members, social and economic factors, and all kinds of other events
and circumstances. But all these influences tend to dwindle in effectiveness, the farther back they have been exerted. Yet, very specific
influences may still persist even if a person's grandparents only
had been directly affected.

Finally, the psychological existence or non-existence of any
member of a person's family constellation may mean very different
things. A mother may be around only very sporadically, say for
the weekends, or she may be omnipresent, unable to let go of her
child even for a minute, or she may be around, but insist that the

children always play by themselves. A father, when at home, may either be available or, in other cases, absorbed by his stamp collection or asthma. Or when he is out at work much of the day, the mother may act as his representative, as his long arm, so that, psychologically, he is never gone. An older brother may grow up in a boarding school, a younger sister may be put up with an aunt for parts of every week, etc.

Yet in order to speak intelligibly about the basic plays of the game of family constellation, these second and third order determinants will have to be ignored. They would tend to cancel each other's effects anyway, with groups of people, and the general features of the basic plays would become apparent. But once the reader begins to try his own hand in this game, he is probably faced with individuals rather than groups, and interpolation will be necessary. In practice, this is the essence of the game. The player learns how to combine the basic types of plays to the best of his knowledge and skill. He may have to consider factors that are not essential to the game in general, but that make a considerable difference in a particular case. He may have to use gamesmanship in every sense of the word. As a matter of fact, I hereby advise the reader to take nothing whatsoever for granted that has been, and will be, said in this book. In rare cases, red shoes, snow, a dime lost or found, or a certain smile, may throw an all-important switch in the game. And we never know in advance whether a particular case is a rare one or not.

The general advice to the reader is this: establish first the sibling position of a person in question and all incidental losses that he or she may have suffered in early life. If the descriptions given in this book do not fit, consider the possibility that a person's siblings may have formed subgroups. Inquire into the age differences and remember that gaps of over six years make for two single children, at least to some extent, rather than ordinary siblings. Or inquire into special events, particularly separations and losses, that might have had effects. If that does not account for discrepancies, inquire about the sibling positions and losses of the person's parents, consult the principal patterns of interaction between parents and children also given in this book, and try to understand what kind of match the parents' marriage might have been and which of their conflicts they might conceivably have transmitted to the person in question. If that is not enough, do the same with the person's grandparents, or establish at least whether they had been lost during the early lives of the parents. If the person in question is married, by all means inspect the spouse too. And if they have children, investigate to what extent the children duplicate their parents' sibling configurations, and how much the children may have added to, or subtracted from, the conflicts already in existence. And if all that does not help, look for persons other than immediate members of the family who may have played an intrinsic part in a person's life. Sometimes, however, the investigation may be shortened by a quick glance at some of a person's friendships and love-relationships. These indicate that he, or she, is acting "appropriately" after all, so that the reader may proceed with the speculations recommended.

It should also be understood that the character portraits of the major types of sibling positions and the sketches of their interaction with different types of parents will tend to mellow somewhat in time, provided all goes well for the persons involved. Psychotherapy would also work in that direction. Under stress or after losses, however, many features may reappear more sharply. The portraits themselves could be considered the major hands of the game. The reader will find various plays intimated and indicated for all of them as well as for the sketches of interaction between a person and his, or her, parents.

While family constellation is being presented as a game or as a theory with exercises, it is actually founded strongly on empirical evidence. The portraits of the major sibling positions are composites of features all of which have been found present in groups of at least six cases for each type of sibling position. Those cases had to fulfill the following criteria in addition: 1) Their parents had to be reasonably well matched. Cases of complete rank and/or sex conflict prevailing among the parents were eliminated. At least one of the parents was to have found a duplicate of one of his sibling relations with his spouse. 2) Neither the person in question nor the parents were to have suffered early losses of parents or siblings. If such a person or one of his parents had lost a parent before they were sixteen years old or a sibling before they were six years old, they were eliminated from the sample. Only the references to losses made in the character portraits of the major sibling positions (as well as those to friendships and marriages that would tend to fail) were drawn in part from the eliminated cases. And only the brief hints at trends shown in the practice of psychological counselling or psychotherapy were taken from other sources altogether: my colleagues and those working under my supervision.

The persons studied (over the past ten years) had been in psychotherapy of various duration or in psychoanalysis with the author (51 cases), in brief contact with him for diagnostic evaluation (58 cases), sought out for psychological interviews in guidance centers and clinics (45 cases), and among his friends and acquaintances (135 cases); or they had been in psychological counselling or psychotherapy with persons supervised by the author (108 cases). From these cases (insofar as they had not suffered early losses) have also been recruited at least two for each of the 64 major types of conflicts that can arise between a person's sibling position and that of his parents (see also page 128).

# PART II

## Major Types of Sibling Position

## CHAPTER 3

## The Oldest Brother of Brother(s)

He is the leader, the master of other men, whether he shows it by force or cunning. He is in charge. He is in control, not so much of a field of work or endeavor as he is of other people in that field. He can tell people what to do, again either directly or by clever soft-sell. He knows how to take them. He is on good terms with other males, especially when they are not older brothers themselves. As a matter of fact, the only one he cannot stand in his immediate vicinity and will have to get out of the way is another oldest brother of brother(s), no matter how well he may understand him otherwise.

He also tends to be a good worker where he chooses to, and a good leader of work, of special enterprises, expeditions, or any condition where work and leadership can be combined. He can inspire others, take the greatest hardships upon himself, and become even stronger as he does so. He can chastise himself and feel the delights of power over his own flesh and human fragility. Yet he will only be the second-most daring, if it comes to matters of life and death. It is as if he felt, unconsciously, that his survival is more important than that of any single one of the people he leads. If one of the people should be in deadly danger, however, he will come to his rescue even if it may cost his own life. Or he may organize the victim's rescue and be active in it, inspiring his followers to do likewise or, preferably, even more. But he does want to get the credit. Not necessarily in simple terms. He does not have to have eye-witnesses, but the public, history, or

ome master superior even to him and in the position of passing
redit should notice and take record.

He can accept the authority of a superior male, his boss, his
teacher, his political, ideological, technical, or literary "father,"
but he will tend to do it in one of two ways. He will either become
like that authority figure. He will mold himself after this image
and conduct his task, whatever it is, completely in the spirit of
his superior. In a sense, he may be more papal than the pope
himself and thereby make the pope superfluous of sorts. It will
suffice for the pope to stand on a pedestal, superb but without
motion, while he, his fervent disciple, does the work. The superior
can safely relegate all authority to him and need not regret it.

Or he, the oldest brother of brother(s), will operate with a
vengeance. This is the alternative. From the very beginning, he
will look for loopholes in his idol's authority and infiltrate his
idol's mind through those loopholes rather than by overall and
whole-hearted identification. He will nag at him secretly, belittle
him, and attempt to discard him bit by bit. When the time has
come, he may get rid of him in a burst, throw him out of office,
or worse. In either case, however, he is ready to assume the role
of authority and competence himself.

One might say that a youngest brother, though his senior by chronological age, would be the more compatible boss altogether. The boss, then, will really want to be guided by his assistant or disciple, although he would get very angry if this became apparent to the latter, or if he merely knew that other people thought so. And his assistant, the older brother of brother(s), will succeed in guiding his chief, if only he does not make it too obvious, renounces some of the credit he might deserve, and listens sympathetically to the meandering ideas of his boss.

The oldest brother of brother(s) is also the person who builds up property—spiritual, industrial, agricultural, financial, or domestic. He likes to keep his environment in order. He is the one who would tend to want a room of his own to begin with, and from early childhood on. His house should be in tiptop shape, literally and budgetwise. He only likes things that are within his reach. He hates to live off capital or to be in debt. To be sure, debts can be very different things in different cases. He may incur debts, but then they will only add up to a fraction of the collaterals at his disposal. Or he may despise finances and everyday reality altogether, but stay far ahead of his moral, intellectual, or spiritual commitments. He is context-bound. He can appraise any contribution to any of the wealths of mankind as to its worth. Generally that includes his own contributions, although secretly he would tend to be somewhat partial and believe that his is really the very best. He has a sense of pragmatism even in the highest realms of theory, an almost unfailing ear for redundancy, a solid memory for relevant facts and events regardless of whether the sciences, the arts, or any kind of engineering, human and technical, are concerned. He spots the people who are his like in those matters, and while he would not want to be too close to them personally, he can establish excellent rapport with them via the pieces of work, thought or art that are at stake. He likes clean facts and tight concepts, and he hates big words, at least as long as they are empty or merely not as full as they pretend.

He is a tough guy with women. He will not fall for any of them, but be delighted and thrilled, though outwardly unwincing, if *they* fall for him. He will tend to treat girls like younger brothers, expect them to live up to his assignments, to do even better than males, to admire only him, or certainly no one else, and to be content with very little in return. Women should be happy to be able to be of service to him; there *is* no greater reward. He wants them to be mothers to him, but he would deny vehemently that this is the case. He will prefer them to be slim and boyish rather than heavy, voluptuous, and maternal, as if to demonstrate even this way that he really is not looking for a mother. But, once he has married, a good portion of his discontent with his wife is precisely that she does not betray her looks. In many cases she really is not much of a mother.

The best match he can make would be a girl who is the youngest sister of brother(s), one who has learned to be somewhat like a boy herself yet admires and adores boys. No, just one boy: him. She should be his inferior in two ways—in being a youngest and in being "only" a girl. She should have learned at home to do everything possible for boys, but not as a mother, rather as a cutie who has been beaten into it. She must be kind and catering out of timidity. And she should be a virgin.

Ordinarily, a girl who has been the youngest after several boys only would hardly buy that, unless she has been struck by losses. Usually she has been spoiled rather than has suffered losses or force. Instead of being coerced to adore and obey males, she has learned to be adored by them. But compromises are conceivable. He could admire her for her (elf-like) beauty and make her into a star for everybody to see and envy, as long as she concedes to this without reserve. And she, who has usually never been short of doting males, may be able to tolerate his reluctance to let her be a woman in every way she has been used to. After all, he lets her be beautiful. He has even taken this most important of all women's concerns in his own hands. What more can she want? Where there are greater difficulties, her brothers may help her get over the hump with him. They may support her and, if necessary, interfere. They may put pressure on her husband to behave toward her as they did, and coming from males (perhaps even from the oldest of her brothers if she has several of them) he may yield. As a matter of fact, he might seek the friendship of one or two

of the brothers, although probably not of the oldest. Yet if his
wife has only one older brother and no other siblings, then even
this brother could be compatible. The brother, in spite of his
greater interest in girls or his own wife, might still find something
in a friendship with his sister's husband. That husband may appear
to him to be more of a male than he is himself. After all, he had
been in control of other male peers. He had not been exposed to
the frustrations involved in dealing with a younger girl whom he
was supposed to protect and be kind to. The brother could learn
from his sister's husband how to be tough with women. So he
thinks. He will plead for compromises, but if the sister does find
her master at last, this is also fine with him.

Other possible matches would be the oldest sister of brother(s),
although both of them would have difficulty accepting their partner's seniority. However, since he is partly and secretly looking
for a mother—the only female he had had in his family—the
older sister may be compatible. This would hold particularly as
long as they divide their empires, so that he reigns, say, in the
business world and on his job, whereas she does so inconspicuously
at home, with their home finances and with their children. Girls
who have been middle siblings would also be eligible as long as
they have had at least one sibling relationship that duplicates what
they get in marriage: a brother who is their senior. The youngest
sister of sister(s) only would have no rank-conflict with the oldest
brother of brother(s), but both of them are in for trouble in
accepting the other sex. This is generally worse than if only one
of them had that trouble. An only child might also be compatible, provided she comes from well-matched parents, preferably
from a father who has been the oldest brother of sister(s) and
a mother who is the youngest sister of brother(s). Such an only
girl would have a little trouble getting used to living with a peer,
but her experiences with her parents are likely to have been
fortunate, and her parents have been peers to each other. Yet in
such cases one ought to wonder why the parents had no more
than one child.

Barring other circumstances, the poorest of all possible matches
that the oldest brother of brother(s) can enter would be that with

the oldest sister of sister(s) only. The spouses would have a full rank and sex conflict, and their quarrels may be unending.

The arrival of children, especially of boys, would make life easier for the oldest brother of brother(s), under all circumstances, and for his wife too, unless she comes from a family of girls only. For the optimal match that he can make—with the youngest sister of brother(s)—the optimal configuration of children would be a boy first, then a girl; or boys first, then a girl or two; or boys first, then a girl, then boys, then a girl again.

Once he has a family, the oldest brother of brother(s) will take pains to care for it with plans ranging way into the future. He will maintain order and discipline and reign somewhat self-righteously. This may earn him the reputation of an autocrat, a Victorian father, particularly if he has a large number of children and if they have not come in the most favorable sequence. Sooner or later, protests against him will be heard, or tacit and overt obstinacy may become the habit. Except for the oldest son, the children will tend to feel poorly understood, and their mother may even confirm them in this attitude and side with them, unless she is an oldest sister herself. In that case both parents may get estranged from their children in later life and assume a common front at least against some of them.

His best male friend is often a youngest brother of brother(s), although he may well achieve the best understanding and unanimity par distance with an older brother or an only child. He will have a feeling of trust in the capacities and competencies of that person, will let him work on his own and merely try to establish the fact, from time to time, that they are still in agreement. With youngest brothers of brothers, however, he can really cooperate. He can guide them, and they will take his leads, socially and at work, even if under the guise of mild protests. An oldest brother of sister(s) would not qualify too well as a friend; he would rather tend to find himself a girl for a friend. But if he had been discouraged in his relations to the opposite sex at home, he might well seek the friendship of this admirable senior of brothers who is so manly, whereas he, thanks to the company of sisters only, does not know too well how to be a male. While his friend has learned to handle and control even boys, he himself did not succeed with a single one of his sisters. But as he is learning from him how to be a male, he may well adopt to some extent the role of a girl, the only role he saw being played by peers at home, and his friend might buy that.

Boys who have been middle brothers may also qualify, especially if they have had an older brother. A youngest brother of sister(s) only would have no seniority conflict with the oldest brother of brother(s), but the latter may find himself transformed to some extent into an admirable and awe-inspiring sister in his friend's mind and be expected to be gentle, kind, and tactful, all things that he would not particularly care to be, least of all when the demands are explicit. Somewhere, though, he might even like that idea. At home he has more often seen his mother than his father treat and handle his younger brothers. In part he must have learned from her what he can do so well: control juniors. But then he must also have felt and acted somewhat like a mother toward them. So he is not entirely unprepared for the present friend, the youngest brother of sister(s).

Generally speaking, friendships tend to be a strong and welcome supplement of marriage. If the oldest brother of brother(s) can keep his friends, he will find it easier to get along with his wife.

The greater the number of brothers he has had, the harder will it be for an oldest brother to settle for a girl, to get married and to stay married. The same will also be true of his friendship with males. One friend might be too little. A gang of friends would appear to be more satisfying. They may be juniors to various degrees, youngest brothers, middle brothers, or close to the top, and brothers of girls as well as of boys. In a group of friends there is room for many kinds of relationships at once. Even another oldest brother of brother(s) might be tolerable, although this could well tend to split the gang in two. Sometimes the success of marriage depends on the male friends his wife will let him be off with or bring home. In other cases, the oldest brother of brother(s) may not even vie for marriage. Nor may he look for male friends. Instead, he may try to have many girls at once, and since he cannot keep up an affair with all of them at once, he may put them to work for him as secretaries, salesgirls, waitresses, dancers, or actresses. Passingly he may consume one or the other of them as women, occasionally feel he has to have had all of them at least once, but even so they would remain "younger brothers." Slim and boyish, obedient, respectful, and efficient, they are hardly real girls. They earn their living by what they put out rather than by what they are, although they should be pretty. The last thing he could stand of them would be their announcement that they are pregnant. They should produce anything whatsoever but offspring, regardless of the fact that women are unequalled in precisely this respect.

Politically the oldest brother of brother(s) believes in strong leadership, elites, even dictatorships, if he thinks they are necessary; he believes in sound investment policies, quality goods, in speed, accuracy, and simplicity of administration, planning for years ahead, lawfulness of actions and procedures, maintenance of principles rather than customs and comfort—of the constitution rather than good sentiments. He may be a revolutionary in his young years, but he will come to terms with the complexities of reality sooner than others and end up a conservative in the better sense of the word. He is reluctant to rely on outside help, whether foreign or domestic. He would rather give help, even if it means hardship and toil for him or those he represents. If antagonized, he may turn into a stubborn and merciless avenger and, if ever put on trial, he tends to ask for no mercy for himself. If active in politics, he will find himself unpopular with the crowd, at least in Western style democracies and while in office. He needs straw men and vote getters. Often he prefers to work behind the scene altogether, as the expert diplomat, economist, lawyer, financier, or master racketeer.

In religion, he is for being without a mediator between himself and God, or for being that mediator himself. He is a deist who believes that God set the world right at the beginning, and that it has been functioning fairly rationally ever since without him. Or a moralist who insists that God's strongest manifestation is mankind's moral code. Or an atheist who recognizes the fair order governing the universe and its miraculous secrets, but who would not have any kind of supreme being in charge of its creation and maintenance. Or a materialist who makes matter his God (or goddess), but claims its laws to be of iron. There is one thing the oldest brother of brother(s) can rarely be: an ordinary pious person.

In philosophy, he is the system builder, or at least the believer in system building. He does not care too much for history of philosophy; there are too many capricious accidentals. Philosophy should be man-made, and in every nut and bolt his hand should be apparent. If there is fault or contradiction, discard the system. Build another one. Or cut off its sick arm, and do not let another arm grow. Make it yourself, of steel, wood, or stone. As a practical philosopher he believes in common sense, clear purposes and relationships, and hard cash. If he should turn romantic, or introspective, or existentialist, he will not merely be the practitioner, but be the attorney, the man who forces feelings and experiences into a creed or constitution.

Death is merely the end of life, as far as he is concerned. There is little, if anything, thereafter, no matter how pleasant, reasonable, or heavenly this non-existence may be. But one's works might live on, or one's memory might, and if he has had a family, they will do so too. As a matter of fact, they may even have to be cared for, and hence one's property will have to be disposed of. The oldest brother of brother(s) tends to draw a will long before his death has become likely. He is seldom taken by surprise. He has not only built up an estate but kept it in good shape and seen to it that its orderly transfer after his death and its good maintenance are guaranteed. Usually he has even taken care of his own funeral and sometimes written his own obituary.

Losses of immediate family members or dear persons will be "handled" efficiently and in good composure, with little overt mourning, although the experience of loss is stronger underneath and more specific than it looks. Guilt will be manifest in proportion to the degree of unconscious ambivalence toward the person lost. Yet the guilt is usually under control. It does not set him up for more losses or punishment, as it tends to do with others.

The most painful loss will be that of his mother or motherly friends. As for the mother, her exit leaves the survivors in the family without a woman. The loss entailing relatively the greatest guilt will be that of a younger brother or a dear (male) friend acting such a part. Yet even that loss can be dealt with more or less consciously, partly because the oldest brother of brother(s) can still remember the time when his wish to be without junior peers had actually been gratified, the time before they had been born. He knows what to wish for. They should go where they came from, to hell, if must be. (In contrast, the younger brother of brother(s) can never quite formulate such a wish.) On the other hand, the loss of a girl, sometimes even of his spouse, tends to affect him less than the other losses. He will observe the conventions of mourning and wait dutifully before attaching himself to another female, but he does not appear to be shaken. He has behaved that way even with temporary losses, with limited separations from girls. They were separations for good as far as he was concerned. He himself would break off relations with girls who "left him" just a little too often or for a little too long.

If ever he gets to receive advice, counsel or psychotherapy, he is inclined to dislike his dependence on another person. This may keep him from seeking it in the first place. If in the position of giving help or advice himself, he tends to take over and manage too much, to fare better with males than with females, and best with oldest brothers or only children.

## CHAPTER 4

# The Youngest Brother of Brother(s)

He is a capricious and willful man, a person who can surprise and amaze his elders but also put them at a loss, annoy, and antagonize them. This may have become apparent shortly after birth; already he began to look more vigorous but also was more difficult to keep in bounds than his brother(s). On the surface he gives the impression as if he would tolerate nobody above him, as if independence and freedom are among the greatest of his concerns. He will give in to no one. Yet on closer inspection it usually turns out that he needs the others in order to react to them. If he were really independent and free, if nobody would curb him, he would not know what to do. He will seek out domains where he can trespass, and people with whom he can pick arguments, or conduct elaborate, although meandering, conversations. He needs elders in order to liberate himself from them, to break out of their control. But almost as soon as he has done so, he will rush back into their arms.

He is an irregular worker, sometimes quite excellent in his achievements, and other times lousy, dragging, or altogether unproductive. Much depends upon his moods, and these depend upon the people he is working with and on his friends and his family at home. He does not hesitate to unwrap his domestic problems right on the boss' table, nor to bring his working problems home. He is good at work, both when he can compete or when somebody superior in status, wisdom, skill, and the like is watching. If someone has an idea, he will have one too, and it may come close in quality to the original idea but seldom reach it. If nobody has an idea, he

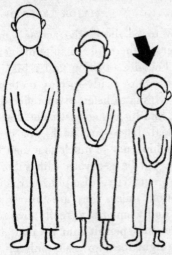

usually has none either, or one that is quite useless. If another person speaks in a meeting, introduces a new subject, wins laughs, etc., he will try to do likewise, no matter how small his qualifications. Or he will burst out with inappropriate truths. On the other hand he may contribute nothing in a meeting where he would be perfectly qualified to speak. He just does not think of it or does not like the atmosphere of the meeting.

He is at his best in free artistic or scientific endeavors, where his external environment and livelihood are taken care of by an impersonal institution, a wise or kind sponsor, or a motherly female. He may turn out to be a genius, if his talents are sufficient and a few carpets are laid out before him, or at least not taken away. Even then he may wonder to the end of his life, whether he should not have chosen something altogether different for a profession. He depends on opportunities, but will do little to create them himself. Sometimes he succeeds as an entertainer or actor, although he is not quite convincing to a part of his audience, most of them women. To them he is somewhat of a fool in matters of courtship, love, and understanding of women.

He is not a leader. If in a position of authority, he will appear to lack stability, justice, and insight into almost all problems involved, although he may get the gist of some of them quite well and establish fairly good relations with some of his "subjects."

The latter are likely to be those who act as secret seniors toward him, as older brothers, fathers, or, in spite of their male sex, as all-accepting mothers. Females working under his authority will have no easy life unless they are ready to play mother in ever so many ways. They must be willing to listen to his reflections, to do personal favors for him—get him his coffee just right, sew a loose button, or remind him of crucial dates—and to be, or pretend to be, thoroughly enchanted by him, not so much as a man but as a delightful genius. In return he will be generous with subordinates, not insist too hard on order, regularity, discipline, or speed, and thereby wreck his own position, unless they are the right kind of subjects to begin with: men and women who really love to take responsibilities upon themselves and permit him by their own sweet persuasion, cunning, or straight force to insist only on those of his ideas and ways that seem really worthwhile. If they are not the right kind of subjects, if they take him at face value, both they and their boss may be fired, or the institution he heads or the business he controls will disintegrate.

He not only can accept but he loves authority, provided it is not too demonstrative. With a kind and understanding senior he may last forever, get into no conflicts at all, admire his idol no end, defend him against any kind of criticism, and still never manage to mold himself after him. He will perpetually want him to his avail as the director of his own life and efforts, as the person to submit to, and even suffer from. If the senior dies, he will not take his place; instead he may enter an excessive period of mourning. Only failure to hit upon such an ideal authority—who might even be a female—will make him rebellious against those imperfect ones whom he can and does find. He will then be an incessant trouble maker, a hopeless dreamer and romantic, a person who wants everything everywhere at all times. He might arouse sympathy and gain a certain kind of following during uneasy times. In a revolution, he may become a leader of some stature, but he will fail as soon as peace and order have been restored, as soon as the revolution has accomplished its aims. The one exception is that the true leader of the revolution, an elder by character, likes and understands him and uses him as his pet executive.

The youngest brother of brother(s) does not create nor even preserve property and estates to any great extent. In all walks of life he takes and spends easily, with no concern where the next donation will come from, or whether he will ever get a return on what he spends. He lightly squanders the savings of others, his family's inheritance, or the money he has been making by his own wits and talents. He will make fabulous presents on the spur of the moment. He hates all curtailments by law, the administration, or "misers." He will live beyond his means and reach far above what he can reasonably hope to get. If sometimes he gets it, it comes as no surprise to him. It matters little that he does get it; physical goods are not important. What counts are people, sympathy, understanding—which means mostly being understood, even though he tries hard, but unsuccessfully, to understand in turn— and the romantic angles of life, of industry, economics, and even the sciences. It is more important to be liked than to be good in the field, better to be noble, gentle, a humanitarian than an expert or an efficient manager. The world is abundant enough to furnish even the most unexpected. Hence debts mean nothing, just as riches don't. You can reach for the pie in the sky, if only you have no trepidation about it. Once you've got it, you can eat it and have it too, he believes. And somehow he gets enough, though sporadic, evidence that he is right. The world is not a pragmatic one. Some of its purposes are always beyond comprehension. Everything may be important, even the most insignificant and boringly familiar detail.

He is a soft one with women, a gentleman, a cavalier, even where he plays the tough one or the cynic. Yet it seems he has little determination to win the most feminine of their favors. He tends to win them anyway, but then he does not quite know what to do with them. He is shy, awkward, almost innocent, and women are often willing to bestow much more on him than he has asked for. They like a man who is not so dead set on making them at all costs, even if they have to teach him what to do with a woman who has consented. Even when he shows the coat of a wolf, he is actually oblivious of women and their concerns. He does not seem to understand them. All he wants is to be understood himself.

His best match is a girl who has been the oldest sister of brothers. She must be able to assume the role of a senior and to handle younger, somewhat dependent and guidance-seeking boys. She need not be very feminine in appearance, although he would like her to be beautiful. Sometimes she really is, although it might be a cool or plain kind of beauty, and other times she really is not, even though he claims it. If she has coped with several boys at home, she can usually cope with this one. However, he may turn reticent, balking, or even antagonistic, as soon as she starts competing with boys in the slightest way, or if a male friend of his makes merely a remark to this effect. Only if she is very maternal and lets him pursue all of his many and often short-lived interests, only if she never insists on taking him to task at home but merely smuggles subtle suggestions into his mind, only if she can guide his professional conduct without his notice and without ever demanding credit for it, or, in other words, only if she is the secret boss, will they be capable of happiness. Looking up to her, he will also be inclined to look up to her family and her brothers, sometimes to the point of appearing to lack backbone. He will try to ingratiate himself, and as long as he does so socially, as an entertainer, as a very nice guy, or by his reputation in his field of work, he has good chances of succeeding. There is one thing they can never count on: reliable help, particularly in business or financial matters. Not that he might not give it abundantly at times. But at other times he refuses to get the point, or finds a principle somewhere in his mind that prevents him from moving a finger. He will not even drop a word with a person whose intervention could make all the difference. He is equally inconsistent in accepting help. He might ask for it when there is no need to speak of, and refuse to accept it even when it could be easily and willingly provided. His wife will often have to mediate in both directions, or do some lobbying behind his back.

Another possible match would be a middle sister, as long as she has had at least one younger brother. A youngest sister of brothers would not be so good. She has been used to the other sex, but she cannot very well act the senior whom he has been looking for. An only child might also qualify as long as she comes from well-matched parents (which is not too likely). For example, if her mother has been the oldest sister of brother(s) and her father the youngest brother of sister(s), the daughter's chances with a youngest brother of brother(s) are not too bad. An oldest sister of sister(s) would provide the guidance of juniors that he needs, although neither spouse will be fully at ease with the other's sex. Worst of all would be a marriage to a youngest sister of sister(s), unless other and especially favorable circumstances would compensate for their difficulties. She would neither provide the guidance nor even know too well how to handle the other sex. (And neither would he). A third party willing to supply them with the guidance they need would be welcome, although that may sometimes also break up the marriage.

The arrival of children would be hard for him to take. He would feel threatened in his own status. There ought to be only one darling little genius for his wife: he himself. But if she has been an oldest or middle sister of at least one junior boy, she will be able to manage. For the optimal match—the youngest brother of brother(s) married to the oldest sister of brother(s)—the best configuration of children would be a girl or two first, then a boy; or girls first, then boys, then girls again, then boys. But it would be wise if there were not too many in all. The poorest match— marriage to the youngest sister of sister(s)—would also be the least prepared for any children of their own. Usually one child is already too much for the parents. Both of them are looking for a senior to guide them, and they may even try to make their child into one at an age when he or she could not possibly oblige.

As the children grow up, the youngest brother of brother(s) will slowly get used to them, but he will do little planning for the future. His wife, if the right one, will do some of it for him and be his monitor for the remainder, urging that he ought to set some money aside, take out life insurance or raise the one in operation, look after the children's education, find a better school, speak to the teacher, or, one day, at last, set up a will. But he will often be busy with the pursuit of his trade, art, writing, science, philosophy, or hobby, and find no time, no money available, no reason, nor even room in his mind. On the other hand he may be his children's best companion and entertainer, inconsistent and careless, always ready with a story, sometimes poking fun at their oh-so-serious mother or their teachers. He will be on par with the children rather than their superior by experience and responsibility. He will have least trouble identifying with his youngest boy, but even here his capacity to understand, to form an integrated picture of the boy's interests and concerns, will generally be limited. When his children have grown up, he is likely to make *them* his confidants rather than vice versa.

As for male friends, he gets along best with older brothers of brothers. He may occasionally enjoy the friendship or company of another youngest brother. There will be empathy between them. Together they may long for the same distant lands and stars, but they will be able to stand each other for any length of time only if the other is the youngest brother of sister(s), or of both brother(s) and sister(s). The most enduring relationship will be with a senior of boys, or with an only child whose father was a senior of boys. The older brother of a sister may also be a possibility, although he may not be particularly anxious to be a steady friend of a boy; he would prefer to spend his time with girls, unless he has been strongly discouraged at home. Middle brothers may also make good friends, provided they have had younger brothers themselves. Sometimes the youngest brother of brother(s) may even be less wary of a middle brother than of an oldest brother, especially if his own brothers have been very close to him in age.

So important are male friends to the youngest brother of brother(s), that he will sometimes be willing to sacrifice a girl in order to keep a boy, if that boy is the right one. He will tend to be quite interested in having his male friend meet his girl, anxious to hear his opinion about her, ready to drop her, if his friend advises so, even ready to pass her on, or merely lend her for a night, to his friend, should that wonderful man so desire. He will plead for his male friends, and make his girl or wife like them and their friendship. If she does not, he will try again and again, for years if necessary, or wish her to hell one day. In that case he would try to get himself another girl who has less trouble being motherly to him and all his male idols.

The number of brothers he has had bears on his marriage. The larger that number, the harder will it be for him to give them up and to give up his male friends of later life; the harder will it be to become and be a man for his girl. If during his childhood his brothers had not formed subgroups, and if they had been inspired by their parents and their own experiences to wish more and more for a sister as the boys continued to grow in number, he may well have gotten the brunt of this wish. He may have been made into a girl of sorts. Consequently he might not marry at all, or marry a strong female who controls him as an older brother would and orders him around for the rest of his life. He may put her on a pedestal and attempt to be her humble servant, trying forever to fathom the depths of her mind, her womanhood, and even her capacity to have children.

Politically, the youngest brother of brother(s) is against monarchy, against dictatorships, even against strong leadership within a democracy. *Laissez faire* is his motto. Everything will take care of itself. Even extreme opposites can be brought together. How? By love and by understanding; by letting people take their own courses; by ignoring all boundaries, laws, and regulations; by adopting a new language, that of the heart. In spirit he will be a revolutionary, way into his old age, perhaps a true Christian, but there is no revolution that could fully satisfy him. Yet, if the president of the bank where he works, the governor of his state (even a king or the council of a radical political party) tells him that they love him and his ways, that he is just fine as he is, that nobody could do the job better than he can, this will be the end of all needs for change. With their permission he may even become a ruthless and destructive executive. He loves to be a member of a power group and thereby get to do and obtain the things that he would ordinarily dare to vie for only by inefficient magic, hypnosis (which sometimes tends to be a fad with him anyway), or endless tours of mere talking.

He will not only look for help of any kind. He will count on it. He will trust that there is always a way out, and that he himself will not have to find it. It will come to him by the grace of God, history, or circumstances. If it does come, that is. But since an essential part of politics in Western democracies is appealing to people, he may be lucky even here.

In religion, he can tolerate hierarchies and mediation as long as priests, saints, and the "One and Almighty" like him best of all. That would be his tacit contention. He believes in God's incessant interference with the world that He has created, in mystic unions, flashes of revelations, miracles, and the brotherhood of all men, especially if he is their dearest brother. He is a pantheist, and the last thing he would like to be called is a moralist. Emotions constitute the world. That holds even when he is an atheist. It is not matter that counts, nor its laws, but what you feel of matter, of nature and its infinite beauty, or of other people. As a matter of fact, there are no laws without exceptions. Hence exceptions are the laws. Both blend forever into each other. To him no stretch of imagination is too long to furnish the proof.

As for philosophy, he is the mystic, the romantic, the experientialist and existentialist. Philosophy is a mood rather than a system. It is reception rather than construction, growth rather than movement, a way of existence rather than a mode of action. Philosophizing is among the essences of life. Even failing may be fun, if he can take his time with it, if expansive reflection is possible. And what is success when measured by the vastness of the universe or the delicacy of a dandelion ball? If active in formal philosophy, the youngest brother of brother(s) would rather be a historian of philosophy than a logician or system-builder. He would be an opponent of methodology, clear concepts, and strict definitions. He prefers to look for the etymological roots of concepts rather than their specific meanings as derived from their contexts. The grandiosity of a scheme impresses him more than its simplicity, genesis, or purpose.

Death is not worth much thinking about. Somehow and secretly he believes that he might not have to die at all. But if it should be inevitable, there will be a wonderful life thereafter, a state of high exaltation in the presence of God. The youngest brother of brother(s) is the person who may forget to draw a will, or who draws a rather imperfect one. In his last weeks, days, or hours he feels even more that he cannot be bothered by such worldly trifles.

The rings from heaven have already reached his ears. By giving in to them, by gazing toward his end with a glow, he may be doing more for his survivors than by disposing of possessions and privileges.

Losses of immediate family members or dear persons will throw him into turmoil and confusion, although the loss of a parent may be lessened in its impact, if he has several older brothers. In that case, the loss of a brother would also tend to be less severe. After suffering losses, periods of deep mourning and forced euphoria may alternate. He will appear overly afflicted at some times or in certain instances, and peculiarly unconcerned at others. Guilt over unconscious wishes for the loss will tend to be "denied" as well as get the best of him, either all at once or in succession. He will fumble repeatedly in various matters and get himself into ever new troubles, at least for a while.

Like the oldest brother of brother(s) he will tend to experience the loss of his mother or a motherly friend as the most painful loss. The loss of an older brother, or a friend assuming that role, may confuse him thoroughly. He has always been with senior (male) peers. They were there before he came to life. So it is difficult for him to spell out any wishes in his mind to get rid of them, to dream up what life would be like without them. Hence the loss will take him by surprise and find him in a considerable turmoil at first. Girls, however, can be foregone without much trouble. Even the loss of a very dear one or of his spouse has little impact unless she was a kind of mother to him to begin with. Often he will not even observe the conventions. He may date a girl and sometimes even marry again soon after he has lost his wife.

He flocks to prophets, advisors, and psychotherapy, and usually loves what he can get. As far as he is concerned, it need never end. If called upon to give advice, guidance or a listening ear, he tends to believe that, for the client, things will take care of themselves. In that case he might even claim that psychological help or counselling should be counsellor-centered. He usually does better with male than with female solicitors of his help, and best with youngest brothers.

## CHAPTER 5

## The Oldest Brother of Sister(s)

He is a friend of the girls and ladies, whether sincerely or with tongue in cheek. Love of the tender sex is the most important of all concerns, no matter how important his other engagements. If necessary, he will undergo stress and hardship, but at the end of the road there must be a woman, or two or ten, all at once or in succession. No trophy is good enough by itself. Obtaining it must help him win the lady of his choice. On the other hand no sacrifice is too high, if it gets him, or merely protects, his beloved. He can get along with men but he prefers to communicate via women, theirs or his own. Sometimes they change partners in the process. Not that he could not negotiate or work with men directly, but what would be the point, if he can get a woman's help. That was how even God had originally arranged it in Paradise.

He may be a good worker as long as there are female colleagues or co-workers, or secretaries, assistants, maids. Work without Muses is barren. Only if his mind is quite definitely on a girl outside of work, if he is happily betrothed or married, will he tolerate the exclusive company of men or purely factual contacts with the women around him. Yet his tolerance will last for little more than a day at a time. He would rather not go on long trips or expeditions, nor join the army, nor get into any other field of work where women are scarce, should not be brought along, or would not go anyway. He prefers a leading position to a subordinate one, not so much because he has felt a calling for it but because he thinks he is more likely to be able to set his own pace, take off for his

44

women whenever he likes to, or use his rank to get them in the first place.

Even so he tends to be a responsible worker. He is not exactly absorbed by his job or profession; he may change it, even in later life, if the new work does not differ too much from the old. Yet he is still interested in doing a good job, if for no other reason than not to lose outside privileges that have already been his. He is a realist. He does not aspire the close-to-impossible. He wants his peace and his fun. That's what life is for. And he does not want to take more than a reasonable risk. Only with a woman to win will he play for higher stakes, be more careless, and even courageous.

He can accept authorities as long as they do not interfere in his private affairs. He likes authority to be technical in character and does not believe in authority per se. Only if the person in the superior position is a woman, will he concede that she may be broad in her outlook and have a say in things other than her field of competence. However, the woman must always keep in mind that she is a woman and that, in this very capacity, she has to be the subordinate, the submissive, patient, and wise friend. If she does, he will not hide his affection and admiration. If she is an older person, she need not even be too articulate in these concessions to men, as long as there is some man superior even to her—if possible, a male to whom she bows in awe.

As for men, he will accept them as his superiors at work, if they work harder than he does, if their sacrifices are greater than his own, if they are better than he is in the field, and if they are neither favorites with women nor favor them too much themselves. An older brother of brother(s) tends to be relatively easy to accept for him. That man will treat him as if he were a younger brother, and he may perhaps behave a little like he has seen his sister behave toward older males, including his father and himself. Or he may take that authority for a "father," particularly when that man is considerably older than himself. He is inclined to be a "good son" to him. He will even permit the girls in their environment to adore that man more than him, as long as he himself is clearly second-most favored.

If in a position of authority himself, he is for live and let live. Work is one thing, and fun, recreation, women, and love is another. His subordinates should partake of both. Let them also have their women. He wants no goofers among his workers, but they should not wreck their brains or bodies either while trying to accomplish his goals. And there should be celebrations from time to time. Let them bring their women, let the women bring their men, let people see whether his own wife is not the most attractive girl and he himself the most gorgeous man of all. Nobody will have to admit that this is so. He merely wants some evidence that he got the best of all wives, and that he is the best man his wife could get.

He is a fair-to-good preserver of property, estates, business, and the like, but he will not expand it greatly nor be anxious to create much himself. Yet, he may create new enterprises, but it will be accidental, more a by-product of his efforts to win and keep the favors of the girl or woman who has attracted him the most, and to care for the children that she has "given him" so graciously. He is much less hurt than the oldest brother of brother(s) would be, if any of his enterprises fail. As long as his family and he himself survive, things cannot be so bad. He will start all over with something else, and if he should fail again, he will start from scratch for a third time. To him it does not really matter what field one is in, as long as one can make a go of it and a living. After all, what is there that matters more than love.

He is kind and considerate with women. He can court for a long time without getting discouraged, go out of his way in order to demonstrate his interest, and is seldom, if ever, ashamed of what he does for a woman. But he can also sense his chances with women better than other men, especially the oldest and youngest brothers of brothers. He will not operate in a vacuum. She must be interested in him, too. Once that is established, he can let her take her time. She should look him over. That's her right. That is what he would want his own sisters to do to their boy friends before they decide or ask him, their oldest brother, for his consent. If the girl of his choice decides otherwise, in fairness, he bears no grudge. They can part as good friends.

The best match he can make would be the youngest sister of brother(s). This match could be perfect. After all, he has been used to girls his junior, and she to boys her senior. They would tend to have no conflicts over sex or rank. He is likely to make his choice more full-heartedly than the oldest or youngest brother of brother(s) could, and she will not have to transform into a bit of a boy or into some kind of mother. External tokens, such as complexion, hair, facial and body build, or the way she dresses, will be secondary to what she is like as a person. He can accept many modes of attractiveness in girls, whereas brothers of brothers only are more particular, stubborn, and narrow in their preferences.

His sisters are likely to agree with his choice and accept the chosen girl. They can identify with her as she will be able to do with them, and the need for competition will be small, especially when they have made their own choice of spouses with the approval of their brother. Only an unmarried younger sister—unmarried for whatever reason, realistic or imaginary—who believes that this is her final fate, will interfere jealously and possibly create trouble. The more younger sisters the oldest brother has, the more likely is it that one of them will be the jealous one. That should not be confused with little jealousies that are inevitable whenever the adored brother takes up dating or is getting more serious with a girl for the first time. These jealousies pass before long.

The prospective wife's older brothers can hand their little darling over with confidence to a man who has been in their position in his own family, who can empathize with what they feel, and whose feelings and thoughts they will tend to understand. They won't have to be close buddies with their brother-in-law. But they also know that he will not be more of a buddy with a gang of boys than with his own wife. He will be their girl's boy, although also her master, and she had better accept it.

There are a few other matches that have fair chances of happiness and success. He could, for instance, marry the oldest sister of brother(s), but he will have some conflicts over seniority rights. For quite a while their problem will be who the boss is. Only the arrival of children, by definition the little ones, will mitigate this. He could marry the youngest sister of sisters only, and she would be happy to submit to his authority, but she is inclined to act and behave a little too prudish and belligerent. She has not been used to a peer of the opposite sex from earliest life on, as has the youngest sister of brother(s). A girl in a middle position may also be all right as a spouse, as long as she has at least one older brother. An only child would qualify, too, especially if she comes from well-matched parents, such as a mother who had been the youngest sister of brother(s), and a father who had been the oldest brother of sister(s). But well-matched parents are not indispensable, apart from being rarer than chance, with only children. She will be the "child," the little one, anyway. The oldest brother of sister(s) may not be quite ready to act as a parent, but he can hardly help acting as a senior. Relatively the poorest match would be the marriage to the oldest sister of sister(s) only, although the fact that he himself has been used to girls will reduce their conflicts over acceptance of the other sex. *He* can accept it. He is not quite that poor a match for her. Occasionally the wife may bring one of her younger sisters with her, perhaps as a frequent visitor, or even to live with them, and that could conceivably improve their situation, although one day he may wonder why he had not picked the younger one for a spouse.

The arrival of children as well as any particular constellation of them are not crucial. The oldest brother of sister(s) would rather have some children than none, but he and his (well-matched) wife are already happy with things as they are. Their relationship will not go to pieces, if they should have no children. They might be considering adoption in that case. It does not really matter either whether they get a boy first or a girl, or boys only, or girls only, or many children, or few. They can take in stride whatever they get .

He will care well for his children. Yet he does not go out of his way to do so. His wife still and always comes first. He tends to be as good a father as they come, neither overbearing nor indifferent, neither too strict nor too soft, and quite a guide, implicitly rather than explicitly, for his children's relationships with the other sex. If he is married to the youngest sister of brother(s), the children are the most likely of all to be at ease with each other, with friends of the other sex, and with prospective spouses.

Male friends matter less to him than they do to brothers of brothers only. Almost all major types, oldest brothers of brother(s), youngest brothers of brother(s), youngest brothers of sisters(s), and only children, would be compatible, even though not eagerly sought. Only other oldest brothers of sisters would not last long as friends. Oldest brothers of sisters are much more likely to get along well with each other's sisters than among themselves. Like other same-sex friends, they cannot do much with a person who is their duplicate, except identify and empathize with him. They have too little to offer to each other in their own rights and by their immediate presence.

The oldest brother of sister(s) is usually not "one of the boys." He is no gang-man. There is nothing in the company of men that could not be had as well or better from women. This is his opinion. Where this is not the case, he may well have inherited conflicts over rank and sex, or over losses, from his parents, or he may have suffered losses himself. He may then go out with the boys for games, sports, beers, pranks, and the like, but to the gang he will appear chicken. He has to be home on time, his wife and his children expect him to. He cannot afford anything too wicked or dangerous because of his family. He lets the boys know that his wife comes first. He might even admit this openly. When it comes to fights

among the boys, he is for mediation and reason, even if it earns
him the reputation of a coward. He does not care as long as the
women know of his strength as a lover. He counts on them to
get him back on his feet after defeats. Yet before such a (troubled)
oldest brother of sister(s) has founded a family of his own (or
when he does not care to found one at all), he may take to being a
somewhat careless dare-devil. He will never play for the highest
stakes, though.

The greater the number of sisters he has "presided" over in his
family, the harder will it be for him to settle for one girl only in
marriage, and also to get along with male friends, except in slightly
peculiar ways. He might relate to men as if he himself were a bit of
a woman. He may prefer those men who would let him do that,
men who, quite likely, are somewhat feminine or unmasculine
themselves, at least in some aspects of their characters. Religious
orders, the ballet, the opera, the stage, and the movie industry
may offer particularly attractive vocations. If he can be a leading
performer, director, or conductor, he will have many girls and
women around him, as well as men with artistic flairs (which—by
some public opinion at least—indicates less masculinity), and he
may be the master of both. He will tend to work in the interest
of a master—a composer or author—if possible an older one or
one who is dead already, but at any rate an authority beyond
doubt. From his creative idols he excludes the newcomers, the
revolutionaries, the chaotic ones who have not yet emerged with
a style of their own. All of this holds also in the lower echelons of
entertainment and even in various branches of business. The oldest
brother of (too many) sisters will tend to go for public relations,
advertising—for the various kinds of "cheer leading"—perhaps
also for industrial design.

In politics the oldest brother of sister(s) tends to prefer a
moderately conservative government, party, or style of administration, as well as non-interference with business, family life, private
and internal affairs, and a person's ways of thinking. Everybody
should be permitted to make up his mind by himself. The forces
of life and society that are already functioning as they should, he
believes, need to be guided and controlled with only a minimum

of effort. The more everybody does and pursues what he wishes to anyway, the greater the likelihood that he is working for the common good. Everything is all right as long as a satisfactory love-life and family-life and education for the children are guaranteed. All other aspects of life and politics are secondary, can be decided on in purely technical ways, and do not have to be his concern, unless they involve the field of his own business, profession, or job.

In religion he believes in life and love. He is somewhat indifferent to, or skeptical of, God. He does not insist on any "ism," one way or another. He may be an atheist, but would seldom make a point of it. He may be a member of a conventional faith, without great fervor but with the belief that some religion is probably good for the children. He is not without opinions, but he likes them to be objective, well-founded, and involving only the fundamental issues of life, certain principles of morality, conduct, and love perhaps, and an ultimate purpose in life which some may want to call God.

In philosophy he tends to be an Epicurean or Stoic. In the first case he believes in the pursuit and consummation of pleasure and happiness, both simple and refined. All values of life are a natural outgrowth of these interests. In the second case he is a heroic and calm non-believer, a fervent friend of spiritual and intellectual discipline over all emotions and accidents of fate. Nothing is stable, except that whatever happens and whatever he might feel cannot throw him off balance. Or he may become a wizard of the Socratic art of discourse which accomplishes, above all, elegant proofs of contradictions inherent in the discussants' opinions. In either case, he does not care much for finished systems. They defy life. Nor does he like mysticism and existentialism which, in his opinion, defies life by autistic preoccupation with oneself, the "philosopher."

Death is serious and inevitable. As a matter of fact, it is built right into life itself. Life culminates in love, love in procreation, and procreation is necessary because there is death. Those who procreate die themselves, but they can live on through their children. Love, if it is really great and sincere, might live on too.

The greatest of all stories and legends outliving their heroes are those of people who loved each other with the utmost of abandon and succeded against their specific kind of adversity.

Losses of immediate family members or dear persons will be felt deeply and sincerely. Mourning comes quite naturally to the oldest brother of sister(s) and he is without feelings of guilt more often than other bereaved people. He has never wished to any great extent for the lost person's departure. Any loss in the immediate family, whether of mother, of father, or of a sister, will hurt him in about the same way, although for him, too, mother tends to be the dearest of all and hence the hardest to lose. If he has many sisters, the loss of one of them will be less traumatic than if he has only one or two, unless it is his favorite sister who dies. Similarly, losses of motherly and fatherly friends, of girl-friends, or of his spouse will strike him severely. Only the loss of male friends will often leave no mark to speak of. Generally he will recuperate in due time from all such losses. He can mourn efficiently and learn to live securely without the person lost.

As for his own survivors, he has usually left a fair will in time, i.e., not made decades in advance nor at his death bed. The will is usually simple and general, leaving much of the interpretation and execution to the good senses of the beneficiaries who, he believes, are in sufficient harmony with each other to avoid feuds and contests. And often he is right. He does not think that he will have to take care of life and people way beyond his death. Life takes care of itself, and people, at least those dear to him, play along with it gladly.

He is not a frequent candidate for psychological advice or counselling. Neither male nor female psychotherapists are too much of an "attraction" to him. What can they offer that real women would not give much more graciously and generously? If called for help himself, he tends to hold a good middle line between the extremes of being over-solicitous and careless. He is usually better with females than with males, particularly when the females have had brothers.

## CHAPTER 6

## The Youngest Brother of Sister(s)

He is a girls' boy. They love him. They dote on him. He evokes all kinds of maternal instincts in them. It does not matter what he undertakes or where he is heading, they will tend to be around, assist him in his endeavors or, more often, take care of his physical needs. They will keep house and cook for him. They will see to it that he has things to wear. They might even tie his necktie. They will clean up the mess he leaves behind when working. They will keep his files in order, do the typing, attend to the garden, make little repairs in the house themselves, and take care of his interests during any of his (erratic) absences. They almost wish nothing in return for it. Being able to do these things is enough in itself.

In reality, he will not always get such service, but this is what he would prefer and for what he will unwittingly tend to set himself up. In one case this may involve the official services of many females, in another only some modest help furnished without much intention by a kind woman, even an old one, who takes pity on him. But even then he will take it for granted. Frequently he retains strong ties to his older sisters, or at least to one of them, sometimes the unmarried one, because only a sister may be willing to do all that he would tend to take for granted. Sometimes it may also be some feminine and motherly male who is to take care of him.

He is not a very regular and systematic worker, but he can keep himself busy forever if his work corresponds to his talents and interests, or if it helps him satisfy somewhat childish goals, such as making a living from playing bridge, the xylophone, or horses,

or establishing himself in a penthouse or way out on a cliff. Where
his talents are great, he is capable of real accomplishments, preferably as an individual or as the star of a team. He can lose himself in the pursuit of his work, provided there is little interference from others, especially males, and provided some motherly
females look after some of the bare necessities of life.

He is much less reactive and competitive than the youngest
brother of brother(s) is in his work with other males, but he may
be erratic too. He may change his plans repeatedly, appear inconsistent and negligent of his obligations, but he is not really.
Though oblivious of the realistic and concrete contexts of his work,
and though believing that somebody will always pick up loose
ends for him, he seems to follow an inner line. In some capricious
and hidden ways he is consistent, at least wherever his technical
competence is good. By intention he does not settle for mere ade-
quacy. But even with good and excellent abilities he will often
be found to miscalculate the nature of his tasks or the degrees of
his competence. He will stumble along carelessly and gaily, sometimes zooming to great achievements and perfect solutions, sometimes procrastinating forever some simple and inevitable problems.
He will often not meet deadlines, nor like them in the first place,
even if he himself has set them, and improvise ingeniously at

the last moment. His work will sometimes be sloppy, though usually adequate, and at other times a masterpiece. He will surprise his superiors forever by these fluctuations and his apparent, though not intrinsic, reluctance to take any orders at all.

Should he be in a leading position himself, he will have similar troubles. If engaged in a field of work that has clear outlines and boundaries and requires specific talents, such as chemistry, corporation law, surgery, radio engineering, banking, or even managing sales of a given selection of goods and services, he can be excellent. Sometimes he seems to succeed in a large variety of fields, but closer inspection will usually reveal that he manages to get by on some specific angle that he knows best, or on some technical communality, say finances, of all those fields. He may spend funds assigned to him as if there were infinite, though perhaps irregular, resources. With trance-like determination he will draw on the services of motherly females and even males, not necessarily for the benefit of his business, but always for his personal comfort. Yet his psychological understanding of people, such as those working under him, is often lacking. He did not have to try very hard for insight during his early life. He also tends to be a little weak on the psychological aspects of his business or job. However, he is quick with compliments, flatters well, especially women, often passes out generous, but not very thoughtful, gifts, and treats personal problems with a certain lofty elegance but often without much concern. What he does sense, though, is the talents and achievements of his employees, provided he himself has enough to show of either. He can select quite well and put to work those who are likely to do a technically good job for him. But he has no way of telling whether the personal problems involved are huge or negligible. Some authority above him may well be able to utilize his services quite efficiently, particularly when that authority is an older brother of brother(s) or, perhaps, an only child of well-matched parents (which is somewhat rare). He, the youngest brother of sister(s), may even be taken advantage of in such a situation. On the whole, he would not make a very good president of an enterprise, but a fair-to-good vice-president, and an excellent expert in his specific field of experience.

He does not ordinarily build up or preserve property too well. He may even squander it. Not infrequently, new assets are coming to him overnight and almost from nowhere. He often finds a female who does the building and preserving for him. It may be his wife who checks his proclivities to waste, ramble, fuss, and get nowhere. With proper management by a responsible female his talents and abilities may well be steered toward highly productive and profitable goals. A fortune may accumulate almost without his notice. It may also be lost without arousing his concern. He will tend to have generous and sweeping plans for his children, but often their implementation will be up in the air. To him there is nothing more important than to follow one's own interests and inclinations. Whether they entail riches, security, and prestige, or their opposites, is of no importance.

He can be nice to women, adore and flatter them, he can surprise them by his tact and care, but he does not always do so. He behaves much of the time as if he could afford to forget what women want and as if they would take to him anyway. After all, he has always had them. He has had sisters as far back as he can remember, whereas for the oldest brother of sister(s) there had been a time when he was alone and a time thereafter when, in all likelihood, his sisters were no more than rivals whose sex he had not yet recognized. Since the youngest brother of sisters has always taken women for granted, his efforts to win their favors and all his courtship are somewhat playful, peripheral, or even mildly sarcastic. He likes to show that he can be an endearing person, and in a way he is. There is a certain careless grace about him. But the woman he wins will have to be very kind, soft, and maternal to him, will have to overlook a lot, and count on little support from him except in real emergencies. She must be willing to suffer. Not too infrequently she has suffered some loss early in her life. She cannot have a career of her own, even though she may be an expert in the very same field of work he is in. He wants her in the house as his faithful wife and devoted mother of their children, and as a sounding board and first sponsor for all he undertakes in his profession. He may refer to her as his wonderful spouse who has made it possible for him to succeed in his work. He may claim that he could not have done what he did if it had not been for her. But it does not sound completely convincing, particularly not to his wife. He is not at all aware of how much an active part indeed she had in his success.

As for marriage, he would do best with the oldest sister of brother(s). This could be a truly perfect match. She has been used to boys her junior, and he to girls his senior. They should have neither rank conflict nor sex conflict, although he will be the more dependent one, no matter how independent and efficient he may look in the areas of his greatest talents, and she will be the somewhat dominant and protective one. She may be attractive and even beautiful, but his choice of such a person appears to have come about by accident rather than by keen eyes or specific wishes for women and beauty. What matters more to him is that she promises unconsciously and instinctively to be good with (gifted) "little" boys.

Not infrequently he keeps up close contacts with his sisters, way beyond his wedding. If they are married, that's fine with him, as long as he remains the little darling whom they love even more than their husbands, on whom they can bestow the favors he is used to, and for whose benefit they may even engage their husbands' means and resources. Unknowingly he might provoke arguments among his sisters and their husbands. Often the latter grow jealous of him. Their wives seem to be fonder, more permissive, and more understanding with him than with their own children, let alone husbands. But whether his sisters are married or not, they will try to get some control also over his wife, to advise her on his foibles and see to it that she really takes good care of him. They may even have the newlyweds live in their house. If he has married the older sister of brother(s), and if the sisters are happily married themselves, they will learn soon that his wife does indeed take care of him and they may "let her have him." The wife's (younger) brothers, on the other hand, will probably behave somewhat like her husband. They tend not to let go of her, and she will retain a special fondness for at least one of them, and possibly evoke her husband's jealousy. Yet since he and her brothers have been in similar positions, they will be able to identify with each other and resolve the conflict after a while. (If their sister were married to the *oldest* brother of brother(s) or of sister(s), they may fight a more serious battle with her husband.)

The youngest brother of sister(s) could also marry the oldest sister of sister(s). She would be willing to act the senior, the dominant and responsible one, but she may not be fully reconciled to the fact that she is married to a man. She may be a little belligerent, especially over his insistence on assigning a female role to her—kitchen, children, church, and playing the charming hostess at parties—and he may feel cheated, misunderstood, treated unkindly, and may not infrequently look for refuge and consolation with one of his own sisters. A middle sister would be eligible, as long as she has had a younger brother. The other peer relationships she is used to may conflict with the one that is duplicated in her marriage, but some close friend(s) could easily substitute for those. An only child might be all right, too, if she comes from well-matched parents, say, from a father who has been the youngest brother of sister(s) and a mother who has been the oldest sister of brother(s). Yet why did they have no more than one child? Should her mother have been an only child, too, then her (the daughter's) chances of treating her husband motherly, patiently, and kindly, are small. She will not be satisfied with her "gifted little boy." She wants to be the child herself.

Relatively the poorest match would be the marriage to the youngest sister of sister(s). Neither of them can afford the other the guidance, support, and responsibility they are longing for. He has at least been used to a peer of the opposite sex. If they find guidance outside their marriage, from one of their parents or friends, or if he finds the work and profession that suits him and his (possibly great) talents, their situation may be somewhat better. (He has an advantage over the youngest brother of brother(s) in that he has at least been the first, or oldest, *boy* in his family, no matter how many girls preceded him.) His specific talents and his work may make him the guide of their marriage, in a secondary sense. Occasionally, his wife may bring along an older sister of hers, either to visit frequently or even to live with them and furnish both of them with the guidance they need.

The arrival of a child may come as a bit of a nuisance to him even in the case of an optimal match. He would feel the child to be a rival for all those favors coming from his wife which he had taken so much for granted. He may lose himself more than ever in his work and profession, or at least pretend to. He may come home rarely or go on extensive business trips. This will be more likely if the child is a boy. With a girl he might feel less threatened —as he is still the only boy in the family—and even come to realize how much his wife has been doing for him without his notice. He might do so with a boy, too, provided he and his wife are optimally matched for each other. The oldest sister of brother(s) can usually handle a child in addition to her husband and even employ his cooperation to a greater extent.

The best configuration of children would be a girl first, then boys, then girls, then boys again, as many as she would care to try for. He would just as soon have the minimum number, say two, one, or even none, but he can take them when they come. He can even grow to like them a lot. However, with the poorest match, i.e., marriage to the youngest sister of sister(s), neither of them would want children. If they should have one, a girl would generally be a trifle better than a boy.

He does not make a terribly good father, but his wife, if the oldest sister of brother(s), would tend to be a responsible, though somewhat oversolicitous, mother. She is the one who raises the children, who takes care of all their problems including those arising later on in school. She becomes the person to whom the children turn for advice and help. He is more of a companion to them, but too busy with his own work to be of much use at first. Only when the children grow up and begin to get interested in his profession or in his hobbies, will they be able to reach him as a father. He may have a lot to offer. He may even be a good teacher, but mostly thanks to his competence in his field of work and his absorption in it. In case of a poor match, however, neither parent may have any interest in their children. They may be wise and have none, but if they do, he will often take this as an excuse to grow even more apart from his wife and possibly leave his family in self-righteous protest. In such cases he is a good candidate for showing up with another woman somewhere in no time at all, forgetting forever to pay alimonies.

Male friends matter, although to a lesser extent than they do for the oldest and youngest brothers of brothers only. Youngest brothers of brother(s) may be among his favorites. In a way he can be a little bit their senior. He has been the first, hence potentially the oldest, boy in his family. At the same time he can learn from youngest brother(s) of brothers about the issues prevailing among boys. The youngest brother of brother(s) may have been dominated by his older brother(s), possibly pampered and even made the girl of the family. But he has also identified with his older brothers, at least with one of them, and there was something to learn indeed, it would seem. The youngest brother of sister(s), on the other hand, could learn from his senior sibling(s) only how to be a girl. Another favorable type of friendship would be that with an oldest brother of brother(s), but they might have more conflicts over seniority than one would assume off hand. Besides, the oldest brother of brother(s) would not like his friend to behave like a star and leave all the mess and trash of real life to him. The youngest brother of sister(s) may, however, collect himself vigorously and build up discipline in order to deserve the friend's favors. Friendship with an only child would be among the less likely to succeed, even though he is an only one himself, the only boy. The oldest brother of sister(s) is also among the less likely candidates for friendship. Both of them would probably prefer to pick each other's sisters in spite of the fact that they would not be optimal matches for the girls. Middle brothers would be more eligible again, at least as long as they have had older and/or younger brothers and/or older sisters themselves. Friendship with another youngest brother of sister(s) is possible too in spite of the trend of same-sex friendships in general to avoid partners of identical positions. (Singletons, to note an exception, often choose same-sex singletons for friends.)

The youngest brother of sister(s) is not too popular with the boys. They resent the ways in which he takes help and support for granted. They claim that he always leaves them the mess to clean up. They consider him neither a very pleasant peer, colleague, or comrade nor a very likeable superior, even where his technical competence is unquestioned. Other males get most annoyed with him when he happens to be younger than they are, or no more than their age. Only where the youngest brother of sister(s) associates with men who are by far his juniors can he ordinarily avoid that kind of trouble and quarrels.

It should be mentioned that he may also establish something like friendships or platonic relationships with older women, or women who have held senior positions among their siblings, or both. These may be his real and true friendships, the ones he cares for much more than he does for all those with males.

The more older sisters the youngest brother (of sisters only) has had, the greater will be his difficulties with friendships and marriage. He may be so used to being unique by virtue of his sex, that potential male friends might have a very hard time with him and his careless and seemingly arrogant ways of relating. And he has been used to so many girls catering to him, perhaps even trying to run his life, that he will have trouble resigning himself to one girl only, as he would have to in marriage. Sometimes he may prefer intimate relationships to males. With three, four, or more older sisters presiding over him, he will have adopted some feminine features himself and might attempt later on to relate to males like a female, but also to pick feminine males.

In politics the youngest brother of sister(s) has either almost no opinions or strictly technical and often fairly efficient, though limited, viewpoints. As far as he is concerned, any of the historic or present-day systems may work, if only certain basic principles of economy and expediency are being observed in government, administration, banking, trade, etc. He might not even like to consider, or talk about, politics as a whole. He would prefer some specific aspects. He may be capable of excellent analyses, ideas, and achievements, but he will try to stay within the more or less accidental boundaries of his skills. He lacks the overall or global outlook and the instinct with which some people can very well appraise, and behave in, situations of which they have only a limited grasp or inadequate information. He may be an excellent advocate of a political party, but will be poorer in his under-

standing of the political system of which his party is a part, or
of the world in which this political system is a constituent member.
He will also tend to take many aspects of his own experience and
conditions of life for granted, to refuse to explore others even
where they might be essential, and to be at a loss where other
people or broad and basic problems are to be traced and understood. Somehow he always manages to keep things going, but he
might not have much of an idea what for.

In religion he is either indifferent or conventional. In the
first case, all religions, ancient and present-day alike, are historical
phenomena, no more, nice to look at but nothing to get seriously
or piously involved with. Nevertheless it may be considered fun
to study all of them, or even to compare them for certain aspects,
morality, imagination, and the like. In the second case he tends
to go along with the religion he has grown up with, to believe
without much doubt what it has taught him, even to lead a life
which, on the whole, the minister of his church would recommend
to his community as a fair (though uneventful) compromise between the pursuits of the world and those of God. The minister
may not know that this particular sheep of his flock may cherish
something rather irrelevant to God and the church more than he
does either. All this may be very different, should the special
field of interest or hobby of the youngest brother of sister(s) be
theology. In that case he may excel in religion in general or in his
special field of interest, and rise to high honors within his profession, not so much as a minister or bishop than as an expert of,
say, church history, canonical law, parish administration, preaching,
international relations.

Philosophy does not usually have a grip on him either. He is
not set on history, nor on system building, nor on existentialism.
Yet he may be an excellent historian, or a top logician, if he has
set his heart on it. Even then he is somewhat impatient with any
so-called philosophy of life. He does not believe in anything that
means to pervade the individual and to make him over. Things
are best as they have come to be all by themselves.

Death will come one day, he realizes, but so what! It may
strike you in the midst of your work and fun, or it may crawl

up on you in the sick-bed. With the help of modern medicine and experienced doctors one can fight it to various and often considerable degrees, but ultimately nothing will help against it. Yet when it comes to dying, or when he finds himself in external danger to his life, he will be quite agitated, unstoical, or even behave like a hysteric. He will cling to any straw of hope and especially to any person whom he suspects to have a say in the matter, preferably to a kind nurse or "big sister." At that point, as ever, he has no illusions about death. He knows how thoroughly it will terminate all of him.

Losses of immediate family members will affect him to the degree that he feels their consequences. However, the news of the loss itself tends to leave him strangely unaffected. He may not even put on much of a show of mourning. Often he surprises his relatives and friends by his expectations that the remaining family members step in and give him the help and support he has lost. It does not seem to dawn on him that the other bereaved could have felt, and suffered from, the loss themselves. His mother and his favorite sister are usually the hardest to lose. Their loss may send him into some mild, but restless and agitated, form of depression. For them his mourning may even be sincere and persistent.

If in need he is a ready candidate for psychotherapy, provided he can get a motherly woman for a therapist. In that case he can usually make good use of it. He is not too eager to become a counsellor or psychotherapist himself. That work may appear psychologically too involved for his liking. If he has become one, he tends to be at his best with oldest sisters, fair with girls, not so good with males, poorest with oldest brothers of brothers, all relatively speaking.

## CHAPTER 7

## The Oldest Sister of Sister(s)

She can stand on her own feet, take care of others, and even boss them to an extent. Where she cannot, she would still like to very strongly. There is a certainty and finality in what she has to say that may not always be justified by actual circumstances, whether they concern people, housework, education, art, or politics. She pretends to be surer of herself than she really is, but usually succeeds conveying that impression. Even where she is far from being an expert, she will still have comments, at least to the effect that there is little to comment about. If something is of no interest to her, she will often present it as something that is of no general interest. She can cut people short who know much more than she does on the subject in question. But she can, and usually will, direct group conversations with a certain (loud or quiet) vengeance. If she cannot dominate, she may be unhappy, angry, or aggressively mute.

At work she is likely to be responsible, competent, and to get things done. This is particularly true where she is in some position of leadership. This position need not always be recognized officially. She will tend to identify with her superior, who must be male in order for her to accept his authority. He will have to be distinctly older than she, or in a position distinguished on other grounds that cannot be questioned. He may be an aristocrat. He may come from a foreign country. He may have had a training and experience or won recognition of a kind that she, or any girl, for that matter, could not possibly match; such a male may even be younger than she is and still retain the right to control

others as well as herself. She herself may see to it that everybody obeys and adores him.

Females will have to bow to her in order to win her sympathy or mere tolerance. She will insist on being the final authority with them, work vigorously to establish her claim, always with side-glances and remarks about the relative inferiority of the others. This includes older women and her official female superiors, if she has any. Secretly she despises them and will not rest until she has surpassed them in rank or in achievements, and until the males around her, above all those in leading positions, have given her full credit for her efforts and accomplishments. Only other oldest sisters, usually of sister(s) only, will elicit her respect as long as they remain at a distance and are no contestants.

Taken in all, she is a kind of queen, both conscientious and self-righteous, who will accept orders only from her king father and very few others, but give orders to all kinds of princes and princelings, expect unconditional submission from all ladies and princesses, and do as good a job as her king father will want her to. Depending on his intentions and qualifications, this may be very good, mediocre, or even wicked and despotic.

Property, wealth, and possessions are secondary when compared to her people, above all, to her siblings, children, or those who submit to her reign. Their existence, growth, and welfare are her real wealth, she believes. If she has no people to take care of and direct, she is unhappy, and may feel useless and depressed. She loves anything they do, as long as she can make out that it is not detrimental to her position nor to the (ultimately male and paternal) authority from whom she derives it. The fact that she behaves somewhat like a male herself makes it difficult for girls under her control to identify with her, and hard for the boys to love her. They rather fear her and sometimes cooperate or obey only in order to avoid her wrath and malice.

As for material realities, she likes to be well supplied and to spend freely. She will not incur debts on her own behalf, but may do so for the sake of those entrusted to her, or in order to stimulate, possibly even to punish, an inadequate provider, father, husband, or boss. At work, she likes to draw big salaries, not as an indispensable condition but as a token of appreciation, and she tends to spend it freely and often carelessly, although generally in the service of her work and obligations. If she has nothing left at the end of her career or at the end of her active family life, after her children have married and/or moved to their own homes, it is just as well. But she would hold on to some form of control over the people of her career, business, or family. She may follow her people, even to distant places, and try to continue to run their lives or careers, at least in some of its aspects. She may wish to be consulted on matters of business strategy, or on some specific issue that has been close to her heart before. Where she is deprived of such opportunities, she will bear grudges and sometimes turn quite hostile in general.

For men she is a hard girl to make. She tends to rebuff advances for quite a while. Often she appears so strong and independent that she discourages them anyway. She may be beautiful, but men simply do not think of her as a woman who would want to be conquered or seduced. She does not encourage flirtation and courtship either, much to her own regret when she has set her heart on a man who does not notice this. In that case she will try to boss him around, to test his interest, to disappoint him on purpose, even to talk disparagingly of him with a certain amount of conviction. As long as he has not declared himself, preferably in some humble and utterly devoted way, she is not sure whether she should like or hate him.

What kind of man will take all that from the woman who wants to be loved by him? Only men who are somewhat passive or feminine themselves, or who have been bossed a lot before, or possibly those who have been traumatized by early losses will take it. They, in turn, may relax her sufficiently to bring her more tender and even motherly sides to the fore. She is not all that cool and belligerent as she appears at first. But even after she has found what she has been looking for, her pride is among her greatest concerns. She has chosen him because he struck her fancy, for no other reason, she claims, and if it was an unwise choice, if he is poor, of low origin, inefficient, or even seemingly unworthy of her love, what does it matter? She takes the liberty of loving him anyway.

The best match she could ordinarily make would be the youngest brother of sister(s). He would tolerate her dominance. He would even seek her out for it. And he would have little trouble accepting her as a woman. He may not understand why sometimes she turns obstinate even in the most physical sense. She won't budge in arguments. She will handle household problems, merchants, and parties in her own (stubborn) way and choke his mere attempts to get in a remark. She won't even let him lead her at dances. But he will not mind as long as she takes care of him and the family and lets him pursue his interests. Sometimes she may challenge him even on that. As she will frequently lack his technical competence and talents, she can interfere only peripherally, although in their personal relations to each other she may top him by common sense, female logic, or occasionally by plain meanness.

The youngest brother of brother(s) may also do. Implicitly he will accept her guidance, no matter how numerous and violent their struggles and arguments may be. Neither of them would be too ready to accept the other sex, but he does not mind her being, or trying to be, somewhat of a man. He may like her as a comrade, and she has been looking for someone submissive, someone to mold, anyway. A middle brother would also be a fairly good match as long as he has had one or more older sisters among his siblings. An only child may often do, preferably when his parents have been the oldest sister of brother(s) and the youngest brother of sister(s), or something close to it. An only child has not been used to peers, but this may sometimes give her the advantage she is looking for. The oldest brother of sister(s) would be compatible only insofar as he has been used to the other sex. But generally he would be looking for a junior female, while the oldest sister of sister(s) would be looking for a junior who is not too obviously, or too much of, a male. Among the worst matches that she (or any senior girl, for that matter) can make would be the oldest brother of brother(s). They would have both rank and sex conflicts and a hard time coming to any kind of terms with each other.

Children would be an important relief even in cases of (relatively) optimal matches. She can then let go of her husband and devote her energy to them. She tends to be a proud, powerful, and protective mother, who will retain a certain belligerence against males. Her husband will have to realize that his role in creating their children was utterly minor, and the boys among the children will learn that there is no difference between boys and girls except that boys wear pants. Most girls can lick boys, and certainly she herself can do that with anybody in the family. She would prefer to have girls rather than boys, or girls first, by all means, before she would put up with a boy, too. It would be better even for the boy himself, if he came after one or more girls. If he were the first, his mother would make a hard try at subduing him, at cutting him down in size, at making him feel sorry that he had not been born a girl. If she were married to the oldest brother of brother(s), children may be a most welcome relief, although both parents would tend to wage their war against each other by recruiting the children of their own sex and by agitating and conspiring against those of the opposite sex.

Her best female friends would be younger sisters of sisters. Ordinarily they would have little trouble subordinating themselves to the big sister. They might supplement each other beautifully, even if the friend happens to be the husband's sister or cousin. Such a friend may do some good for the marriage too. The youngest sister of brother(s) would not care too much for what the oldest sister of sister(s) has to offer. She would be more interested in, and freer with, boys anyway, and the oldest sister of sister(s) could not easily let her have such an advantage. She would rather forego her friendship. Oldest sisters of sisters would make friends all right as long as their fields of work and interest do not overlap too closely. She can empathize and understand their problems (with others), but she cannot be too intimate with them, at least in the long run. Middle sisters may make good friends, provided they have had older sisters. Generally, she will tend to act as a kind of fatherly friend to her girl friends, and be aware, if tacitly or unconsciously, that no friendship with a female can match the one with a male. She will use her girl friends as welcome supplements to her marriage or friendships with males. She will even pretend that she lives for girls, but for that pretense she needs men.

The larger the family she comes from, i.e., the greater the number of her sisters, the greater will her difficulties with marriage tend to be. She may not get married at all, or make a very inept match that could not possibly work out even under more favorable circumstances. Nevertheless she will stick to it with fatal persistence, as if to prove to herself and the world that she should never have married, even though she did. If she stays unmarried, she sometimes steers toward nursing or the monastery and is likely to land in a leading position, that of a director of nursing, a chief of the city's social work, or a mother superior. She can preside over many females. In point of fact, there she may be at her best. But the competition of males must be kept from her. Otherwise she may become quite unreasonable, no matter how competent and efficient she had been until then. Again, this does not preclude that she may not do all that for some superior and distant male whose authority she accepts blindly. Occasionally and under opportune circumstances, she may become promiscuous from a position of power. She may take and discard men, in rare cases use them even to generate children. But she will remain the sole authority in her own domain and the sole parent for whatever offspring she may have set her mind on. She may even hire help, including criminals, to get rid of a man she is done with if she cannot otherwise achieve the separation.

Politically she tends to be a conservative, even an outright anti-revolutionary. She believes in legitimate authority, no other, and legitimate is what has been around ever since she can remember. Above all, she believes in her father. Only if he should have been a rebel, may she adopt an unconventional creed, but even then she will be conservative in her own ways. She cannot permit, nor see any need for, change of what her father has left her as a legacy. She will see to it that his will—or the will of somebody like him, of some man vastly superior to everybody around her in age, status, or competence—is being fulfilled. She will believe in the letter of his message rather than in the spirit. The oldest sister of sister(s) as well as her conservativism will be feared rather than loved by the people over whom she reigns, but she will not mind. This is what she wants. All leadership and government must be lawful, and the law must be obeyed under all circumstances. If she does not get what she wants, or if she has been severely disappointed by her father or some other ultimate authority, she may turn into an avenging suffragette, an advocate of women's participation in politics, a supporter of female candidates, or just a belittler of men and their achievements in general.

Something similar holds for religion. She is a theist believing in the absolute reign of God but also in her own infallibility, as long as she lives by God's commandments. God takes an active part in everything that is and happens, but He also puts to work every man and woman alike. He helps nobody who cannot and does not help himself. Justice and morality are His important areas of concern and of His interference. If He strikes by means of fate, He does so justly. The person struck had better look into his past for faults. If He strikes her, the oldest sister of sister(s), the story may be different. She might accept it and love Him even more dearly. Or she might protest violently, especially when she compares her own afflictions with those of others, supposedly much more deserving of punishment than herself. In rare cases, she is an atheist, but then she follows the founder of her brand of atheism or its contemporary high-priest with the same fervor as she would have followed God.

Her interest in philosophy, provided she has it, is likely to be an interest in a great philosopher or wise man, in the principles that guided him, and in their consequences for her. She wants to make him her idol and object of identification, although she will do so only in a restricted sense. It may never dawn on her to study his biography; she may ignore his relations to women, even if they have been a crucial issue in his philosophy. She wants a gospel, and whoever is strong and persuasive enough to have produced one can be her potential hero. His gospel must be articulate and clear-cut, and it must have an effect on people's actions. Romantics, existentialists, or mystics have practically no chances with her, unless they, too, are able to introduce a simple and handy system.

Death will have to strike her by surprise. She cannot be had by it otherwise. She won't lie down for long illness, nor will she pay much attention to her health earlier in her life. The mere thought that something could happen to her, or that she would have to submit to irrational and impersonal forces stronger than herself, is repugnant to her. Death is to be ignored, and where it cannot be she will often put up a primitive and violent fight against it. She may refuse to fall asleep for days in order to keep up vigilance over her failing life. She may even lay hand on herself to evade the grip of death.

Losses of immediate family members can be borne by her without too much suffering as long as she has not yet felt fully responsible for the lost person. Only father must never leave for good. When he does, she will be close to despair and take a long time to recover. Her father's death or loss is the only "punishment" that would really make an impression on her. The loss of her mother, except when occurring in her earliest years of life, would usually be less upsetting, and not too much guilt would be attached to it. She may even admit consciously her own wishes in that direction. The father, however, has frequently been perceived as so powerful and strong that his departure, through death or otherwise, can only have come of his own accord. But then, why would he do such a thing, unless she has not at all lived up to his expectations, or has done something very much against his wishes. As a matter of fact, having left her is not enough punishment. He should have killed her. If it was death that took him from her, oh, how much would she have loved to die in his stead. Yet, once she has recovered from such a loss, she will be the most adamant executor of her father's will.

She is not usually too upset over the loss of any of her sisters either. She can handle whatever guilt she may feel quite well; better anyway than a youngest sister can handle the much more diffuse guilt over the loss of an older sister (see also pages 33, 43, 114). Only when the lost sister has been her favorite, or when she herself, the oldest sister of sister(s), has already begun to consider her sisters her legacy, may she suffer more severely. She has failed in the eyes of her father or some superior authority, if she has let any of them die or get lost. Her task had been to hold the family together, to take care of everyone who needed care, and the little ones have been the most precarious, almost by definition. Such had her father wanted her to do, and she has failed him miserably. The same would hold for her own children, for all people who have submitted to her rule, and even for her husband. Their losses will appear to her as personal failures, sometimes even the result of her own doings. She believes she can never forgive herself.

Should she seek counsel or psychological advice, her problem is often her conduct with men, whom she seems to scare away, and her blind devotion to her father and to strong father figures, but she cannot benefit too easily from such counsel. Her invincible pride is in her way. As a counsellor herself she may sometimes appear to be too domineering and bossy, particularly with men, and possibly not too deep or sensitive in her understanding of women.

## CHAPTER 8

## The Youngest Sister of Sister(s)

She likes an adventurous and colorful life. She wants entertainment and change, and if it does not come quite as she desires,
she may seek it actively, though haphazardly and often on the
spur of the moment. With her nothing ever seems fixed and set-
tled. She is ready to throw her beliefs, achievements, and friends
overboard and go for new sets of them altogether. She is likely
to retain a certain youthfulness way into her old age. As a
matter of fact, she has often looked more dynamic and sparkling
than her sister(s) already at birth or soon thereafter. Men can
challenge her forever to compete with them on almost any issue
that they happen or care to introduce. She is even more competitive with girls, but men will be the most important issue. She has
an advantage over other girls. She can seduce men better, partly
by her greater inclination to submit. She is likely to appear more
feminine than oldest sisters of sisters (who may be too bossy)
and oldest sisters of brothers (who may be too motherly). Although
at first she is more successful with men than other girls, she is too
capricious, willful, competitive, or distractable and unstable to
hold her conquests after a while, or even to stay interested herself.
So she may lose.

At work she can be anything—excellent or erratic in her
accomplishments, a good sport or a sissy, a reliable colleague or a
vicious tattletale. She may be any one of these for good or change
from one to the other depending on external and internal circumstances, both of which are almost never under her complete control. In her attempts to correct them, she will often overshoot the

target. In almost no case would she be a good leader and boss of others. Only with a male boss who knows how to take her as a worker and as a woman, who is fatherly enough to overlook her little flaws and faults and old enough not to qualify as a potential lover, may she be in a position to utilize all she is able to do, and this can be a lot. Perhaps older females, used to positions of seniors from childhood on and willing to guide inconspicuously, if possible without claiming any credit, may be capable of doing likewise, that is, keeping her well and productive at work. What threatens to get her down is her dilettantism. She may be able to do many things reasonably well and incapable of deciding which to embark on. Her preference will be to embark on all, but on none of them for good. She would be at her best at jobs that require high, but somewhat automatic, skills and no decisions to speak of. She makes a good typist or interpreter, she may be an expert on fabrics, in special services, in routine functions of banking or selling, in fashion or advertising. Yet with all her craving for adventure and distraction, she is frequently unoriginal in her contributions at work. She may aspire to be creative, but her aspirations are usually too rushed to do her much good. She may be most creative where she has the least intention to be. She might seek, for once, to be deeply and truly understood, but she would not know for sure when she has been understood and when not. She may be a sucker for anybody pretending empathy, only to end up even less understood and more willful than she had been.

Taken in all, she is a charming, quick, capricious, and yet gullible brat. Her family and friends must always be ready for surprises and ready to pay for them if they entail costs.

Possessions and property may mean a lot to her, but she cannot be expected to create or preserve it. She may marry into it. She may find a rich husband with no trouble at all. Yet she may waste it all with him, if he lets her, or do so by herself, should he die or divorce her with a portion of his wealth as a compensation. Or she may leave him to marry someone richer than he, or richer than an (older) sister's or girl friend's husband. In other cases, however, the youngest sister of sister(s) may not care for riches. She may marry a poor and/or incompetent person out of spite, perhaps because one of her sisters, or all of them, hit it so well financially. Very seldom will she contribute directly to the build-up of any kind of estate, even when she is in a field where this can easily be done and she has the talents. She is too fond of gambling and too ambitious to be able to hold on for long to whatever she may succeed in accumulating.

She tends to be quite attractive to men and fairly inventive in getting places where they come in crowds. She can sparkle in conversation, impress by her dresses and make-up, although both may be a little loud. She can intrigue two, three, and even many more, men at a time, keeping them in expectation for days and weeks—a femme fatale, almost—especially when she is truly concerned with someone else whom she wants to make jealous. She can even be graceful about this, but gradually the men notice that they are not getting very far with her. They begin to suspect that they are chasing a phantom. When she submits to their wishes, probably because she notices the dangers to her interests, her giving in turns out to be just a bit phony. There is a speck of pretense and connivance in the way she lets herself be carried away. When the men notice, and she notices that they do, she may rush to new people or make a desperate move toward her true love. That

may get them together, at last, and if they should decide on the spur
of the moment to get married, if they have children soon, and if
he should be a compatible match to begin with, she may be over
the hump. But if he or she wavers, she may fall into her pattern
of teasing and evasion even with him, discover in her own mind
that perhaps he was not the right one either, and begin to flirt
with others again. Unconsciously she would love to be coerced
by him to give up all that nonsense, but on the surface she is, or
has pretended to be, sufficiently impulsive and arrogant to dis-
courage force. Her true love may believe that if he would try to
take her by force, or any other device of his, she would slap him
in the face and leave.

Her best match would be the oldest brother of sister(s). Indeed, that person is the most likely one to see through her maneuvers and her inner difficulties. He would know what a junior
girl wants, although he may be a little puzzled by her urge to
compete with him on all sorts of issues. If he recognizes that she
does not really have to win, that she merely wants to have a hand
in the matter and get acknowledgment for that, or if he lets her
win at times and in certain respects, they may arrive at a very
good understanding. After all, she is rather willing to submit to
a senior anyway. But she is not used to a male. Getting used to
him, however, may well dispel whatever reservations she had
retained about being guided and even ordered around. He is a
man. That makes the difference. What may have been wrong
coming from her own sisters or oversolicitous girls in general, is
all right coming from him.

The oldest brother of brother(s) would not be quite as good
in marriage, although they would supplement each other for rank.
She would have little difficulty accepting his leadership, and he
is able to provide it. But they may not come very close to each
other as man and woman. They may plan and agree on financial
aspects of their marriage, on the house they want to live in, and
on business matters, but he is less likely than the oldest brother
of sister(s) to awaken the woman in her. They may still get along
all right, but in times of contemplation they may find they are
missing something that they cannot quite name. The arrival of

children, particularly when they are of both sexes, will often make a difference. He will be able to empathize and side with the boys, and she with the girls, and possibly both of them will recognize their spouse's share in the creation of their favorite children. Even before that, the event of birth, the birth of *their* child, may help to bring them closer together as man and woman.

A middle brother or an only child may also be compatible, but the middle brother should have had at least one younger sister among his siblings, preferably one right next to him in age, and the only child ought to come from parents who have been the oldest brother of sister(s) and the youngest sister of brother(s), respectively, or close equivalents. The poorest match she could make would be the youngest brother of brother(s). Not only would both lack experience with a peer of the opposite sex, they would also be in a rank conflict. Either one would try to be the little one and look for leadership in the other, and neither one of them would be able to furnish it. What is worse, not even children would make a difference. They would not be welcome, even if, consciously, both of them believed the opposite. They are likely to try to make a senior out of their child—and one child is usually plenty once they see what it means to keep it—but they are bound to fail for quite a while, possibly forever. Even after their child has come of age and could conceivably be a senior to them, i. e., their guide, their confidant, he will only be able to pretend. He has not learned it from them. Hence he has not learned it at all, unless they have put him up with another family that had been more optimally matched.

Even if she marries most favorably, the youngest sister of sister(s) may have some trouble with her children. She will often talk her husband into hiring someone, a nurse, a maid, a governess, and the like, to take care of the children. Or she may hand them over to him more often than he would like her to; at any rate, more often than other wives would do. Only if he is prepared from the very beginning to take a share of the burden off her shoulders will they get by without arguments and quarrels. Sometimes, if he assumes principal responsibility for the children, she may be able and even eager to take care of them all by herself. At other times

(and more often than with other wives) her own mother may be
called upon and do pretty well with the children, if this does not
conflict with other obligations. The wife wants to remain the child,
together with her own children. Even if she can get her mother to do
as little as some of the cooking, things may already become tolerable for her. The sequence of the children does not matter much,
as long as at least one of them is a boy. She really wants a boy,
not so much per se as for the prestige and implications. She wants
to emulate others who have had boys, or must outdo them. Nevertheless, she would do best with a boy first, then a girl, or boys
first, then girls. But more boys than girls, please, would be her
sentiment. One might think that a series of girls only would also
do, as that is what she had been used to at home. Yet she would
often fall short of an understanding of her daughters except,
maybe, the youngest. If her children fail to arrive in the order and
kind she has planned, she may get quite angry and jealous of other
mothers. She may blame her husband for it, even divorce him,
but at the same time try to deprive him of the children whom she
does not really want herself. So, once she has got them, she may
discard them for another husband. In rare cases she may come
to love her children at last, especially when she does not remarry,
and does not have to compete with a male peer. Needless to say,
all these features will be more pronounced, the poorer the match
she has made.

Her best female friends would be older sisters of sisters. If
there are no men at stake, or if men are not much in contact with
them, they may get along beautifully with each other. Her friend
will guide her and take over many of her responsibilities. She
herself likes to be guided and to serve her friend with devotion.
One or both of them may be married, but they will still get along
with one another as well or better than they do with their husbands.
In fact, their husbands had better leave them with such supplements. Having their friend, the wives may be more fully happy
than with their husbands alone and, this being the case, the husbands will benefit indirectly. Other likely girl friends would be
the oldest and the youngest sister of brothers. Generally, however,
the first one will be less eager for the friendship of a girl than of a

boy, at least as long as he is a junior sibling, and so will be the second one, if the boy is a senior. After a while both types of girl friends may lose interest in her, the youngest sister of sister(s), yet she would continue to seek them out. She is feeling comfortable with the senior girl and senses unconsciously that her friend knows how to handle boys. So she, the youngest sister of sister(s), may learn that from her. She is usually not aware, though, that such an older sister will prefer her to boys only if her relationship to her brothers has not been too lucky. Normally, that oldest sister would be interested in her to the extent that she can furnish her with boys whom the youngest sister of sister(s) has a gift to attract. If the oldest sister of brother(s) would let her be around even after she has got her boy, the youngest sister of sister(s) may still learn little from this, because the boy is likely to be a junior himself. He would be the wrong kind of boy for her. In that respect, the other type of girl friend, the youngest sister of brother(s), would have a little more to offer. She could show her how to treat senior boys, because those would be the ones she would prefer. Even in their direct contact, the youngest sister of brother(s) and the youngest sister of sister(s) are better off. Although the former is a junior sibling, as a girl she is the first one, i.e., potentially the oldest. Hence she may be able to give a little bit of the guidance that the youngest sister of sister(s) is longing for.

Middle sisters who have had younger sisters among their siblings may also qualify as friends. So may an only child, preferably if her mother has been the oldest sister of sister(s). Without knowing why, the youngest sister of sister(s) may like the fact that her friend has not been used to any peers. In that respect she herself has something to teach to her friend, whereas the friend, in turn, may have less need to control others than an oldest sister of sister(s) would. The singleton could let her live beside her more freely and show her how to be a little more independent and how to enlist even the support and sympathy of much older persons, of fatherly and motherly friends, rather than peers.

The greater the number of sisters who preceded her, the greater will her predilection for girl friends tend to be, and the smaller that for boys and marriage. That does not mean that she may not try hard, perhaps even desperately, to meet boys and to marry them. This is not a good condition in which to find the right ones. She may marry just to get away from girls, and then she may have to divorce her husband for lack of too many things, above all love and understanding, and return to girls. She is often sought out by strong women, chairmen of women's clubs and sometimes by manifestly homosexual females or by feminine and artistic men, to be their darling, pet, or little child on whom they may squander tenderness and affection. They will permit her to be willful, moody, and irresponsible. In point of fact, they will be delighted about it, since it proves how much she needs them. She may even arouse jealousies among those females, and one or the other of them may set out to wrest her from the fangs of men to whom she might fall prey, in spite of all protection and warnings.

Politically the youngest sister of sister(s) may be anything. She can switch from one to the other extreme or declare to have no opinion at all. She will support strong and weak leaders, left and right parties, democracy, dictatorship, monarchy, the workers, businessmen, whenever it suits her or, just as often, whenever she can oppose someone else, say, dominant women or arrogant, erratic, dependent, men. When left alone and unchallenged, her tacit preference would be for change, mild or even radical forms of revolution, the rule of feelings, sympathy, group and community spirits, and understanding. Even if she favors a political system, party, or faction, her motive will rarely be clear-cut egotistical. She does not want to benefit personally, say, financially, or in terms of her husband's promotion. She may not be able to benefit, even if she wanted to. She will support a cause, because she likes the man, or has been insulted by one of his opponents, has always had a preference for the poor or for redheads, or because she thinks that justice can never be achieved except in heaven. She may start a campaign one day and refuse to accept the very idea of such campaigns the next day. She may strongly argue for women being in the forefront of politics, instead of just operating from behind the scenes, as the wives of politicians, diplomats, businessmen, industrialists may be content to do. Yet she may also shrink from such a position and even deny women any such rights. She is not sure about how much women really can, or should, do.

Her attitudes to religion are not too different. They may range from utter indifference to fervent concern, from theism to deism and atheism. She may believe in direct contact with God, or she may prefer mediation of all degrees. Yet in all forms of belief she will rather feel than reason about the implications: "God could be remote, hiding way beyond the most distant stars. But God might also flicker in a match that is being lit, or make two people fall in love. God is innermost and omnipresent, and His presence has manifold disguises. If there is no God, His absence is innermost too. There is indeed no God, and God is forever nowhere." All of this may pass in a process of erratic debate about God and for or against him, with moods changing even on the part of God.

In philosophy, should she ever spell one out, she tends to go out on a limb. She believes in the basic goodness of man. Therefore everything should be permitted to man and—more often —to herself. Or she argues that man is governed by greed. There-fore she herself wants nothing or only very little, and it does not matter much whether she gets it or not. It matters even less, though, whether other people get what they want. Occasionally she may be interested in something like the history of philosophy or in logic, and do pretty well with it. In her daily life, however, she may stay singularly unaffected by her philosophy. She might lack that sense of history or that minimum of logic without which a person cannot really manage his or her daily life.

Death is capricious, she would feel. It is dormant for years, yet gnawing away on all of life with invisible persistence. Suddenly it strikes, either to take another long rest again, or to finish all of them off—relatives, friends, and perhaps even herself. Death can be argued with, though. She may find herself talking to "him," bawling him out, or summoning him by superstitious de-vices. Death may even be a lover, his embrace and kiss a sensuous experience, and his permanence a sweet lull.

Losses of immediate family members or dear persons will nevertheless upset her greatly and rather conspicuously. She may be in hysterics. She cannot quite make up her mind as to what to think of the loss. Is it punishment? If it is, can she rage against it, or must she bear it? Is it a blessing? A gift from God so that she, the youngest sister of sister(s), will grow stronger? An omen of worse things to come? A sacrifice? No more than an accident?

The father would generally be the hardest to lose. The mother could be replaced somewhat more easily, unless the loss occurs in her early years of childhood. One of her sisters may take over, especially in cases where that sister had begun to assume the mother's part before the loss occurred. This is more likely, the more sisters there are. With their father, however, they would lose the only man in the family, unless another man gets himself re-cruited fast. But how can he substitute for him who loved her, the little one, so dearly? The mother or the favorite one among her older sisters, the one who has been another mother to her, would come next in impact, should they leave for good or die. But one of the remaining sisters will usually hurry to replace the loss, be a mother to the other children, and (in the case of loss of the mother) even a kind of wife to the father. If he takes another wife, there will be protests from all of them. Even the youngest sister of sister(s) won't like it.

Concerning psychological guidance or psychotherapy, the youngest sister of sister(s) is almost a sucker for it. According to her, it could go on forever, especially if her father, her husband, or a friend of hers is paying the bill. If she should become an advisor or counsellor herself, she would tend to be a little sloppy, careless, and convinced that things will take care of themselves anyway. She would be better with female than with male clients, and probably best, although still not always too successful, with another youngest sister of sister(s).

## CHAPTER 9

## The Oldest Sister of Brother(s)

She can take care of men, at least she could, if one would let her. But usually she does find the opportunities. She is independent and strong in an inconspicuous way. Often one only notices in retrospect how well taken, foresightful, and competent her actions have been. She does not insist on the credit, at least as long as the men whom she did things for get it. She is practical, concrete, of a healthy egotism, and sometimes self-effacing, although chiefly for her men. It's important to her that there is some prospect of retaining the men she has, of finding new ones, or of winning old ones back. Everything else is unimportant. And men tend to like her. They flock to her. They come to her parties and gatherings. They know that she will always have an ear for them, and that she is a good, no, an excellent sport. There is almost nothing in which she would not join, if the men request it, hint at it, or merely need it. Yet she would not participate as a man. She would not wish to compete in what is men's business. Rather, she would assist them like some sort of mother or big, wise sister.

In regular working positions, she does not exactly excel in speed and diligence, but she is fine to have around. She creates an atmosphere that is conducive to good work. She will mediate between quarreling parties. She will even see to it that areas of friction are being worked on and removed. She is the one who undertakes it of her own accord to speak to the boss about it. He will listen to her, because she does not challenge his technical or administrative competence. He would say that she acts and speaks as is becoming to a woman. She gives him the benefit of

her womanly advice on what he would tend to consider side issues. He may find himself following her sentiments which she did not consciously express, and he may decide matters in her spirit, even when she has no technical qualifications to have an opinion on the issue in question. If he should be against women, particularly when they encroach on men's domains, he can still be appeased by *her*. She knows how to take the wind out of the sails of a belligerent male, especially when he rages against women in general and her own boy protégés. Officially in a leading position, she is, in general, tactful and unoffensive to those working under her, shows a strict, yet kind, efficiency, and is able to relegate work gracefully and expediently. If her subordinates fail, she may step in herself, but she is seldom tempted to do it all by herself or insist that she is the only one who can do the job. Such an attitude would be more frequent with the oldest sister of sister(s). In one respect, though, the oldest sister of brother(s) might arouse reluctance and antagonism: she tends to be patronizing. She relegates work because she considers it unimportant, not worth her time. She is often unconvinced of the objective significance of her employees' contributions at work. She lets them make them, of course, but more often because they want to, because they would be unhappy otherwise, rather than because there are deadlines, obligations, factual challenges. What really matters is to keep them happy and herself quietly on top of this lucky condition. If there is urgent work to do, if there is an important commission, if completing the work would be a magnificent achievement, she may very well question the urgency, importance, and magnificence of the issue. "Does it really deserve a change of the pace of my boys," she will ask.

With girls the story at her place of work is different. Their happiness is not as important, to say the least. They can be put to work whether they like it or not. And they will have to accede to her motherly leadership of boys whether she herself is officially in a leading position or not. They are the fillers in her professional life, and they had better accept that. They are of direct interest only insofar as they themselves have a hold on boys or men of interest. Under such circumstances, even friendships between her and the girls may develop.

Material possessions are insignificant compared to the possession of boys or men. If one or more take to her strongly, rely on her, or cannot even live without her, she has got almost all she wants. She may prefer her boy or man to be a money-maker, or rich to begin with. She may remind him of things that ought to be done. Not in detail. After appraising what he has and what he can do, she will simply let him know, explicitly or implicitly, what general landmarks she has in mind for their life together. Depending on her man's qualifications she can be content with much or little —with wealth or nothing but a certain earning capacity on his part. She may possess more money than he does, and his assets could be of another kind, e. g., he could be a great artist or scholar. She would respect his profession and abstain from all direct interference. But she would undertake to run the household, the finances, even the business part of his work. If their assets lie in the same field, she will almost never compete with him or try to outdo him. If both of them should be trained in the same profession, say medicine, she will gladly renounce her career for him and direct their home and community life. Her esteem extends also to her children. Next to men they are the most precious possessions. They may even be more important than men, and for their ultimate benefit she may decide that there will have to be material wealth.

She will have to leave something to the children to draw on in real emergencies. On the whole they will develop their own assets. In fact, they will get all the possible education they want and can take. They will even be pressed through its first stages if they should balk, and she will shy away from no expenses.

The man who gets her for good will usually find himself in very good hands. She wields no great power of fascination. She is no star and no difficult puzzle. She does not baffle her suitors by crazy demands and huge bills. If she is beautiful, she is usually not stunning. Other girls, even those less beautiful than she, may be more attractive to men. She looks so reasonable, responsible, and often friendly, so uncomplicated—but capable of handling complications—and acts with such common sense, that men sometimes do not notice that they are in love with her. The whole situation reminds them so much of home and mother, that it does not occur to them to ask her to marry them. Consequently she usually does have a fairly good choice, but she herself may have to do the proposing. She will have to see through the motions and maneuvers of her "suitors" who may sometimes bring other girls, real dolls, into her house and expect her to take care of both themselves and their dates.

Her best match would be the youngest brother of sister(s). He would be the ideal person to accept what she has to offer. She would love to furnish him with all the things he needs in order to remain a bit of a little boy, a genius of sorts. Both of them have been used to peers of the opposite sex. They will have little trouble accepting each other as man and woman, and they supplement each other in rank. She will lead, and he will love to be led in all but his favorite endeavors; even there he may need some help, at least on their practical and everyday aspects.

Another possible match would be the youngest brother of brother(s). He is likely to have conflicts about accepting her as a woman. He may waver between submitting to her and rebelling against her sex. How can he give in to a woman? Yet, how could he give in to a man? As a matter of fact, men may be the ones to outdo and defeat. He knows that much from his experience at home. With his wife, however, there is no need to, because she is

only a woman. Even so, the oldest sister of brothers may be able
to help him overcome these conflicts, if for no other reason than
that she does not have them herself. She can buffer his outbursts
and usually comfort him unswervingly so that he may ultimately
mitigate his stand. A middle brother may also do, preferably if he
has had an older sister among his siblings. So may an only child,
especially when she has been the oldest sister of a long row of
brothers. To her youngest brother, she may have appeared almost
like a mother, and that is what her husband who had been an only
child would love her to be.

Among the poorest matches, relatively speaking, would be the
oldest brother of brother(s), although he himself would be even
worse off with an oldest sister of sister(s). He would have a conflict
over her sex as well as over her seniority. All her tolerance and
understanding may sometimes not suffice to reconcile him on
either. She would not be induced to retaliate, to be sure, but would
hardly get very far with him. Unconsciously he would like a motherly person, but it should not be as obvious as it is with her. The
oldest brother of sister(s) would also be among the poorer matches,
but he would at least have been used to a peer of the other sex.
Both matches, however, that with an oldest brother of brother(s)
and that with an oldest brother of sister(s), are likely to be helped
by the arrival of children, the first match particularly when the
children are boys. Children would be the juniors that both kinds
of men and she herself have been longing for and that they did not
get in their marital choices.

The oldest sister of brother(s) would like children regardless
of the match she has made. She is willing to take care not only of
her husband but also of any number of children she decides to
have. She is usually the one who makes up her mind about children, and her husband may be expected to agree readily with her.
The order of children that would suit her best is a girl first, then
boys, but almost any sequence is fine with her. If she gets only
girls, she would be the one who has had her boy, her husband,
all along and she need not be afraid of losing him to them, at
least not in optimal matches. If she gets only boys, she will simply
extend to them what she has already been giving to her husband.

Her children will tend to come to her rather than to their father with all their troubles. She knows all the remedies there are, and if there are none on a particular issue, she can console them beautifully. Her husband will usually leave it all to her and enlist her help himself. Unless he is fighting her over seniority rights (as he may be, should he be an oldest brother), he will be either largely unaffected by his children and out of the house a lot when they pester him too much, or he will appear like one of the children himself.

Female friends are less important to her than they would be to the oldest and youngest sister of sister(s) only. Her friendships would be on condition. Her friends would have to serve a purpose. This need not be to their disadvantage, but they would not be loved for their own sakes either. If they have a man on their side, it may be because of that man that the oldest sister of brother(s) takes to them. She believes that she would know better than her girl friend, what this man, or any man, wants. The two of them may share him, or she may even take him away, which would often be the end of their friendship. The oldest sister of brother(s) would not need her girl friend except after the girl has picked herself a new boy. If she is the youngest sister of sister(s), she may have good chances of doing that soon. She can interest and win men easily, but she is a little weak in keeping them. Well, she, the oldest sister of brother(s), is going to help her on that score. The youngest sister of brother(s) can also serve this purpose, but she is less likely to lose her boys, once they have taken to her. Besides she would probably pick boys of senior positions, oldest brothers of sisters or of brothers, and those would not care too much for the oldest sister of brother(s). Or they might, but it would not last very long.

If the oldest sister of brother(s) chooses a girl friend for what she is rather than for what she brings along, she may still prefer the youngest sister of sister(s). That girl will look up to her, the oldest sister of brother(s), as an idol. It will come naturally to her to submit to this big sister, especially since that person has learned how to take care of, and hold on to, boys. She can learn from her how to do likewise, she believes. But there is another side, too.

The oldest sister of sister(s), used to relating to junior boys, may treat her girl friend somewhat like a boy, and if the youngest sister of sister(s) happens to be the one who was brought up to be the boy in a family of girls only, she may like just that. The oldest sister of brother(s) will not ordinarily play that role, though. Only if difficulties at home had prevented her from taking care of younger boys (because of troubles among the parents, or because of losses of, and separations from, the father or her favorite brother, and the like) may she be tempted to take the friendship with the girl for the final thing.

A middle sister may also qualify as a candidate for friendship, preferably if she has had an older sister and perhaps also a younger brother among her siblings. The oldest sister of sister(s) may sometimes seek her out too, although she, the oldest sister of brother(s), would not care too much for her friendship. As a matter of fact, her chief attraction for the oldest sister of sister(s) would be her ease with boys. The latter would also try to learn from the oldest sister of brother(s) how to win them, but she cannot usually count on one thing: getting a boy from her. On the contrary, she may lose a boy whom she has picked to her man-wise girl friend, the oldest sister of brother(s). An only child may be a little more inviting as a friend to the oldest sister of brother(s), particularly when the singleton is willing to be not only the pampered child but also obedient to her friend in all matters that really count, i. e., boys. The chances for friendship are best when the only child's mother has been a youngest sister or a close equivalent.

If the oldest sister of brother(s) has had many brothers, it will be proportionately harder for her to ever settle for one man only. She may still marry, but keep a whole flock of men around—old friends of hers, friends of her husband, or her own brothers. She may be the great woman to whom men come for advice, consolation, and comfort: the haven of their ambitions, longings, and sufferings. She may be the maternal and indirect manager of their artistic, literary, and scientific pursuits, sometimes of no more than their hobbies. She may set up a home where she houses and nurses budding or broke writers. She may be the patron of great scientists; she knows that underneath their brilliant surfaces they are children. She may be hostess to men's business and political gatherings; or the professional hostess in men's clubs, military units and outposts; or the only woman in a parish, taking care of its clergymen's earthly needs. She may do just that for her own brothers: keep house for them or administer the family's estate so that they will always have something to come back to. The more lopsided her sibling situation has been, the more likely is she to take all such ventures seriously, more so than marriage, prospects of children of her own, or any relationship with one man only.

Politically the oldest sister of brother(s) tends to advocate moderation above everything else. She will be more sympathetic to the opposition's point of view than her fellow partisans may like her to be, but she will not really be on the opposition's side either. She believes that, through mediation and discussion, if possible under her auspices, everybody on earth could come to an understanding with everybody else. If they don't, they have not listened to their wives. Because if wives were all like her—and she cannot quite see why they should not be—they would guide their husband politicians, governors, mayors, senators to do the right thing that will bring peace and comfort to everybody. If she happens to be a politician's wife herself, she will often excel in advising him cleverly, even in running a good portion of his affairs, yet all of it unofficially and without demanding public recognition. She is content to govern from behind the scenes, *merely* as a wife and woman. She almost could not do it any other way. If put in a responsible position and prevented from picking younger, talented men with fast minds and a devotion to somewhat senior women to help her, she may have very few ideas of her own.

In religion she tends to be above it all. Her brothers may have had to be religious, and she may have watched that they were, but she would not be sure whether she believes what she preaches. Religion is good for them. She knows that much. However, religion has been made by men much like those whom she directs, she thinks. Religion is a matter of inspiration and genius, but neither would amount to much without kind and caring females. They have always helped the prophets, demigods, and gods along. Proof is

that in many religions women play a secondary role and can assume
only inferior status. Who can make that up but some man oblivious
to the services of women that as much as keep him alive? He is
oblivious because he has had the services all his life. They have
come to him without asking (usually from older sisters, or from
mothers, especially from those who had lost, or never had, husbands). That is why he knows only half the story of life, and that,
in turn, is why all men should be helped and educated to be
religious, why religious men must be helped in order to survive,
and why even God himself can be really understood only by loving
and responsible women.

She may reveal all those attitudes about religion to none but
the scrutinizing eye. As for philosophy, however, she will usually
feel free to express her point of view. Where would the philosophers
of all times be, were it not for women who looked after them and
enabled them to sit back and think it all up? If they had men to
look after them, servants of one kind or another, please, take notice
of the barrenness of their philosophies. Not even philosophers can
do without muses, muses who do the cooking, sewing, cleaning,
nursing, together with sympathetic listening. Those things are the
"kiss" of muses that spells productivity for them. Which goes to
prove that all philosophy starts in the kitchen. If married to a
philosopher herself, she may feel that she has to make demands
on him, say, for a large house, fur coats, or jewels. Yet, her reasons
are pedagogical, she would claim. If she makes these demands, he
will have to write books that sell better than others, and that will
force him to produce a salable philosophy, which will be the better
philosophy anyway. This may be her reasoning, unless she has
brought her means of sustenance into the marriage and happens to
prefer laurels of a less tangible kind.

Death, wherever it occurs, calls for her help and support. She
may find herself consoling people over losses that are harder to
her than to them. She can take almost any loss without being
shaken, except that of her mother in early childhood. She is the
one to whom the mourners will turn with their wails. And when
she herself is dying, she will still do the consoling. Even during
her last minutes she will see to it that her boys are being taken

care of. She will deny pain and fear in order not to aggravate them. She will show them how to die, so that they have something to go by when their own bells are tolling.

The person hardest to lose in her early childhood would be her mother, as already mentioned. She needs her guidance as to how to take care of her brothers and her father. Without it she does not really know how to satisfy their demands, particularly in an emergency, although even then she sometimes rises to it by sensitive inference. At a later time in her life, however, neither the loss of mother nor of father can shatter her. She has already caught on to her responsibilities, which are her brothers, and will grow to almost any stature that their situation may call for. She can stand hell and do miracles as long as she has her brothers. Only if she should lose them too, together with her parents, will she be at an utter loss, no matter how comfortably she may have been put up with foster parents (except maybe those who want her to be the oldest sister to their own little boys; but how many potential foster parents would want just that?). In later life her conscious suffering from a loss of her father will be greater than when losing her mother. Apart from the mother, she was the only girl in the house, a good, reasonable, and responsible one at that, and he (usually) a doting father. The loss of the mother, however, might arouse some guilt, no matter how benign and apparently without conflicts her attitude to her mother may have been. The loss gives her all the men in the family, and that is more than she remembers ever wanting. She doubts that this can go well. Hence, the mother's loss may still be the more difficult one to bear even now. The loss of any one brother can be taken in stride, as long as it was not due to any conceivable fault of hers, and as long as the others remain. Again, the conscious experience may be violent, but not too protracted and consequential. Guilt does not bother her too much either. She may have had strong feelings of rivalry, when her brothers first arrived, but as soon as she realized they were boys all was fine. Even if she has continued to hate one of them, she can take care of her pangs of conscience, should he be the one lost. Her hatred has been articulate. She remembers the time when the little brat had not even been born. She knows what she wishes, and she can bury it efficiently once the wish has come true.

Ordinarily she must be very hard up in order to seek psychological help or guidance. At most times and in most cases she can take care of herself as well as of others. She would much rather act the counsellor or become a psychotherapist herself. If she does, she is usually better with males than with females, particularly when the males have had sisters; on the whole, she is rather easygoing and good.

## CHAPTER 10

## The Youngest Sister of Brother(s)

She can attract men better than other girls can. This holds for most men. She is usually everything a man wants a girl to be: feminine, friendly, and kind; sensitive and tactful; submissive without being subservient, devoted; a good companion of men or at least a rather good sport. In some cases she may be on the extravagant side, or somewhat oblivious of a man's feelings, and occasionally quite selfish, but seldom on serious issues nor ever when she has committed herself to a man. She is a little nondescript in other respects. Even with rather special talents she does not tend to make a career with them. She may start one, but any worthwhile man can sway her into marriage and motherhood—and the latter may come about by accident.

She is in no hurry. She can wait gracefully. Things are often working in her favor without her efforts, at least without all but the very feminine ones. She does not seek mediators, people in power, with services and benefits to give away. Yet she may still find such people. To a greater extent than other women, she is guided by her feelings and instincts but not too infrequently she may be their victim. If a man has got hold of her, she cannot let him go. He may be a notorious no-good, a lousy provider. When drunk, and even when sober, he may beat her, and yet she will take it all. She will even defend him against others. Sometimes her brothers may have to rescue her by force, and even then she may use the first occasion to return to her villain, who, she feels, has got something that no other man she met had. Usually, however, she can be protected by her family from making a poor choice

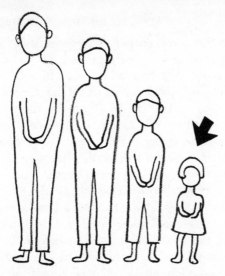

like that although she hardly needs that protection. She senses the
kind of trouble she may be in, and if she could find a man who
is similar but more able and composed, she herself would prefer
him.

At work she is the ideal employee, the best person to work
under somebody's guidance. She is an excellent secretary, particularly to men. She keeps track of everything she is supposed
to and does not have to be told in detail. She senses what is at
stake, even when she does not understand it in all its aspects.
And she serves the purposes of her work by serving the men from
whose minds and hearts those purposes have sprung. She gets
along well with her male fellow workers. They find her nice,
charming, considerate, and trustworthy, although a little too loyal
to her boss and her duties. Women do not always like her. Yet
they are seldom able to put their fingers on what they are griping
about. She is not friendly enough to them. She is not on their
side. She goes after the boss—that's all she ever does. Such may
be their comments, and they contain a speck of truth. The youngest
sister of brother(s) does all this but she does not do it on purpose.
These things are just happening to her. She does not play the
cutie. She really and naturally is one, at least in many cases.

Material possessions mean almost nothing to her, even though they are usually bestowed on her more generously than on others. She is the little one and the only girl among the children in the family. So it is not only her father who chips in a large chunk of property. Her brothers may feel like doing the same, or if they have any influence on her choice of suitors, they may try to get her the richest of them all. Material possessions mean so little, because they seem to come so freely and easily. She has not had to work for them, and she will readily sacrifice them, if this is what her beloved man wants of her. Hence, what she retains or builds up will depend almost exclusively on the husband she gets.

Once married she would want to get a housekeeper soon, even to take her parents' maid along to her new house. She would want to entrust the household chores to her, so that she herself can be the beautiful and devoted wife of her husband. Yet she will just as happily do all the chores herself, if circumstances should demand it. Her greatest material possession is her husband, and if she has found the right one, this holds without reservations. She will go along with him faithfully and graciously, whether he mounts to the highest ranks in his career or in wealth, or has one stroke of hard luck after another. She will often, indeed, be so faithful and gracious that it may move other people to tears. They might try to help her selflessly, and that includes men—even the wolves, at least after their attempts at seducing her have failed. The youngest sister of brother(s) is likely to have a lawyer, a doctor, a pharmacist, a decorator, and an architect among her friends whom she can call upon for advice, appraisals, and help.

Men tend to adore her. Without wanting to, she is likely to attract suitors wherever she goes, and she will never abuse an easy conquest. She is nice and charming with everyone, even those who are not too popular or skillful with girls. Not infrequently she does make men really crazy about her. They love her, even if they can never get her, and she has her ways—literally as well as implicitly—of promising nothing that she would not ordinarily be willing and able to keep. She has learned to take her time with her brothers, and she continues to feel that the supply of men is ample, even if it is not. She is convinced that it is never too late, so that it may occasionally happen that she becomes an old maid.

But she will still retain her charm and rarely be without some kind of suitor or lover. Old or married men fall for her, dote on her, and may ruin themselves, if they are fools. Even then, she is no femme fatale. She is not out to destroy them, although she may do so, by accident. She may feel that if a man is old, he should be able to take care of her like an indulgent father. And if he is married and will not marry her, that she is entitled to an awfully good time. This is not asking very much, is it? She wants a really nice apartment, one of those fancy cars, vacations in some famous resort, and enough spare time to enjoy the company of a few other men. Not that other unmarried girls may not do or wish likewise, but they tend to act with a vengeance. Deep inside they may be quite bitter. Or they may wrest money from one man in order to waste it senselessly on another, who does not even like them. The youngest sister of brother(s) remains friendly and innocent, if not careless, but she is not likely to be anybody's victim who is not pretty much in love with her.

Her best match would be the oldest brother of sister(s). So secure is she, indeed, in matters of men, that she is the most likely of all girls to make her optimal match. Her instincts will tell her soon that an oldest brother of brother(s) is too tough (although he might still be the second-best choice), that the youngest brother of sister(s) is off on a tangent, professionally or otherwise, and that the youngest brother of brother(s) is too erratic and awkard with girls. Subtly and appropriately, she will respond to her boy friends' sibling positions. What is more, their attraction for each other will be mutual. She is the kind of girl that the oldest brother of sister(s) is looking for anyway, and he too knows enough about girls to sense who is good for him and would suit him just right. By character she is a true woman, he would tend to feel, and he could not change that even if he tried to. In all other matters she is like wax and honey. This is what attracts the oldest brother of brother(s) too. He adores that. He would want their love life to be at his discretion too. In fact, she should not have a will of her own. She should be like a timid doe, as far as he is concerned.

A middle brother who has had a younger sister among his

siblings, or an only child whose father had been the oldest brother of sister(s) would also qualify as marriage candidates. Yet even an only child with such an origin may be too much the only one to satisfy her needs. She had been the only one, too, the only girl, that is. She would continue to like that role, but he may not let her have it. The poorest match would be that with the youngest brother of brother(s). Neither he nor she could do very much with a junior. They need the partner to guide them, but cannot find that guidance with each other. Besides, the youngest brother of brother(s) has not been used to a female peer. He will have trouble accepting her sex. The youngest sister of brother(s) will enter such a match only if external circumstances limit her freedom of choice or if losses of family members in early life have shaken her in her confidence.

She will have children either because and when her husband wants her to, or when she feels strongly like presenting her husband with a child. She does not want children for herself. She does not use her husband to have her own children. She wants to delight him with them, and to the extent that he is delighted she will be a good mother. She is neither strong nor domineering, but she will tenderly, patiently, and in some cases with great grace represent him at home, interpret his wishes to their children, and see to it that they are being fulfilled. Not by force. No, she *seduces* the children to be obedient in freedom. She does so by being that herself. By demonstrating in every minute of her life, how wonderful it is to love and submit to a husband, and how wonderful a man that husband of hers is. She will teach her daughters how to be feminine, wise, patient, and yet very much at ease with men. She will be the beloved darling of her sons. They usually have few conflicts about their mother and try to choose a girl of their own after her model. Sometimes they might have trouble disengaging themselves from their adorable mother for a life of their own.

Female friends matter very little. Even if she would like to be friends with girls, men will usually take her away from them, or she will arouse the girls' jealousy and suspicion. But more often she does not seek out other girls. They seek her out, and frequently they do so for obvious reasons, for the boys that she has at her command. Yet neither the oldest sister of brother(s) nor the girl who had been an only child are likely to be able to wrest a boy away from her. And neither the oldest nor the youngest sister of sister(s) are quite as wholeheartedly interested in boys; they may also be trying, unconsciously at least, to win her away from boys and substitute themselves for those, no matter how unlikely the success. The youngest sister of brother(s) just is not interested enough in girls per se. The only one with whom she might get along adequately would be the youngest sister of sister(s). That girl will try to learn from her how to deal with boys, and she herself may, at the same time, be able to utilize her friend's uncanny ways of arousing the interest even of the fanciest boys. What is more, the youngest sister of sister(s) may let go of the boy she brought along more easily with the youngest sister of brother(s) than with other kinds of girl-friends.

If the youngest sister of brother(s) has had many brothers, she may find no other situation but that of home sufficiently attractive in order to give it a try. She may be the one to stay in the parents' house even after all her brothers have left. She will remain the little darling of her parents, particularly her father, and the even greater darling of most of her brothers regardless of whether they are married or bachelors. They will return to her ever so often in order to report, but also to cherish and indulge her. Or she may try to repeat outside the family (more closely than others would try) what she had at home. She may get herself a number of lovers, either at once or in so quick a succession that marriage would not really be possible. She may be mistress to a number of men or masters who would all tend to keep her comfortable and well supplied with the commodities of life. She herself would pick these men, at least as long as she is still relatively young and pretty. Under traumatic conditions—when her family has broken up during her early life, or when some of her brothers have been lost through death or otherwise—or if she should be of low intelligence, she may become plainly promiscuous or a prostitute. Yet even then she will not be bare of a certain grace that may sometimes be sufficient to win her a husband after all.

Politically she is anything that her brothers, her father, her boy-friend or her husband are. Beyond that she believes that women should support their men in their theories and convictions, that they should assist them in their tasks and obligations, and that their own virtues should be feminine above everything else. As a matter of fact, women should not even utter any such beliefs. They should simply have them, implement them in subtle and un- obtrusive ways, and further the causes of all those men who want such women (as well as the causes of all women who are known to have acted in this way already). Often all they can do is be good, faithful, and attractive wives to their husbands. Other men may envy the husbands for the possession of such wives, and people in general may respect these husbands even more. If they succeed in getting such wonderful wives, they must be tops. As long as men will stay in love with their wives and adore their beauty, women have done them the most essential of all favors. In addition the wives would have to take care of the house and their children, and the youngest sister of brother(s) is usually the one who would be completely happy and satisfied with just that. She has practically no ambition beyond it. She does not want a husband who *needs* to be taken care of. She wants to serve him according to his directions, even in matters of kitchen, church, and children. He should be the leader, and never, never the baby.

In religion she is similarly conventional. She believes in God, in submission to God's will, and also in prayer, in humble ap- pealing to Him and in the necessity to please Him by her appear- ance. God wants her to look beautiful, she might well believe. She is no great moralist, no historian, no prophet, and, of her own accord, almost never a fanatic. She feels comfortable in her reli- gion, she loves her church or social engagements dearly, she may even be able to reflect some of her feelings in discussions, perhaps even in poems. But charming and delightful as they may be, they would tend to lack originality. Neutral observers may not find the tiniest spark of genius. They may even deny that her religious experience could possibly have depth, although this would be a little unfair to her. What she lacks most, even in matters of reli- gion, is the urge to excel, to be striking in what she does or says, to stun and surprise people by insights and unusual viewpoints. For her, even very simple statements are filled with feeling, but the statements themselves, when isolated from her personal appearance and from context, tend to be flat, if not trivial. Sometimes, however, she strikes people by the very simplicity, common sense, and instinctive certainty with which she can find the right word or make the right comment.

She has no outspoken philosophy, but she may well have that inner, thoroughly feminine wisdom that can outdo all philosophy no matter how ancient or articulate it might be. She will not be anxious to take care of a philosopher's household, but where she happens to be in that position, she may well add a new dimension to his philosophy rather than slave for him. She will not let him be a bookworm, moving in lifeless, barren thought. She will bring gaiety, fun, and love into his life, again not as a thought-out device but as the thing she cannot help. Even with an amateur philosopher—and not a few men are among those—she will ferment softness rather than discipline of philosophical pursuit, sensuality rather than system, and practicality rather than aloofness. Not that she will show him how to be practical—she is not at her best in that—but her general demands on life will forever tend to force him down to earth. Only if he is already there, his feet on the ground, can he hope to tame and subordinate her. Only then will he succeed in making a patient little lamb out of her that will eat from his hands and be grateful for anything that he cares to give her. To be with that man, for better or for worse, that would then be her philosophy.

Death can really throw her. She has loved so much and so deeply that she can be badly hurt by the loss of the loved. She has put all her stakes on one great bet. She had not even a choice. It all happened as if, in a wonderful fairy tale, the gods saw to it that her happiness was not spoiled. When fate cuts into such a bond, she may be so completely lost, so utterly dejected, that she would want to die herself. And if others are not looking after her, she may well succeed. Very rarely, though, by laying hands upon herself; she just won't do anything to keep living, won't get up, won't eat and drink, won't mingle with people. That's all.

Among those who share a loss, she is likely to be the most severely affected. She is the one whom the others will have to console. Directly, she can do little to soften the loss for them. Yet by the abandon with which she suffers and mourns, by the "recklessness" with which she summons the other losers' support, she may help them after all. It sometimes looks as if she were doing the mourning for all of them, but also as if the others could not conceivably let themselves go to the extent that she does. Who would otherwise take care of this poor little darling?

The loss of any family member will have about the same impact, and in all losses, except that of the mother, there would be boys or men around to substitute. They might even compete with each other to do the most for her and, in the course of this, succeed in both forgetting their own grief and atoning for whatever guilt feelings they might have over the person lost. For the youngest sister of brother(s), the father's loss would tend to diminish in severity and come closer to that of a brother in proportion to the number of brothers she has. They can soften the blow. The loss of the mother will be more severe than that of the father only if it occurs during her early childhood. Even then—and certainly when she is older—she is likely to be successfully mothered by her father and her brothers. Although they may hire a woman or governess to fill the mother's role, or the father may remarry, they themselves will be doing the major share for the girl. Strangely enough, from the ways they behave toward her she will learn what her mother was like as a woman. Although she may have lost her mother so early that identification with her had not yet progressed very far, her father and her brothers carry the mother's image with them and will convey it to her. Since she is quite sensitive and alert to what men want and need, she will sense most of it, all provided that father and mother had been rather optimally matched.

Only when she loses a vastly preferred brother, or father who, in her appreciation, outdid all her brothers, or her beloved husband who had dethroned them all—father and brothers, her favorite among them—only then may she not find enough support among the survivors. She may perish, at least mentally, or, in some cases, wake up to a new reality of life in which she has radically stopped being the little darling girl. Yet no matter which loss it is, there are practically no guilt feelings. She has been sufficiently free of conflict about her dear ones to be free of all self-accusations, should she lose one of them. If it happens that she has hated him, she will take the liberty to express that she did not mind his passing.

Partly because of her ease and good luck with men, she is not too likely to look for psychological guidance or to get into psychotherapy, and if she is in trouble, psychotherapy cannot usually help her either. She rarely becomes a psychotherapist herself, and when she does, there is some danger that she may get herself into extra-therapeutic tangles, especially with men, or that she may be forever on the defensive in order to avoid precisely that. She understands men instinctively and as a woman, but not necessarily as an objective counsellor and listener.

## CHAPTER 11

## Intermediary Sibling Positions

There are other typical sibling positions. A person may have both brothers and sisters. If he is the oldest of them, his character, his interests, and his relationships to people should be a mixture of the character portraits of the oldest brother of brother(s) and of the oldest brother of sister(s). If he has had more brothers than sisters, the first would be more pronounced with him. If he has had more sisters than brothers, the second would be stronger. The same holds for the youngest brother of both brothers and sisters. His character should be a mixture of the portraits of the youngest brother of sister(s) and of the youngest brother of brother(s). Analogous relationships would prevail among girls, oldest as well as youngest, who have had both brothers and sisters. In all these cases the preponderance among a person's siblings of one sex over the other will bias the picture approximately in proportion to the preponderance (see also Part V). Yet all this may be complicated by the parents' own sibling configurations. They could, in principle, sway a person's character even more strongly in the direction of sibling preponderance, but in other cases could also compensate for such a preponderance and annul or counteract its effects (see also Chapters 14-23, and Part V).

A person may also be in any of a large number of middle positions among his siblings. He may be next to the oldest, or next to the youngest. He may be the third one of altogether four, five, or six siblings. He may be precisely in the middle. In all but the last case there tends to be some predominance in one or the

other direction. He may be slightly more of a senior or of a junior, or he may be predominantly a senior or predominantly a junior. Consequently his character tends to lean either slightly or strongly in one direction, and tends to be counteracted strongly or hardly at all by the opposite portrait. If he is precisely in the middle, both character portraits, that of a senior and that of a junior, would blend into each other. As a matter of fact, that person may be a little confused as to *what* he is.

But sex ratio and rank are not the only thing that may vary with middle siblings. The sexes may be distributed in a variety of ways (to be precise: in $2^{n-1}$ ways, where n is the number of children in the family), and the sex distribution must be considered too. It will make a difference whether the middle sibling, say, a boy, has been a junior to two girls and a senior to two boys or vice versa, whether he had both a boy and a girl above him and below him in his family, or whether he had only brothers or only sisters. In the first case his character portrait should be a mixture of that of the youngest brother of sister(s) and that of the oldest brother of brother(s). In the second case it would be the reverse. In the third case he is everything, older as well as younger brother to both boys and girls, and he may indeed be quite baffled, confused, or at least nondescript in character. If he had only brothers, his portrait would be a mixture of that of the oldest brother and that of the youngest brother of brother(s). If he had only sisters, his portrait would be a combination of that of the oldest and that of the youngest brother of sister(s).

If he was not precisely in the middle, but, say, the third of altogether seven children, the same relationships as above would hold, but with a bias. If he has been a junior to two girls and a senior to four boys, the portrait of the oldest brother of brother(s) outweighs the other, that of the youngest brother of sister(s), and vice versa. If he has had one boy and one girl for seniors, and two boys and two girls for juniors, he would be somewhat confused again, but tend to assume more of a senior than of a junior position to both male and female peers. (His next younger brother, however, would be even more confused than he himself.) If he has had only brothers, the portrait of the oldest brother of brother(s) would tend to suppress that of the youngest brother of brother(s) to some extent, and correspondingly, if he has had only sisters.

The same would hold for all other positions and for all girls as well who happen to be in comparable intermediary positions. Heeding further precautions, outlined on page 111, the reader will usually be able to interpolate for these complications intuitively and gauge the degrees to which the basic character portraits should be considered valid. If he is interested in more formal and logical ways of dealing with these complications, he may find Part V useful. Short of this, the following rules of thumb should be observed:

If a *boy* has been the *oldest of* both *brother(s) and sister(s)*, he combines characteristics of an oldest brother of brother(s) and of an oldest brother of sister(s). He is on good terms with boys and girls alike—somewhat softened in the perfectionism that he would demonstrate as the oldest brother of brother(s), and softened, too, in the dislike of the oldest brother of sister(s) for comradeship, male gangs, or simply being one of the boys. He is a relatively kind and tolerant leader of men. In fact, he need not have a leading position at all and may sometimes still be happy. And he will not be, nor feel, quite as cool and irresistible to women as the oldest brother of brother(s) often does.

If a *boy* has been the *youngest of* both *brother(s) and sister(s)*, he tends to be a blend of both types of youngest brothers. He is somewhat less competitive with males than youngest brothers of brother(s) are, but also more successful in securing a steady female to take care of him, if nothing else. He also gets along better with boys, particularly seniors, and is less oblivious of all but his work or hobby than the youngest brother of sister(s) often is.

If a *girl* has been the *oldest of* both *brother(s) and sister(s)*, she tends to be less of a despot, but also less in need of a fatherly male in whose name she can rule over her peers, than the oldest sister of sister(s). She will usually have more specific ideas about what the men obtaining her care and affection should be doing than the oldest sister of brother(s) does. She is less indifferent to the ways in which they achieve happiness at work or play. She may even be reasonably adept in their particular work or play herself.

If a *girl* has been the *youngest of* both *brother(s) and sister(s)*, she will frequently be more truly feminine and submissive than the youngest sister of sister(s) ever is, but she will also have some ambitions other than marrying out of attraction and love alone, regardless of geographic, financial, ethnic, etc., circumstances. She would be less prone than the youngest sister of brother(s) to marry a no-good just because he and she have passionately fallen in love with each other.

If a *boy* has had *older and younger brother(s)*, but no sisters, he usually shows features of both an oldest brother of brother(s) and a youngest brother of brother(s). He may even be somewhat confused about his position. What he would have in common with both the older and the younger is, of course, his lack of experience with girls. With the sex roles reversed, the same would hold for a *girl* who has had only *older and younger sister(s)*, but no brothers. Yet boy and girl alike may find it slightly easier than their oldest or youngest siblings to compromise with, or even settle for, the opposite sex.

If a *boy* has had *older and younger sister(s)*, but no brothers, he tends to be like both an oldest and a youngest brother of sister(s). He will have trouble making friends with men. They will consider him pampered. In some cases, especially when he has had a great many sisters, it may be hard for him to relate to girls other than his sisters, or ever to get married. It may look to him as though he could not possibly do better than he had it at home. If a *girl* has had *older and younger brother(s)*, but no sisters, she tends to be like both a youngest and an oldest sister of brother(s). She too would not be very popular with her own kind, girls, and is very choosy with men, so much so, indeed, that sometimes she stays unmarried, or when she marries remains closer to some or all of her brothers than she appears to be to her husband.

If a *boy* has *older brother(s) and younger sister(s)*, he is somewhat like a youngest brother of brother(s) and like an oldest brother of sister(s). These two portraits may even be in conflict within himself. He may be most comfortable with a split of the sexes in his family and even among his friends. Boys and girls should be separate and he permitted to move back and forth between them. Otherwise his oldest brother, or oldest brothers of sister(s) among his friends, may outdo him with the girls, he feels, and he is often correct.

If a *boy* has *older sister(s) and younger brother(s)*, he, too, has to assume a different rank for females and males, and may also tend to wish, or keep, them apart while being with them, although he usually feels somewhat less urgent about it than the middle sibling of older brother(s) and younger sister(s). After all, he is the first, and oldest, boy. The girls are his masters only as far as they behave like little mothers.

Middle siblings who are *girls* would show analogous trends. If they have had *older sisters and younger brothers*, they tend to be submissive with their sisters and girls in general, but protective and motherly with the boys. If they are in the company of both sexes at the same time, they are likely to feel uneasy. If middle girls have *older brothers and younger sisters*, they will be in a similar conflict, but it may be less pronounced. They lead the girls' submission to the boys, so to speak, and there is usually little doubt in their minds that such a state of subordination is in order.

If a *boy* has both *older brother(s) and older sisters(s)*, but only *younger brother(s)*, the portraits blending in him are that of a middle brother of brother(s) and of a younger brother of sister(s). In fact, he may sometimes appear to be the latter, but he is a little shy and timid about girls and would not take their services, if he can get them, quite so much for granted.

Analogously, a *girl* who has had *older brother(s) and older sister(s)*, but only *younger sister(s)*, will behave like a younger sister of brother(s) as well as like the middle sister of sister(s). Yet she too may impress others more as a younger sister of brother(s), but would tend to be less comfortable with boys than a true youngest sister of brother(s) would.

If a *boy* has had both *older brother(s) and older sister(s)*, but only *younger sister(s)*, he will show features of a middle brother of (older and younger) sisters, but also those of a youngest brother of brother(s). In fact, he is usually able to get along with men somewhat better than an only boy growing up in the midst of girls might. There would also be less danger for him of remaining single for the reason that he could never have it so good again. He did not have it that good at home. He had not had all the girls to himself. Some of them were taken away by his brothers.

Similarly, if a *girl* has had *older brother(s) and older sister(s)*, but only *younger brother(s)*, her character will be a mixture of the portrait of a middle sister of brothers and that of a youngest sister of sister(s). She too has less trouble than the middle sister of brothers making friends with girls and settling for one man only in marriage, but she is also considerably less erratic and competitive than a youngest sister of sister(s).

If a *boy* has had *younger brother(s) and younger sister(s)*, but only *older brother(s)*, he will partly act like a middle brother of brothers and partly like the oldest brother of sister(s). In fact, the latter may be his stronger role, although compared to an oldest brother of sister(s) he would tend to value higher, and enjoy more, the company of males. He may also be a little less sure and less at ease in his conduct with girls.

Likewise, if a *girl* has had *younger brother(s) and younger sister(s)*, but only *older sister(s)*, she is ordinarily a blend of a middle sister of sisters and of the oldest sister of brother(s). But she will be somewhat less insistent on taking care of men, and be on better terms with girls, than the oldest sister of brother(s) would tend to be.

If a *boy* has had *younger brother(s) and younger sister(s)*, but only *older sister(s)*, he combines features of a middle brother of sisters and and an oldest brother of brother(s). However, he is usually on better terms with men than the first and has less need to control or even to make over the girl of his choice than the second. He would also tend to be less irritated by the fact that he can marry only one woman at a time than the first one.

Similarly if a *girl* has had *younger brother(s) and younger sister(s)*, but only *older brother(s)*, she will partly appear like a middle sister of brothers and partly like the oldest sister of sister(s). She will also be on better terms with her like, i.e., girls, more content with conventional monogamy, and more likely to marry, no matter how large the number of her brothers, than the middle sister of brothers tends to be. She would also be less difficult to entice or conquer by men than the oldest sister of sister(s) often is.

Finally, if a *boy* or a *girl* have had both *older and younger brothers and older and younger sisters*, all major character portraits tend to blend in them. Such persons will be the least descript of all. They are prepared for practically all possible types of friends and marriage partners, and yet in a way for none. Whatever relationship they have with one person, they would already miss other relationships. They cannot choose utterly wrong; some sibling relationship will almost always be duplicated by their partner. But they cannot choose altogether right either. A multitude of relationships, a sort of clan of couples with a few single men and women mingled among them, preferably when representing all types of character within the group, may make such a person more fully happy. This holds, provided that this person has not been too unhappy with the sibling configuration to begin with. If the parents were in severe conflict with each other as well as with some of their children, or if losses have struck either the parents or the person and the siblings themselves, he or she may be unhappy indeed, confused about what he really is, male or female, the guide or the guided, boss of males or of females, or rather their subordinate, etc., and even anxious to leave the family as soon as possible—sometimes in order to emigrate to a distant land and start all over, sometimes to help others help themselves.

What should also be considered and may well make a difference on the grounds outlined before (see page 15), is the *age difference* among the siblings. The smaller it is between any two of them, the greater and more inextricable is the influence that they would be likely to exert on each other. The greater the age difference, the smaller this influence. A difference of six years or more may make semi-singletons of the siblings involved, provided there are only two, or if the others are separated from them by even wider age gaps. In a larger number of siblings, those that are closer to each other in age are likely to form closer ties than they would with the rest.

Even mere *proximity* in sibling position may tip the balance. The sibling who is a person's immediate neighbor has a greater effect than a sibling farther away. Thus, if a boy has been followed by a younger brother and by two still younger sisters, the character of the oldest brother of brother(s) would dominate to a degree over that of the oldest brother of sister(s). By the same token the younger of the two brothers may be a more even blend between a youngest brother of brother(s) and the oldest brother of sister(s), whereas the youngest girl would show more strongly the features of a youngest sister of sister(s) than of a youngest sister of brother(s). What might happen in this constellation is that the second brother and the older of the girls form one couple, and the oldest brother and the youngest sister another, willynilly. Before the last child had arrived, the oldest brother may have adopted the baby girl in the family. After he had put up with his younger brother, she was not threatening him as a rival, especially since she was of the opposite sex. (As a matter of fact, such a combination may be something like an exception to the proximity-law. The sibling once removed from the person in question may be like a direct neighbor, if the sibling in between is of the same sex as the person in question.) If, however, as in the example given, there is still another sibling of the opposite sex following, proximity may win. The middle two form the stronger of the two pairs, and their characters get built accordingly.

With a larger number of siblings, there is always a tendency to *split up* into smaller groups. Age gaps, proximity, sex distribution, but also special events at certain times, such as migration, substitution of a parent, who has left or died, loss of a sibling, etc., determine the subdivisions. Uneven number of boys and girls may still lead to the formation of couples, but leave out the rest. Any such sibling may be a mild kind of outcast or a member of the peer group that is merely not fully in on things that matter. Even a sibling configuration of boys only, or of girls only, may split up into subgroups. A physically stronger and more vital child may pair off with the more passive, feminine, or pretty among his, or her, siblings, and a more artistic child may find himself inclining toward the scientist, the leader, the football player, or the engineer among the siblings.

Physical resemblances, related talents and interests, but certain mutual experiences, too, such as school, summer camp, a trip (in which other siblings did not participate—yet, one would wonder on what basis did fate or, more frequently and particularly, the parents single them out for such an experience in the first place), or even traumatic events, accidents, losses, etc., may also make for closer bonds between some of the siblings. In case of a person coming from a large family and holding an intermediary position among his siblings, it may be wise to establish by some means who his closest siblings were. But merely asking him who he was closest to or who he liked best may not always do the trick. Firmer and more chronic criteria, such as frequency and duration of actual contact, sharing rooms, common residences away from home, etc., may have to be traced before the observer can judge a relationship. Otherwise the person questioned may well be referring to the siblings he would most want to be *like* rather than to be *with*, i.e., to a relationship of identification rather than one that is complementary and mutual. All of these considerations would hold likewise for females.

It should also be mentioned that in rapidly growing societies intermediary sibling positions are bound to outnumber those at the ends. Families with five or more children may be frequent. Yet, in the modern and more industrialized societies, families of four or three children are more likely, and in cities the average is even less. Therefore, one could say that the sibling positions which are discussed more fully in this book are in the upsurge. Apart from that, the major portraits outlined are likely to recur more frequently than expected even in large families, not only as blends of two or three portraits, but even in fair purity. A sibling configuration of, say, twelve children will inevitably split up, usually in a number of ways, and identifications may cut across them. By age and otherwise, the oldest sibling of such a family could potentially be the parent of the youngest. There may be two or three older brothers, one of them specifically of sisters, because two girls followed him. Then there may have been an age gap, and still another girl may lead the rest of the siblings. Analogous considerations would hold for younger siblings.

## CHAPTER 12

## The Only Child

Trivial as it may sound, the chief characteristic of the only child is that he is the only one of his kind, and that he remains a child often way into adulthood. He or she has not been used to the omnipresence of other children at home. Neighbors or cousins cannot make up for it, because they are not around the house at almost all times and occasions as siblings are. With foster siblings it is a different story, but even with them it will be established shortly in his, or her, mind that he, or she, is the only *true* child. The others are secondary fixtures. They seldom have the impact that real siblings would have on a child who has been the only one merely until they arrived. In fact, all oldest siblings have been single children for a while. It has been indicated (pages 33, 72) therein lies even a certain advantage over their siblings, at least those of the same sex. When the oldest siblings recognize that their position is being contested by the newcomers, they have a clearer idea of what to wish for than their siblings ever will. They want to get rid of them and reinstate the original condition. Hence they can curb, control, and even "forget" the wish, better than younger siblings of the same sex can. Hence the irresistible urge of the latter to compete with, outdo, overcome, or dispose of, seniors or all those supposedly better than themselves.

For the only child, even more than for all other sibling positions, it is hard to imagine, let alone assume, any sibling position but the one he or she has *actually* held. Hence what might have happened to the only child—the thought that he, or she, might have become the senior sibling—will dwindle in its effectiveness

about as fast as a senior sibling forgets that he ever was an only child. Time works in favor of what happened in reality rather than in favor of any possibilities that remain imaginary.

In case of a *male*, the only child is used to being the favorite of two adults, his parents, their pride and joy. He is used to winning acclaim, arousing sympathy, concern, sorrow, and the like, and getting all possible support on a moment's notice. Hence he will tend to believe at work that, here too, he should be the center of his peers' and his superiors' attention. He does not admit to it but may believe, notwithstanding, that his entire work situation has been arranged so that he may display his talents. Yet he does not mind revealing his faults and shortcomings either. He may even be blandly ready to make a fool of himself, as long as he succeeds in capturing everybody's attention.

Material possessions are of little importance in and of themselves. Implicitly he knows that his greatest assets, other than his own actual—and sometimes great—talents, are his parents or those who come after them and are willing to take their part. But he will take whatever they bestow on him for granted and have it end right there. That is, he would not of his own accord tend to think of improving the estate and finally passing it on to others, such as his relatives or children. Yet if, for one reason or another, material possessions have captured his fancy, or if they turn out to be instrumental to longed-for pleasures and experiences, or if they throw the necessary light on the stage of his existence, things may be different. If, indeed, his talents do make him a star, he can be found dictating his own prices arbitrarily and accumulating possessions or money in conspicuous quantities.

In his relationship to women as well as in his friendships with males, one could say that he is prepared for all types of partners. Yet he is not really ready for any peer relationship at all. He will rather be looking for mother and father figures respectively. They may have to let him be the infant prodigy forever and may have to take care of his wordly affairs. The spouse had better see to it that there be no children (especially when she is an only child herself), or perhaps just one child, and that she can take care by herself of everything involved (or, in cases where she is an only child, that adequate help and support by a parent or parent figure is guaranteed). Her husband does not have much use for children except maybe for one that turns out to be the spitting image of himself. The friends of an only male child had better count on no great sacrifices, although, for the heck of it, he may sometimes make them. Then, however, they usually come not because of their need, but because the sacrifices matter so little to the benefactor.

The only way in which he can assume features of a sibling position other than that of a singleton is by *identification* with his parents, mostly his father. And since there is no sibling around, no brother or sister to practice his identification on, he will have to turn to his mother. There, however, he gets into conflict with his actual age. He would act a part that is beyond him, no matter how composed, how much like a gentleman, he may look on the surface. After all, he *is* a child (and his parents may want him even to stay one). What may also keep him from adopting more of his father's sibling position is the fact that, if he were to have siblings, he would be their senior. They could only come after him. If they came before him, they would already have been

there by the time he was born. This possibility, however remote
it may seem to him, might make the male singleton take after
his father somewhat more easily when the father had been an
oldest brother of brother(s) and/or sister(s) or a singleton himself. All other paternal sibling positions would be in conflict with
what he, the son, might have been besides a singleton. The spouse
to get along better than others with such an only child would be
a junior, preferably of brother(s). In fact, of all comparable
matches with *strict peers*, psychologically speaking, that any male
singleton can make this might turn out well as often as the
logically best: an oldest sister of brother(s). Sometimes a middle
sister who combines both features may also do.

In case of a *female*, the only child would show similar trends.
She would tend to be somewhat more capricious, extravagant, and
even selfish, than other girls. It is rather difficult for her to
understand what really goes on in other people's minds, except
for those few who seem to understand hers. She may be obedient
and responsible to her parents, but only if they are crazy about

her, and if they do on most occasions what she wants them to. She comes to believe, tacitly or even loudly, that she is the most precious of all princesses, and there is hardly a prince who would be good enough for her. He may be subjected to every kind of humiliation for a test. Yet even after she has condescended to marry someone, she is prone to run back to her parents one day and have them comfort her effusively, while she pouts.

At work—if ever she gets around to it—she is often a nuisance. Not that she could not work. She may have excellent capabilities. But she won't do it for the purposes that her employers have in mind. She is often ready to find thousands of excuses for not doing or doing things that she is or is not, respectively, expected to. She will be a poor sport with her colleagues. And she will exasperate even the most tolerant boss, sometimes because her father or mother may have had a hand in getting her the job in the first place. Her father and her boss may be business friends. So she can't be fired. Only where she finds a congenial milieu, preferably with older, kind, and extremely tolerant, superiors, may she live up to their expectations and actually do quite excellent work, at least for stretches of time.

She wants everything on which she happens to have set her mind, but her mind appears whimsical. Material goods may not matter in detail, yet by the carload they may fascinate her. She may ask for the most fantastic presents and favors, along with very trivial ones, and she can get equally upset, if either kind does not arrive. She is not competing, though. It does not occur to her to ask for more, or less, or as much as friends, cousins, or peers in general might be getting. She does not compare herself to them. She wants what she wants. She makes her demands known, needs her parents and some parent-like friends or even "lovers" to satisfy them, and is totally indifferent to what others are getting from other sources. Only her parents or paternal protectors must not seriously be solicited by anyone but herself.

Friendship and marriage will usually work out only if she finds kind, tolerant, mature, and preferably (much) older partners. She is at her best with someone who loves her whims as part of the display of her beauty or charm, somebody who does not mind suffering all kinds of little tortures at her hands. This will hold particularly for her husband. Friends of the couple may sometimes think of him as a fool or masochist. If she is to have any children at all, he will have to take care of them or provide her with nurses and servants. For her part, she could do without children. Should her husband be an only child too, they will, with great likelihood, remain childless; the few exceptions tend to prove that they should have. As a matter of fact, such a marriage would hardly work unless both of them have powerful outside or professional interests in common. Like her male counterpart, she too is prepared for all types of friends and spouses and yet for none, because she cannot really stand a peer. She can only stand parents.

She too has a chance of turning into a peer herself only to the extent that she identifies with her parents, primarily her mother. She can learn from her how a woman with her sibling position would relate to a man, and she has chiefly her father on whom to try it out first. Yet just as with the male singleton, she would have to do more than her age can possibly give. Hence she must appear quite precocious and sophisticated in some respects, and at the same time remain very much the child in others. She may look quite mature in discussions of literature, fashion, politics, or even a particular science or profession, but be utterly dependent upon guidance by benevolent superiors or parents, if put to work. Also she may develop a very good psychology (psychological insight, that is) of her parents and other mostly older people, but she can utilize very little of it in her own affairs, particularly with people of her own age. Since she too would be a potential senior—all siblings she might have had would have had to come after her; otherwise they would have been there already—she would pick up her mother's sibling position more easily, if the mother had been an oldest sister of brother(s) and/or sister(s), or a singleton, than if she had been anything else. The difference is likely to be slight, though. Yet it may be responsible for the somewhat equal likelihood of female singletons in general to match adequately with a spouse who had been a junior himself, preferably to sister(s), or a spouse who had been a senior himself, also to sister(s). A female only child would also do fairly well with a middle brother combining the characteristics of both sibling positions.

The overall characteristics of the only child, male and female alike, tend to hold up as drastically as outlined in cases where the same-sex parent has also been an only child. More often the parents have come from larger families and will convey to their own child whatever they are by their own sibling position. Hence it is more imperative with appraisals of only children than all other sibling positions to investigate the parents' family constellation, especially that of the same-sex parent. An only child, male, will be different depending on whether his father had been the oldest or the youngest brother of brother(s), or of sister(s), or whether he has been in any of the intermediary positions. He will partly duplicate his father's traits, interests, and kinds of relationships. He may indeed appear to be himself whatever his father had been in his own family. Yet on closer inspection, some features of the only child will usually reveal themselves too.

The same holds for the female only child. Her mother's sibling position plays an important part in her own psychological make-up. She may behave somewhat like an oldest or youngest sister, or somewhere in between, and it may look as if she had been used to peers of the same sex only, or to those of the opposite sex, or both. It will somehow seem as if she could get along with peers after all. Yet in a situation of stress, under conditions of fatigue, boredom, extreme external, physical, or social restriction, etc., she may turn into the impatient, egocentric, and moody singleton after all, at least as long as the special predicament lasts.

At any rate, with singletons the same-sex parent's sibling position is the one to be considered, and if that parent happens to have been a singleton himself, his own same-sex parent will have to be investigated. His sibling position would descend on his grandchild only in dilution, to be sure, but there may still be traces that can make the person in question look not quite like a single child.

Under all circumstances, however, one should ask the question why there has been only one child. What was wrong with the parents? In many cases of only children, conflicts prevailing between their parents, losses suffered, but also illness, late marriage, etc., would all tend to account for some of the difficulties that only children seem to be having.

## CHAPTER 13

## Twins

They are a twosome that is different from that of any other two siblings. They were together from birth on. There is no real senior or junior, although one will have been born a little earlier than the other. The parents may sometimes expand on that issue, using it to account for other differences they think they have discovered and that they are taking issue with, such as resemblances, looks, intelligence, and the like. As a matter of fact, the parents may be transplanting their own conflicts into their twins.

If the twins are the only children that the parents have, they will behave like brother and sister, like two brothers, or like two sisters, depending on what their sexes are. Yet ordinarily there is no senior-junior problem. They are of the same age and the same rank. Hence, the character portraits of the oldest and the youngest brother will blend for each of the twin boys, and that of the oldest sister and the youngest sister for the twin girls. In the case of two boys or two girls, the pairs will eventually have some trouble separating and taking the step into marriage. Sometimes marriage to another set of twins may do the trick—get them married—but twins do not come frequently enough to allow for such a solution as a rule. In the case of a pair, i.e., boy and girl, the twins will have the same trouble of ever letting go of each other and could benefit similarly from marriage to another set of twins. They would be used, though, to a peer of the opposite sex. Marriage would be easier for them. Supplementary contacts with same-sex friends will be less urgent.

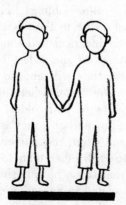

Identical twins have an even more intensive problem. They have been not only a twosome, as far back as they can remember, they have been the *same*. Hence separation for the sake of outside friendships or marriage may be even harder, and the urge to marry other twins, preferably identical too, will be comparatively stronger. But for them, too, twins just do not come frequently enough to offer them adequate chances, although twins or their parents may go out of their ways to provide the opportunities. Sometimes identical twins may find themselves with one common friend, lover, or beloved, and of all same-sex siblings they may mind such a situation the least. Since they are so much alike, and since they have learned to identify with each other so thoroughly (in lieu of becoming one single person altogether, which unconsciously they are likely to wish for with all their heart, more so than other siblings and even non-identical twins), they can empathize with each other and be content with the other's satisfactions to degrees unknown to other siblings.

In some respects it might be easier for twins, than it would look at first, to marry two people who are not related to each other. The newcomers, who ordinarily have had no appreciable contacts with each other, may find it fun to join this twosome. In turn, they might help wean the twins from each other for real life and adulthood, so that they could eventually separate, even go to different parts of the world, if necessary, without any great upsets.

If twins do have other siblings, the picture sketched will be overlaid by that belonging to their position among them. If they are same-sex or even identical twins and lead their siblings, they will also show features of the oldest brother or oldest sister. If they have come last, they will appear like youngest brothers or sisters. And if they were somewhere in the middle, they would combine characteristics of both oldest and youngest siblings. If they are a pair, i.e., boy and girl, they will be like oldest, youngest, or middle brother and sister, respectively. Yet in all cases they will tend to be closer to each other than to the rest of their siblings; for this they will sometimes be punished, sometimes envied, and occasionally even isolated in an active effort by the others.

If twins who have lived and grown up with each other for any length of time are separated, their loss will be greater than any comparable loss of a sibling suffered by others. In fact the twins may work so excruciatingly and radically toward forgetting each other, after such a loss, that they may really succeed, and live on as if they had never had a twin. Which only goes to show how much they have lost. Milder cases of that sort would be something like voluntary breaks with each other in later life, as they might also occur among siblings in general. Yet while siblings can usually be reconciled, those who have been inseparable at first, the twins, may never get together again upon separation. Usually, however, twins tend to be glued together more tightly than ordinary siblings, and more often stay attached to each other for a lifetime.

What holds for twins, is true of triplets, quadruplets, etc., too. Since these are so rare and usually considered (and thereby often made) a specialty where occurring, they can be foregone in this context.

# PART III

## Major Types of Relations to Parents

## CHAPTER 14

## Methodological Considerations

It has been said before (see page 10) that parents are the most important people in any person's life. Yet nearly everybody's parents are considerably older than he is himself, at least chronologically speaking, and they are always a man and a woman. Thus compared to the large variety of possible sibling configurations of which a person may have been a member as he grew up, his parents offer little diversification in those crude aspects.

Yet the parents' characters as well as the nature of their relationship to each other and to the person in question will still be quite different in different cases. In our game of Family Constellation, these differences can be treated analogously to the ways in which the person himself has been handled. The parents' sibling configurations predispose them for certain character portraits rather than others, and their relationship to each other can be established as compatible, conflict-laden to various degrees, or incompatible. In this game, parents are, above all, former siblings. What is more: their influence upon a person may agree or disagree to various extents with the influence which a person's own sibling configuration exerts on him.

A multitude of types of parental matches can come to combine with any of a multitude of configurations among their children. This is one more reason to call Family Constellation a game. If it would not allow for a broad variety, it would be a scheme or tabulation rather than a game. As it is, the variety possible looks infinite. That means that only the most important patterns of interaction between the parents' sibling configurations and that of the person in question can be outlined.

The patterns discussed are those of *identification with the same-sex parent* and of the conflicts resulting therefrom. Although there will always be some identification with the opposite-sex parent too, the former outweighs the latter in most cases, and where it does not, there are usually plausible reasons deriving straight from the principles of the game.

The patterns discussed are also those of *direct relationships to the opposite-sex parent*. These are determined by the relationship prevailing between the parents themselves, and co-determined by, as well as reflected in, a person's relationship to his opposite-sex siblings. A sibling of the opposite sex, however, will generally identify with a person's opposite-sex parent and also have conflicts of various degrees in proportion to the difference between the parent's and his or her own sibling configuration.

The relationships between fathers and daughters as well as between mothers and sons are, in a way, implicit in all that has been said about compatibility of spouses. A parent and his opposite-sex child are compatible, or in various degrees of conflict, with each other by the same rules. One difference is, that nothing can come of the parent-child relationship, no marriage, that is, and no children. Yet, this relationship tends to make all the difference in the world for those heterosexual relationships that *are* allowed to develop fully.

If there are no siblings of the opposite sex (if there are only boys or only girls in a family), the relationship prevailing among the parents decides more or less all by itself what kind of relationship to the opposite sex the children learn to envisage. It has been emphasized all along that persons coming from monosexual sibling configurations are better prepared for friendships with persons of their own sex than for love-relationships and marriage, but whatever training and experience for the latter they can accumulate in their early lives depends ordinarily on what they see their parents do to each other.

The amount of conflict prevailing among the parents will, under all circumstances, tend to aggravate proportionately the problems a person may be heading for in marriage. These problems include conflicts between a person's own sibling position and that of the same-sex and opposite-sex parent. Hence the patterns of relationships, outlined in Part III, tend generally to be the more pronounced in their complications the more conflict there is among a person's parents, and patterns without complications may get some from these conflicts.

On the other hand, time will be a mitigator and healer. As parents and children grow older, their conflicts tend to stabilize, and overtly there may be little trouble. Underneath the surface, however, they continue to be active. If they break into the open, often over an unreasonably small provocation, they may be more severe than anybody in the family or among friends had of late been expecting. Readers who have been surprised by such outbursts in their own families may find some special comforts and consolations in the following chapters.

As for research method, each of the sixty-four basic types of conflict between parents and children has been empirically derived from a minimum of two cases for which the following criterion had to be fulfilled in addition: neither the parents nor the person in question had suffered early losses of parents or siblings (see also pp. 20, 21). It will be noted that one half of these basic types of conflict is somewhat like a mirror image of the other half.

## CHAPTER 15

## Father the Oldest Brother of Brother(s)

If a father had been the oldest brother of brother(s), his relationship to sons will generally tend to be better than that to daughters, although he is inclined to over-control both of them and manipulate them beyond necessity. In some cases, however, particularly in those where there are only daughters, the father may learn belatedly, and from scratch, what a female is like and how she would want to be treated. His daughters would slowly grow on him.

If a *son* is the *youngest brother of sister(s)*, he develops trends in two directions, that of an oldest brother of brother(s) and that of a youngest brother of sister(s). Hence he may be in some conflict with his father. The latter would want him to be a responsible leader, loyal to his same-sex friends and tough with women. The son, of his own accord, would pursue his talents, be taken care of by girls, and not give a damn about boy-friends. There are likely to be arguments. The father resents the oblivion which makes his son pursue only what he likes, and the abandon with which the son has the girls in the house, and other girls too, cater to him. Thus the son often tries to evade the father's influence or anger. The mother may even help him do so, and as a consequence arguments may prevail also between father and mother. He, the boy, will appear to be the chief cause of these arguments.

If a *son* is the *youngest brother of brother(s)*, he has little trouble learning from his father how to be a man. It may well be that the two of them can get along splendidly with each other. The father may treat him as if he were his own younger brother

129

rather than his son. He may treat him better, in fact, than he ever treated any of his own brothers. This may bring the son into conflict with his older siblings on various grounds. They may be jealous of the father. They would want to play the seniors for their brother and, if can be, learn from the father how to do that. Instead, the father will do it himself and not give them a chance. On the other hand, if they would try to be like this favorite youngest son of his, they will usually fail to win the father, feel rejected by him, and sometimes come to hate, and conspire against, their little brother. However, the more older brothers there are intervening between father and the youngest brother, the less outspoken will be the relationship between the two.

If a *son* is the *oldest brother of sister(s)*, he may learn how to get along with girls better than his father ever did. The son may even make a considerable impression on his mother. She may find him kinder, gentler, and potentially a better future husband (unfortunately to a woman other than herself) than her own husband had ever been. So the father may be quite jealous of him, resent his easy ways with girls, despise him for not being enough of a man, worker, and leader, and part with him in anger. Yet the father has tended not to grant him even the slightest status of that sort at home. Indeed, he may not grant him anything that is coming from the girls in the family, and thereby intimidate his boy, sometimes to the point of incapacitating him for marriage. Once father and son have parted they may grow closer to each other again, but while together, there is a stubborn struggle over who is boss, in spite of some, occasionally even considerable, agreement on life and work as a whole.

If a *son* is the *oldest brother of brother(s)*, just like his father, there will be little conflict between the two, at least as long as the son tries both to stay out of his father's way and to model himself after him. The latter would come naturally to the son anyway, and the father could well accept his son's efforts to emulate him. He may eventually want him to take over some of his own business affairs, at least in all those cases where the son has given ample evidence that he can think and act in the spirit of his father. The old man may send him out as a representative, ask him to set up a branch office, or relinquish some of his tasks in order to make room for the son. The mother will be somewhat left out from such a team, but one or more of the younger brothers who will be in protest against the leader pair, may side with her and carry her banner. The greater the number of younger brothers, the more likely is it that the oldest brother and the father can divide their authorities even right in their home.

If a *daughter* is the *oldest sister of brother(s)*, she tends to antagonize the father by her interest and concern in her brothers. The father may argue that they should grow up and become men first before making the demands that his daughter seems to be fulfilling for them. On the other hand, being a grown man himself, he cannot ask of his daughter to take care of him, no matter how much he would secretly want just that. Therefore, he is often somewhat ambivalent. She irritates him in a way that he cannot quite spell out. He resents what seems to him like a claim of hers to leadership. He is jealous of her success with young men, and worries that she is being too kind to them, yet if they are taking advantage of her, he is often reluctant to offer her the help she may need. Sometimes he cannot even bring himself to say a word of consolation. This might be her complaint, but actually she is not likely to get herself into such a situation.

If a *daughter* is the *oldest sister of sister(s)*, she tends to get along with the father fairly well. She is not terribly close to him, but desires to execute his will and his intentions with respect to his daughters, and usually manages to do so. She is the most obedient female in the family, but also the most taxing and adamant with respect to all others. She enforces her father's discipline. She may even remind her mother of it at times. The father, in turn, tends to rely on her blindly, without ever giving her much credit. Sometimes, he may be outright inconsiderate and nasty to her, but she does not seem to mind too much nor for too long. She has his permanent confidence, and that is all that matters. She may hate her sisters, though, for his greater tolerance of, and patience with, them. As if it were their fault rather than the father's.

If a *daughter* is the *youngest sister of brother(s)*, she and the father are generally on good terms with each other, although as she grows up she may begin to get along even better with her brothers. In fact, if it were not for his sons and later on for his daughter's suitors, their relationship might be called perfect. She is feminine, submissive, and invites a man's help and protection in ways that can hardly be resisted. Only she should not invite so many men. She should be choosy, spare herself for just the right man and reject all others. The father cannot quite see that this may be precisely what she is doing of her own accord. She is in no great hurry to get married. Secretly the father wishes that she would never marry but stay with him. He would deny such a charge vehemently, though unconsciously he may still be rigging the situation in his favor. Usually, however, the girl will find her husband after all.

If a *daughter* is the *youngest sister of sister(s)*, she tends to be father's (capricious and even vicious) little pet. She can get away with almost everything. In fact, the oldest sister may receive the verbal spanking that the youngest deserves. The father dotes on the youngest. He may behave like a moon-struck fool, make her lavish presents, and pay extravagant bills for her. Unconsciously he encourages her to run them up, in the first place. Sometimes it appears as if he were looking for punishment and had singled her out to inflict it—punishment perhaps for his anger that all his children were girls. His last child was his final disappointment in that respect, but she is also the last one he should blame for it. He is aware of that. When she has come of age, she delights him particularly with her treatment of suitors. She seems to tease them forever, and that suits the old man just right. He does not really want to let go of her. He also loves her spark and irridescent ambitions at work. She is among the few persons who could outdo him, or beat him to something, without his minding it. He would even love her to do it.

## CHAPTER 16

## Father the Youngest Brother of Brother(s)

If the father had been the youngest brother of brother(s), his relationship to his children tends to be less than paternal, to say the least. He gets along better with sons than with daughters, especially with those sons who are disciplined and willing to assume responsibilities of all kinds—in business chores, routine work, the household, and school. If he has several daughters, or daughters only, he may find himself catering to them, mainly because they, or at least the older among them, are inclined to cooperate with any of his moods and erratic endeavors, to chip in the work that is necessary, and never really to egg him on to compete with them. Why not? Because they are *only* women, he would feel, although somewhat with a chuckle.

If a *son* is the *oldest brother of sister(s)*, he is likely to be in conflict with his father. The son would, on one hand, be willing to take responsibility and act as a guide for a junior. But this junior should be a woman. As a matter of fact, this is precisely why he resents taking care of his father's affairs. The father should be able to handle them himself. Besides he should understand more about women. He is old enough. The father, in turn, will neither notice that he is not handling his affairs independently, but looking for guidance instead, nor approve of his son's ease with women and power over them. The father may resent him particularly for his luck with his own wife, especially when she is a younger sister herself. Indeed, not even his own mother, i.e., the boy's grandmother, may be immune to the boy's charm. Yet the conflicts pre-

133

vailing among the parents, if both of them are juniors, may also serve to wear out, or stifle from the start, that charm of his.

If a *son* is the *youngest brother of sister(s)*, father and son may be fairly good friends. Not only because with the son's birth there was a boy at last, but also because the son grew up to realize that he was the first, and potentially the oldest, son. The father will feel much less competitive than he would with a senior peer. And the son would be able to pick up from his father what the father had been—a younger brother of brother(s)—and what the father must have identified with to some extent: his older brother(s). In fact, the arrival of such a son may even do some good, retroactively, to the father's relationship with his brother(s). As regards the mother, it would be helpful if she were an oldest sister, preferably of brother(s). She could furnish down-to-earth guidance for both, father and son. And her daughters might help out, if they see the mother provide guidance.

If a *son* is the *youngest brother of brother(s)*, like his father, they may have an intrinsic understanding of each other—as far as they are capable of understanding other people, in general. But they have trouble acting on this understanding or even making sense of it. What they have is probably a mutual feeling of being understood. If the father's older sons have not succeeded in taking care of him and helping out in his responsibilities, business, home, and family—being merely children, they cannot really at first— he tends to pin all his hopes on the last son. He feels encouraged in that, because he recognizes himself so much in the little boy. Yet this is exactly what he has no use for: a little boy. It hardly makes a difference whether he keeps him intimately around or sends him off on obligations all his own. He does not even have a well-defined task for his youngest son, to begin with. The older brothers will have to take both of them, father and youngest brother, under their own wings. Otherwise the two may forever be off on tangents.

If a *son* is the *oldest brother of brother(s)*, he may find himself getting along with his father quite nicely. The father will tend to relegate to him all sorts of decisions and even his business as soon as he possibly can. He usually continues to have a hand in it, but his son is the secret, or even official, leader. The father may well be able to accept from him what he would not dream of taking from his own older brother(s). With his son, there can be no doubt about seniority. He, the father, has been the first one, chronologically. He has even been his son's creator. And the boy does not seem to go for women, including his mother, in any great way. He does not seem to need them. So there is no reason for jealousy either.

If a *daughter* is the *youngest sister of brother(s)*, she and her father have trouble getting along with each other. He would want his daughter to understand him in all his many (erratic and often irresponsible) pursuits. She should even understand the personal problems he has with his wife or with his colleagues and superiors at work who, he claims, do not understand *him*. He may even bear a grudge against his sons on those counts and expect her to side with him. She, on the other hand, may be receiving such pleasant and kind attention from her brother(s), that the father is not very attractive to her. She too wants to be understood, to be sure, but by men, and as a woman. Anyway, she is so much more graceful about it than the father, and she seems to be getting understanding, courtesy, and affection without having to ask for it. Men just give it, and her father resents that she gets it. He would want it for himself.

If a *daughter* is the *youngest sister of sister(s)*, she and the father have one thing in common: they feel misunderstood by other family members and even people outside the family. They are in agreement on that issue, but they cannot furnish each other with the understanding they long for. It also suits the father that she is not serious about any of her dates and male friends. That way she could stay available to him, say for long sessions of general gossip and philosophy in which they can bewail the world's and man's shortcomings. Even so, the father does not like nor quite understand the effort and time she is spending on young men. If she does not really want them, why doesn't she cut them out of her mind altogether. Sometimes father and daughter may be scurrying after their many goals so fervently that they do not run into each other for weeks and months. As soon as they do, though, they seem to be in their old rapport at once.

If a *daughter* is the *oldest sister of brother(s)*, she and her father tend to get along quite well. She can do something for him. She can take care of him, and he loves that. Only she should not take care of her brothers, too. *They* do not need that, the father feels, the older brothers because they *can* get along by themselves and the younger ones because they should be able to. They should take *him* for an example; he, too, had to learn how to stand on his own two feet. The father's jealousy will be more pronounced in cases in which he had not found his optimal match, i.e., a wife who had been the oldest sister of brother(s). In case of an optimal match, however, the men in the family may divide the girls between them and even switch the girls, on occasion. Under such conditions it may not be too difficult for the father to let her marry. Her optimal match, a youngest brother of sister(s), would be fine with the father, too. In fact, he and his son-in-law might become good friends in their own rights.

If a *daughter* is the *oldest sister of sister(s)*, she would tend to take responsibility for the girls and the father, but she would not find in her father the guidance she needs in order to take over. If her mother has been an oldest sister herself, she may get the guidance from her. Yet it might not be quite right that way either. Much would depend on whether the mother's father had been an oldest brother himself. In that case, the grandfather's authority may, directly or via mother, serve as the guide that the oldest sister of sister(s) is looking for. If the mother had been the oldest sister of brother(s), she would know how to treat, and cater to, men, so that the daughter could learn from her. Yet neither mother nor father would tend to help her much in the task that she feels has been carved out for her: leading and educating her sisters. Usually she takes care of her father all right and does him a lot of good, at least subjectively, but often she will be somewhat baffled and, unconsciously, may harbor pity and disdain. The father does not seem to mind this subtlety as long as she produces effects he can rely on. And he likes it that, partly out of responsibility, she is not eager to marry quickly or waste much time on men.

## CHAPTER 17

## Father the Oldest Brother of Sister(s)

If the father had been the oldest brother of sister(s), he tends to be on better terms with daughters than he would be with sons. They are his darlings and, sometimes, can get away with almost anything as far as he is concerned. His wife, however, generally sees to it that the limit is something more tangible than the sky. With sons, he is prone to show less patience, and they had better catch on. Their identification with the father concerns above all his relationship to women, their mother in particular, rather than his relationship to men, work, property, etc.

If a *son* is the *youngest brother of brother(s)*, he is often quite confused about his father. He may try to relate to him with devotion and submission, a thing he would resent doing to his brothers, but the father is not much interested in him. The father does not understand him, the son feels. He wants so much of him, but the father seems to give so little. Besides, the son is too confused about women—the mother is the only one in the house—to be able to benefit from his father's ease with women and the delight he takes in them. Sometimes, however, particularly when the father did not marry optimally (did not marry a younger sister of brothers), the youngest son may be chosen to be the darling, the baby, even the girl of the family, and if this agrees with the boy, things may look all right, for the time being. Even the mother may like a child, at last, who is a little bit like herself. Later on the son may have trouble turning into a man and choosing a woman for marriage.

If a *son* is the *oldest brother of brother(s)*, there will be conflict between him and the father on two issues: their authority position in the family and elsewhere, and the treatment of women. The son can learn from the father how to treat juniors as if they were women. Yet his own juniors, his brothers, are male. So who is the leader of the boys? The father, who does not quite know, or care to know, how to handle them, or he himself who knows almost nobody but boys? This is one of the problems father and son will have to work out. The son's other problem is, how one impresses a woman. In spite of all his efforts to excel in work, leadership, and courage—more precisely, to outdo the father on all those counts—the father still seems to hit it off much better with the mother and other women than he can. Sometimes, much to his chagrin, even his own fiancée or spouse may develop a peculiar affinity for his father.

If a *son* is the *youngest brother of sister(s)*, he and his father are somewhat in conflict over how to treat women, although both of·them have been used to them from childhood on. The father is their master—considerate, but firm—their admirer, and connoisseur. The son takes the care and help from his sisters for granted and sometimes hardly bothers to look up from his work or fun as they serve him. If the father has not made his optimal match, the mother may aggravate the conflict by siding with the boy. On the other hand, father and son may still be pretty good friends. Ordinarily, a friendship between males of these types would dissolve almost as soon as it had formed, because both men are more interested in girls. In this special case, however, they are held together by circumstances, and their complementary rank relationship is even enhanced by their chronological age.

If a *son* is the *oldest brother of sister(s)*, he and the father are in identical, or at least similar, positions and may have a very good understanding of each other. But they will have to beware of getting into the same waters. They need clearly delineated separate fields of pursuit, even though, or just because, their pursuits are so much alike. Since their chief interest and attraction is women, they will have to divide those between themselves. The father gets the mother and perhaps one of the daughters, and he, the son, gets a little bit of mother, too, and another of the father's daughters. Or the father gets the mother, and the son gets the daughters. Or the father may get his daughters, and the son may have the mother to himself. Such would be their deals.

If a *daughter* is the *oldest sister of sister(s)*, she and the father have trouble with each other, even though he knows how to treat girls, and though she would ordinarily be most willing to take his orders. She is not the right kind of girl, he may feel. If she were not his daughter but just any woman, she would leave him strangely cold or strike him funny, although he respects his daughter's intentions. And she, in turn, may rack her brains in order to extract instructions from her father, without succeeding to her satisfaction. He will usually give her some instructions, but mostly just to please her. She cannot quite understand what is missing between them. She may notice sadly that one of her sisters, often the youngest, has hit it off so much better with him. Under the father's influence, she may turn quite feminine later on and become rather popular with the boys. And the father does not even mind it. He loves her to have that kind of fun, which to her only proves that the world is not just at all.

If a *daughter* is the *oldest sister of brother(s)*, she and her father may struggle over their rank. She does not want to bend or bow. She tends to believe that men are little boys who need to be taken care of. Otherwise they could not even survive. The father does not agree at all. If he has married optimally, i.e., the youngest sister of brother(s), he will often refer the daughter to her mother, or praise the mother as the person from whom she should learn. The mother, however, is not very obvious or impressive as an example. It might happen, though, that the daughter tacitly assumes a somewhat parental role with both of her parents. Her mother may let her do that in any event, but the father will too, if the daughter can muster an ally, such as the father's mother. Besides, the father will notice that some of his male friends, colleagues, business partners, and the like, seem to be quite impressed with his daughter, and since he is a ladies' man rather than a great pal of the boys, this may come in quite handy. She could help out there, or even take over.

If a *daughter* is the *youngest sister of sister(s)*, she and the father tend to get along nicely. Not that he would approve of all her high-flying and frequently changing plans. And he does not like her conduct with the boys; she is overdoing it. He may feel sorry for a guy whom she has mistreated. But even so it looks as if she could do no wrong with him. In fact, she may actually *do* less wrong than youngest sisters of sisters who have other types of fathers. He may refine her ambitions, so that she will not drive so ceaselessly and insatiably for higher honors than the men in the race, nor try to entice and have more men than all other girls. Thanks to her father, she may even be able to settle for one man only all of her own accord, not merely out of fear or coercion, as might be expected of a youngest sister of sister(s). If the father has not married optimally, though, it may happen that the two of them, father and daughter, form a sort of inseparable couple, and that their rapport with each other may even work to preclude her marriage.

If a *daughter* is the *youngest sister of brother(s),* she and the father tend to have a very good and mutually satisfactory relationship with each other. She will usually love "her daddy" dearly, and he is fond of his little darling. He teaches his sons to be exceedingly nice to her. He can and will entrust her to their care with increasing confidence as she grows up, but it will always be clear to all of them that he is forever available to her when needed. Sometimes he likes to single out his daughter and leave the mother to his sons. Yet, if he has married optimally, there is generally no question that his wife comes first. She and father love each other the most, it seems. That is also why father and daughter, in spite of their great affection for one another, can separate gracefully when she is taking the man of her choice for a husband.

## CHAPTER 18

## Father the Youngest Brother of Sister(s)

If the father is the youngest brother of sister(s), he tends to prefer his daughters somewhat to his sons. He is forever likely to press his childhood advantage, whether consciously or unconsciously, that he was the first and only boy in his family. As such, he was catered to and spoiled by women to an extent that makes it hard for him to be whole-heartedly a father to any of his children. He relies on his wife for that, and she had better be an oldest sister of brother(s). If she is, she can handle the children, and him, too.

If a *son* is the *oldest brother of brother(s)*, he and his father may not be too much in each other's way, but the father will also offer very little guidance for his son. The opposite happens: as soon as the son is barely ready, the father literally expects him to do the man's work in the house, to take responsibility for daily chores, for helping his wife, even for guiding or taking care of the rest of his children. Hence, before the oldest son has learned to meet such thoughtless demands, he will live through a period of considerable uncertainty and insecurity, during which he has largely his own resources and experiences to draw on. Only in cases of optimal (and close to optimal) matches among the parents will the mother furnish the guidance that the father fails to provide. But how can the mother teach him to be the leader of his brothers? And, if she is able to, how can he help but become somewhat motherly, hence also somewhat feminine? In that case, he may find it hard to return to full masculinity one day and look for a suitable spouse.

If a *son* is the *youngest brother of sister(s)*, just like his father, the two are likely not to contest each other. In fact, if the father has married the oldest sister of brother(s) and is intent on

141

keeping her for himself, and if the son sticks to his own older sister(s), father and son may not even notice each other very much. And if the son should not be getting quite the care and the service from his sister(s) that the mother seems to be squandering on the father, the son may be watching his father for clues to his success. That is about all that the father can offer him. He cannot usually guide him out of his plight or even explain it to him. Nor may he notice that he is being looked over by his son. This holds for the father's areas of work and interest, too. He is often quite absorbed by it, but still does very little to help his (eager) son along.

If a *son is the youngest brother of brother(s)*, father and son tend to get along fairly well with each other. Although unlikely to be as paternal and protective as other fathers, the father will be aroused by this type of son just about as much in that respect as he can ever be aroused. He is a youngest himself, but he has been the first and only *boy* in his family. Hence he has something to offer to his son who is a junior of boys. He can show him how to pursue his own interests, regardless of circumstances and other people, and thereby possibly help furnish him with a professional attitude that he would not have otherwise. And the son might even pick up from the father what his older brothers failed to learn: how to make mother—and other females, for that matter—cater to him and offer their devoted, self-effacing services. He is the least likely of all the children in that family to become a kind of mother for other boys, or to stay so, to his own disadvantage, as an adult.

If a *son* is the *oldest brother of sister(s)*, he and the father have no trouble appreciating women, but they are prone to do so in different ways. The father takes them as a matter of course, whereas the son begins almost from childhood on to court and protect them. The father's principal goal is frequently something other than women. The son's ultimate striving is for a woman. The father may find his son uncanny at times; he may wonder where he learned to deal so well with the ladies. Yet, since the father's wife is likely to be the oldest sister of brother(s), if he has chosen optimally, she may not like her son's sovereignty over women nor his assurance with them, at least not for her own part. The son's sister(s) tend to feel neglected by the father, but adored and pampered all right by their brother. Hence, father and son may have less trouble in dividing their empires fairly than would this father and a son who is the youngest brother of sister(s); they find them divided before they make up their minds. What is more, the father may discover that his son could even help him put his daughters under their father's control. The daughters can get from the son what does not occur to the father to give to them. In turn, they may give to him a bit of what his son does not particularly want to get: their unconditional devotion and service.

If a *daughter* is the *youngest sister of sister(s)*, she and her father tend to have not too much in common. The father has been used to maternal indulgence and continues to expect it from his wife and daughters. His youngest daughter, however, would be the spoiled one in her own right. She may ordinarily be permitted to compete *with* men and *for* men with a vehemence and abandon impermissible, if not inconceivable, to her sister(s). But the father has no use for either kind of competition. All he wants is to devote his time and energy to his favorite subjects, work, or hobbies, and leave the household chores and children—even boys, if he has any —to his wife and his daughters. Only the mother, preferably if the oldest sister of brother(s), can narrow that gap a bit and mediate so that the daughter does not feel quite as powerless and discouraged with men as she did with her father.

If a *daughter* is the *youngest sister of brother(s)*, she too gets to know little of her father, although she probably misses him much less than the youngest sister of sister(s) would. She has her brother(s) to pamper and adore her, and her mother to show her how to take care even of a man who has been spoiled, such as her father. Not that she would ever practice this daily, but she may rise to an occasion and earn the father's fleeting praise. While the father is not too concerned with her, on the whole, the mother would be, especially if she is the father's optimal match, i.e., an oldest sister of brother(s). She would envy her daughter because the brothers dote on her. Yet she would resent these sons, should they try to give her, the mother, a bit of the same treatment; she would not quite believe that they could do it, even if they actually did. If the mother were an oldest sister of sister(s), or a youngest sister herself, she would, again, figure more in the girl's mind than the father. He is a little too out of the way for her.

If a *daughter* is the *oldest sister of sister(s)*, she and the father may get along all right. She would want him to offer her guidance, though, and he may fail her on that. But not infrequently his competency in a field of work—competency that is partly the result of the abandon with which he pursues his work—may furnish that guidance after all. He may not be a very good father, but he often is an expert in a science, in law, in a business, sometimes even a genius, and that would imbue him with the authority that he lacks otherwise. His daughter may have been floundering for quite a while in her search for a god, but at last she catches up with her father and finds some leadership. however specific and technical. From there on, she may even come to her father's full attention, join him in his work, and take charge of the rest of his daughters.

If a *daughter* is the *oldest sister of brother(s)*, she and the father are usually blissfully happy with each other. She takes care of him as she has seen her mother do it, and as she has practiced it with her brother(s). She even steps in for her mother, when the latter is busy with her sons, or substitutes for her mother altogether, if the mother should be out of the house or otherwise off duty. The father can get along all right as long as his wife is an oldest sister of brother(s), and as long as he has at least one of the two, his wife or his daughter, look after him. He may be perfectly satisfied with his daughter's marriage one day, especially when his sons have married before her. He knows that, should he lose his wife, either temporarily or for good, he could always count on his daughter. She would take him into her and her husband's house. Even his sons, more likely to marry oldest sisters of brother(s) than other types of girls, may provide him with substitutes for his wife; in emergencies he could count on his daughters-in-law, at least on one of them. The father does not even think about such things in advance. Implicitly, he takes them all for granted. And his daughter often buys every bit of it; all this apparent selfishness, that is.

## CHAPTER 19

## Mother the Oldest Sister of Sister(s)

If a mother is the oldest sister of sister(s), she will ordinarily get along better with her daughters than with her sons. However, she may tend to exercise too much power and control over both of them, and thereby either impose herself too thoroughly as a model of identification, or drive the daughters away much sooner than she would want them to leave the house, whether for careers or marriage. Her effect on her sons may be more clearly on the negative side. Somehow she seems to resent them. This is at least what they would pick up, and if she is the only woman to go by, such as when the children are all boys and still quite young, they may be intimidated for keeps.

If a *daughter* is the *youngest sister of brother(s)*, she is prone to digress from her mother's plans and wishes in various ways. The mother would want her to be devoted to a worthy cause, and the mother would determine which one. She would also wish her daughter to stick with the girls rather than the boys. And, by all means, she has to stop her inadvertent seductions of boys or she will end up badly. The daughter, on the other hand, may be puzzled by what she (justly) feels is undue rigor, if not malice. To escape her mother, she may get married haphazardly or run away from home, usually with a man. In most cases, however, the brothers or even her father know how to prevent that. They may act as buffers, and mother may not like it. Even if she does not mind, she might still argue persistently that they are spoiling the daughter.

If a *daughter* is the *youngest sister of sister(s)*, the mother may get along with her rather well, if not splendidly. She will

145

behave toward her as if she were a younger sister. In fact, she may be much more at ease with her than she was with her own sisters or her older daughters. Her urge to subordinate them under her will (which tends to derive from some older male's authority—her father's, boss's, or God's) may have worn off by then. Her older daughters would have taken the brunt. On the other hand, the daughter will have trouble learning from the mother how to be a woman. What is more, her own sisters may reject her out of jealousy, and if—in lieu of *relating* to them—she would try to *be like* them, she may adopt their attitude toward the mother, offend the mother, and end up in neither camp, so to speak. Ordinarily, however, the mother does not let this happen.

If a *daughter* is the *oldest sister of brother(s)*, she has no trouble at first picking up from the mother how to treat children. Sooner or later, though, the two begin to disagree on how boys should be treated. The mother will try to control them just as she controlled her daughter, or more so, because they are boys. They should learn even better how to obey a woman. They should learn who is really wearing the pants. The daughter would disagree, of her own accord, but may not be permitted to get enough experience or backing from other sources, such as the father or her brothers. She would be in doubt and conflict over the treatment of boys and men, may stay so way into adulthood, and find it difficult to choose a partner for life. Some form of an ultimate break with the mother may help her on that, though.

If a *daughter* is the *oldest sister of sister(s)*, just like the mother, they tend to understand each other quite well. This type of daughter is relatively least in conflict about her identification with this type of mother. She can adopt from her how children, girls as it happens, should be handled. In fact, to the extent that she has become like her mother, she may be permitted to take over, with the mother content to exert her unconditional power over all of her children via the oldest. The mother is more likely to be satisfied with this, if she has married a youngest brother herself who submits to her will in all things that matter. She may let her daughter have the girls, while she keeps an eye on her, and a hold on her husband. But there may also be a subdivision, such as the mother taking care of her second-oldest or other younger daughter, and the oldest daughter assuming responsibility for the rest of them.

If a *son* is the *oldest brother of sister(s)*, he and his mother will usually be on no good terms. She resents his ease with, and command over, the girls. Who does he think he is? And why do my daughters take to him? Such may be her somewhat belligerent questions. He, on the other hand, often sees her as an unduly harsh and domineering woman who presides imperiously over much or all of the family without much inspiration. At least she does not inspire *him*. She may pressure him into turning out top work, but it does not matter to her what kind, and how he likes it. She may force him to quit girls he is interested in, to invite or take out others whom he does not care for (but whose parents are the mother's friends, or rich, or influential, or all of this), to marry the girl she approves of, or even to remain single. Sometimes his sisters cannot counteract the mother's influence on him even if they try. They, too, may be intimidated. And sometimes he might have to run away and go far to escape her adamant and barren regime. His father will do little to help him, either, if he is mother's optimal match, i.e., the youngest brother of sister(s).

If a *son* is the *oldest brother of brother(s)*, he and his mother do not get along too well. They have a rank and a sex conflict, so to speak. Neither of them has been used to a peer of the opposite sex, although, to be sure, both of them have ordinarily grown up with a parent of that sex. Mother and son are not treating each other as what they are: an adult woman and a young or even little boy. They are rather treating each other as powers. Both want to be bosses and rule over the other, and their fight may be a tough one, indeed, even if much of it remains under the surface. As a fighter, the oldest brother of brother(s) is in a better position with (this type of) mother than the oldest brother of sister(s) who does not really want to fight a woman. The former, on the other hand, does not quite see his mother as a woman. Hence he can fight more freely, and if he loses, it is because of his tender age rather than because a woman beat a (little) man. The father could be of real support only if he, too, were an oldest brother of brother(s). In that case, however, he would be among the poorest matches the mother could have made, so that the son would learn little more about his parents' marriage than that it is an incessant war. Mother and son may become allies of sorts, after all. For the mother, there is one thing in her son's favor: he cannot and does not request actual sexual submission as does her husband. Unconsciously she may never forgive her husband for that.

If a *son* is the *youngest brother of sister(s)*, his relationship to his mother could be reasonably good. He has little trouble submitting to females, as long as they let him do in his work and/or his entertainment whatever he wants. The mother would be even more qualified to care for his physical comfort than his sisters are, but she will not always give him the freedom he wants. She is too authority-bound to make much of an allowance even for herself. Yet, with her daughters buffering her impact and, in case of an optimal match, with the father able to identify with his son, things may turn out quite well. The mother might learn to abstain from too much managing, and her daughters could not help teach her that, provided that the mother has not stupified them as they grew up. If, however, the mother had married an oldest brother, she may force her daughters to gang up with her against men, including her son. In that case his prognosis would not be quite so good.

If a *son* is the *youngest brother of brother(s)*, he and the mother may get along quite well. The older siblings may function even more as buffers between him and the mother than they do with the youngest brother of sister(s). After all, his siblings are all male, and any gripes the mother has had against men will have landed on them first. After having had this experience several times over, the mother may have softened and refined her approach, or, if she has not, her sons may have wised up to her and offer the youngest brother better techniques of dealing with her. Yet, whether the mother has failed to have her way, or improved her conduct of her own accord, reasonably she could take the least offense with her youngest son. Of all her sons, the youngest is the most likely to develop a good relationship with her, and to get to know her even as a woman. This may not be enough to prepare him for an optimal choice in marriage. In fact, the mother may be the one who undertakes to set him up with a wife. But the mother's and his relationship may be good enough in itself. They may even depend on each other more than outsiders would consider good for either one of them.

## CHAPTER 20

## Mother the Youngest Sister of Sister(s)

If the mother is the youngest sister of sister(s), she is not too likely to be very maternal, or at least to be so consistently. In effect she prefers daughters to sons, especially older daughters whom she expects to assist her in the chores of motherhood and the household as soon as at all possible. Only in cases where she has had help all along, either by her own mother or somebody kind and motherly hired for the purpose, may her daughters escape that pressure. Boys will be puzzled by the ways in which she mixes maternal affection with caprice and somewhat fabricated seduction. They find it hard to figure her out, but if they should, they would be well prepared for almost any kind of woman likely to attract their interests.

If a *daughter* is the *oldest sister of brother(s)*, the mother and she may look compatible on the surface, but they are not. The daughter may be ready relatively early in her life to play mother, but she would not have learned much of it from her mother. Besides, and partly because of this, she would be reluctant to cater to her mother. She would cater to the boys, though, in spite of the mother who will often interfere and foul up her work and accomplishments with them. The mother may do this out of mere jealousy, she suspects. The mother does not like her daughter to be on such good terms with the boys of the family, including her own husband, particularly in cases where the latter is a junior by his own sibling position. Her preference has always been to keep men breathless and surprised, but in family life the boys might get tired of it sooner or later. With all her caprice, the mother may run out of new schemes in her own family. Her boys have worn her out, she may claim.

If a *daughter* is the *youngest sister of brother(s)*, she is often at odds with her mother, particularly over the boys. The mother will notice before long that much to her chagrin, they adore the little girl, that they go out of their way doing her favors, and that they may not even be jealous of each other. What is worse, the little girl seems to be doing nothing to elicit or deserve all that. How different from her own experiences with boys. So the mother tends to disrupt this harmonious love club, to challenge her sons, tease them, play one against the other, and be quite hostile to her daughter until everybody's life has become miserable. This is less likely to happen, if the mother has been married optimally, say, to an oldest brother of sister(s). The father, then, may intervene on behalf of his daughter and teach his sons how to be more diplomatic with the girls, both the big and willful one and their sweet little darling who does not seem to know what the turmoil is all about.

If a *daughter* is the *youngest sister of sister(s)*, like the mother herself, they may develop a deep though somewhat puzzling sympathy for each other. They agree that being understood is among the most essential things in life. They also agree that this is the hardest thing to get. They understand each other perfectly in their longing, but they are about as unlikely as anybody to be able to quench that longing. The mother may not realize it, but she is getting more actual understanding from her older daughters than from the little one. She is the little one herself, no matter how ambitious and driving she may be. The greater the number of older daughters, the greater the likelihood that both of them, mother and youngest daughter, will receive guidance and understanding of sorts from one or more of the older daughters. Those will be helped, if the father has been a senior himself, preferably of girls.

If a *daughter* is the *oldest sister of sister(s)*, she and her mother may get along with each other quite well. Although the daughter will have a hard time guessing and recognizing what it really is that the mother wants her to do, sooner or later she is likely to succeed to some extent. She will take the lead in the household, with the children, even with purchases or the hiring of household help. Yet she has to do it quietly, preferably even behind the mother's back, in order not to challenge her. Otherwise, the mother may set out to prove that she is still the best of all mothers, often to the disadvantage of the entire family. What helps the mother accept her daugter's lead is the knowledge that she is, of course, the real mother. Nobody can doubt that.

If a *son* is the *youngest brother of sister(s)*, he and his mother are hardly on common ground. She is the capricious and ambitious one, used to being helped in all the little things of life. He is the distracted one, the boy who can become completely absorbed in his engagements, while the girls take care of his physical comfort. But his mother will not do that. Instead she may take to competing with her son on certain issues. He does not get the understanding and consideration from her that he would expect from women. And she is hoping and waiting for her son to grow up as a man, to become that kind, paternal, and patient person who is willing to take a lot of nonsense and to chip in money, presents, and work in order to catch up with a girl's extravagancies. Well, her wait is usually futile. She even gets in conflicts with her daughters who are spoiling the boy, she feels. On this she receives support from her husband, provided he is an oldest brother. In that case, however, the son may pick up some features of an oldest brother himself and become more compatible with his mother.

If a *son* is the *youngest brother of brother(s)*, he too has trouble with his mother. Both of them are looking for guidance. But the mother is not able to give it in spite of her greater age, and the son is not going to furnish it either. However, he may get guidance from his father, if that man happens to be the mother's optimal match, i.e., an oldest brother of sister(s). He may also learn a little from one of his older brothers, usually the oldest, although quite often he is too competitive or too anxious to be different from his brothers to utilize their example. There is one aspect, though, on which he and his mother may be in agreement: both of them do not quite know what they *really* want. Both of them may be under the spell of moods, sudden changes of mind, and an unconscious urge to surprise people. To the extent that they fail to get what they think they want, or to receive sympathy for what they are actually doing, they tend to be of one mind: they feel misunderstood. They may meet each other on that issue in unexpected moments, say in the kitchen, in letters written from afar, or in instances of hard luck.

If a *son* is the *oldest brother of sister(s)*, he and his mother are usually getting along quite well. In fact, the son may sometimes understand the mother better than she does herself. He may be able to predict what she will be doing before she would know it herself, but he would not actually make such predictions, or aim at earning credit for them from other people. He simply knows how to take her, and he may even mollify and soften her ambitions and extravagancies. If she has not married optimally, she may sometimes appear to be on better terms with her son than with her husband. With an optimal match, however (i.e., an oldest brother of sisters), she need not be jealous of her daughters, as she might be otherwise. If she cannot have her husband to herself, say, because he is occupied with his daughters, she can often count on her son; and if her son is unavailable, she is usually able to draw on her husband. Even so, she is somewhat envious of her daughters' greater calm and certainty of which they can avail themselves in meeting the men in the family. On the other hand, she may console herself with the fact that she can fascinate or exasperate her husband and her son, who may both consider her the most interesting of the girls they happen to have in the family. She seems to be glittering in ever new lights, just as she must have done before she got married. Because of this characteristic of hers, no girl, no matter how extravagant, will surprise the son much in his later life. In some cases, though, he may find himself tied closer to his mother than would be good for him.

If a *son* is the *oldest brother of brother(s)*, he and his mother are mostly on very good terms. Neither of them has originally been used to peers of the opposite sex. Hence they would tend to be somewhat shy about girls and boys, respectively, and that may suit their own relationship quite well. After all, mother and son are not supposed to be too close to each other under any circumstances. The son would be eager to lead and control others, and the mother, in turn, may like her son's unusual manipulative skill. She appreciates the ways in which he dominates his brothers and relieves her of some of the details of daily life in the family. She likes, too, that he does seem to make a distinction between boys and girls. At least he is quite lenient with her. Hence she does not have to be jealous of the rest of her children (as a mother would tend to whose son is the oldest brother of sisters). In fact, her relationship to her son may be better in some respects than that to her husband, even where she has married optimally, i.e., the oldest brother of sister(s). In some ways, however slightly, she might not be used to *all* angles of the life with a man to this day. Well, with her son she has no such problem, and he himself does not create one either.

## CHAPTER 21

## Mother the Oldest Sister of Brother(s)

A mother who is the oldest sister of brother(s), generally appears to be, and even is, the most motherly of all. She can handle and take care of boys very well, and she can show her daughters how to do likewise. They cannot ask for quite the same favors as the boys, and wherever they realize and accept that, things are fine. Only the youngest child, if a daughter, may give the mother a little trouble, if for no other reason than that there is nobody, i.e., no junior, on whom that girl could practice how to be like mother. If the mother has married optimally, namely, a youngest brother of sister(s), her sons and her daughters tend to carry with them into the world an image of an inverse authority relationship, of a strong wife and a somewhat dependent husband, and that image may well sway their own choices of a partner for life. The girls may be looking for little boys, and the boys for mothers.

If a *daughter* is the *youngest sister of sister(s)*, she may have some trouble with her mother. She tries to be ingratiating and submissive to her, an attitude she might be quite reluctant to assume toward her sisters. Yet even so she finds the mother slightly, but strangely, unresponsive. It is as if something were missing in their relationship. But what? Well, the devotion would be worth more, if it came from a son rather than a daughter. At any rate, the daughter feels not quite understood by her mother. When it comes to men, this feeling may be even stronger. She knows little about them. The mother, on the other hand, seems to be up to them. They eat from her hands. Father does, for instance.

155

Yet the mother seems unable to answer the daughter's many questions about men. Only in case of a poor match of the parents, particularly when aggravated through losses suffered by mother, may the daughter be sought out by the mother and let in on her secrets, including those about men. Their gist, according to such a mother: Men are no good. Stay clear of them.

If a *daughter* is the *oldest sister of sister(s)*, she and her mother are likely to fight, no matter how covertly, over the leadership among the girls in the family and over the treatment of men. On the first issue, the daughter has an advantage over the mother. Girls is all that she has been used to, all she has ever had. The mother, on the other hand, has originally been used to younger boys. She does not quite know what to do with all these girls that she has now. She may even bear a grudge against them for their failure to turn up as boys. As a matter of fact the oldest may get the brunt of it. About the second issue, men, the daughter knows little, except that the only man in the family, father, is, or should be, the supreme authority, particularly since the mother is not—she does not seem to know enough about children. She, the oldest daughter, wants above all to obey her father, train her sisters in his spirit, put them to work for him, and make good, good girls out of them. Unfortunately, it takes a less than optimal match of the parents for the father to be that authority. Only if he is an oldest brother himself, especially of brothers, would he furnish that authority. If he were a youngest brother of sisters (i.e., optimally matched), he may forever fail to guide or even inspire his daughter. He may disappoint her no end. How can he take all that from mother? Why is he not more of a man? Yet if she is lucky in her own choice, she may one day be married to a youngest brother of sister(s) herself, and she may notice with surprise that he would want her to be more or less like her own mother had been. He might even take unduly to that person, his mother-in-law.

If a *daughter* is the *youngest sister of brother(s)*, she and the mother are unlikely to have conflicts over their authority. The daughter readily concedes it to her mother; it is not their major issue of life anyway. For both of them the major issue is boys, but their viewpoints differ. It is the mother's opinion that boys should look up to the woman, whereas the daughter would rather look up to them herself. This, precisely, may be the bone of contention for them. The mother would want her daughter to learn from her how to treat men. She would tend to think that hers is the only way, and may notice with misgiving that, at least with some of the boys, her daughter is successful in her own right. They cater to her. They dote on her, something that may never have happened much to her, the mother. Partly because of that, she insists that the only kind of people worth being cared for and indulged are (junior) boys. Her daughter is not supposed to be pampered by anybody. But sometimes, particularly in cases of poor matches of the parents, the mother may not mind that. She herself may even give to her daughter what her own mother *should* have given more generously to her.

If a *daughter* is the *oldest sister of brother(s)*, just like the mother, they get along fine with each other, as long as they learn how to divide the beloved subjects. Mother can keep father, and she, the daughter, will care for the sons, or vice versa. Or both of them keep the father, each in her own way, and divide the sons evenly between them. Mother and daughter understand each other quite well. At times of temporary or even lasting absence of one of them, the other can take over, almost as if nothing had happened. As for her own marriage plans, the daughter is more likely than oldest daughters of other types of mothers to repeat her mother's match, or at least to make a strong try.

If a *son* is the *oldest brother of brother(s)*, he is usually having difficulties with his mother. She would want to take care of him as she would of a younger brother, and expect him to be delighted. He, on the other hand, is eager to exercise control himself, and to be taken care of by nobody. Least of all, he wants to depend on a woman, especially since his mother stopped taking care of him when she had more, and utterly uncalled-for, boys. As things are, his mother may even have picked out one of his brothers, often the youngest, to be her favorite, her pet, her beloved. It gives him the creeps to think of it. He may try to challenge her authority over his brothers and even his father. He would try to make men out of them rather than sissies. Or he may give up altogether and stay aloof from the rest of the family, particularly from his mother. Well-matched parents, however, tend to convey something of the happiness of married life even to him. If the father should be a poor match for the mother, an oldest brother of sister(s) or even of brother(s), the son may find the father siding with him. But it will also become apparent to him that his parents' marriage is not the happiest one.

If a *son* is the *oldest brother of sister(s)*, he and the mother are likely to be in some conflict over leadership. The mother has been used to treating boys like the little ones who could not survive, however gifted, unless girls were handling their problems for them, whereas he has learned early in life that he is a kind of master of girls. The girls may be pests at times, particularly when they are feeling the mother's support, but he is the boy, the only one like the father, and they must admire him for that. He helps and protects them in return, and they ask for it. Even the mother requests that he be nice to them, but little does she know that he enjoys that anyway. His trouble is with her, and he has some trouble with his father, too, if the father has been a youngest brother of sister(s), i.e., her optimal match. The mother does not let the son be her loving friend and protector, whereas the father would let him be his. But he is a man and prefers affection from females. And this is exactly what his father could teach *him:* how to entice women into catering to you. As a result of these troubles, the parents sometimes grow even closer to each other and leave the children more to themselves than other parents would. Which, in their case, may do no harm at all.

If a *son* is the *youngest brother of brother(s)*, he and the mother are usually getting along quite well. Of all males in the family, he is most in need of her care, and the most worthwhile recipient as she lavishes care on him. She will not overdo it but go about it inconspicuously, so much so, that her sons, particularly the youngest, hardly notice what they are getting used to. At any rate, the mother and her youngest son supplement each other nicely. In the course of time the son may even overcome the chief predicament of his sibling configuration: the absence of female peers.

He may learn from his mother what a (motherly) woman is like, and how she would like to be treated. At least he is more likely to learn than his brothers are. Not infrequently he marries at an earlier age than do his brothers. Sometimes he is even the first one chronologically. In cases where the father has been an oldest brother of sister(s) or even of brother(s), the parents tend to be in conflict and unhappy with each other. Consequently the mother may turn to her sons, more specifically to the most co-operative and pliable of them, her youngest, and the two of them may form a couple more intimate than will be good for either, particularly for the son. He may be handicapped in his own choice of a wife. The father might, of course, contest the mother, so that the parents become engaged in a tug of war over their sons.

If a *son* is the *youngest brother of sister(s)*, he and the mother are prone to be on excellent terms. At last, she has her youngest brother. He is all her own. She has given birth to him herself. And he has not only sisters who pamper and spoil him, but also a mother who can show them how to do a perfect job. If the father is the youngest brother of sister(s) himself, the family will probably live in harmony ever after. On occasion, the mother and the daughters may switch the males in their mothering feats, and the men may switch the girls. If the daughters do not always cater to their little brother, they can learn from the mother how to suppress their selfishness. And if the son is not completely suc-cessful in luring girls into his service, he will be able to snatch a few more of his father's secrets. Not consciously, though. Nor does the father intend to give them away. So great may be the harmony in the family, that neither the daughters nor the son are seriously trying to win one parent away from the other. They know that father and mother really do belong together and love each other the most. They sense that this is even for their own good. Therefore they can usually leave the family quite easily for marriages of their own, at least as long as they are heading for optimal partners. For the son, that means an oldest sister of brother(s) who is as anxious to sponsor his pursuits and to take care of his earthly needs as his mother and sisters have been.

## CHAPTER 22

## Mother the Youngest Sister of Brother(s)

A mother who has been the youngest sister of brother(s), tends generally to be the most feminine mother of all. In most cases she is a very good wife, but she may not excel as a mother, nor does she make too much of a show of being one. Psychologically she may sometimes appear as one of her husband's children. To her children she offers sympathy rather than explicit guidance, companionship rather than authority, charm rather than competence. Her daughters can learn from her how to entice men, how to submit to them, even how to serve them. With her sons she evokes their masculinity more than other mothers do; she is seductive with them. But she has been even more attractive to, and seductive with, her suitors and has usually selected a wonderful husband who loves her dearly. This fact as well as her husband himself imposes (graceful) limits on their sons' love of mother, and sets a favorable paradigm of what they should try for themselves once they have come of age.

If a *daughter* is the *oldest sister of sister(s)*, she may wish most for guidance from her mother, but never get it in any of the ways she can envisage herself. By her own sibling position she is supposed to lead her sisters. They require it, she feels, and they do, especially since the mother seems not quite willing to give it. But how can the daughter do it without some guidance from the mother? The father could conceivably step in and help, but in case of an optimal match of the parents he would be the oldest brother of sister(s) and too busy being in love with his wife and even with his daughters to offer any real guidance on his oldest daughter's problem. Sometimes it looks as if she should have been a man. The mother secretly wants her to take over like a man, and father *is* a man. Whatever she picks up from him is tinted by his masculinity. Hence she may lead and direct her sisters as if she were a bit of a man herself. This may be a solution for the time being, but it will tend to handicap her choice of a spouse. She may be looking seriously for a feminine man.

If a *daughter* is the *youngest sister of brother(s)*, just like the mother, they are getting along nicely, provided their interests stay parallel and do not converge on the same objects. Their chief interests are boys, but as long as mother has father—who often is an oldest brother, preferably of sisters—and she herself has her brothers, everything is fine. She may be father's darling too, but there are limits. If a situation boils down to either mother or daughter, he favors mother. The mother, too, will permit her sons to adore her, to give her presents, and even to protect her, but there are similar limits. And there are also some, though fewer, restrictions on the brothers' devotion for their little sister. This common devotion may prevent one or the other of her brothers, particularly if there are many, from ever marrying himself. It may be that unconsciously he stays faithful to his sister. Almost without noticing it, the daughter will learn from her mother how to be a boys' girl, and the daughter's own experiences tend to confirm what she has learned.

If a *daughter* is the *youngest sister of sister(s)*, she would be the most likely of all daughters to elicit clearly maternal behavior in this type of mother. For one thing, the mother will have acquired more and more of it, as she continued to have daughters. Secondly, her daughters have sensed her desire that they should step in as little mothers wherever needed, and have soon begun doing so. Thus the increase in the number of children may have relieved the mother rather than burdened her. In any case, the youngest daughter has not only had more of her mother, but also more than just one mother. In fact, her sisters have even adopted some of the father's characteristics too. The older sisters have learned to relate to their mother in a somewhat manly way, and the youngest is the most likely of all sisters to let them do that. She has the least chances of practicing this hybrid masculinity and is more prone than the others to become sincerely feminine and eventually to make a good choice for marriage.

If a *daughter* is the *oldest sister of brother(s)*, she and her mother are in agreement on their general appreciation of men. Yet they appreciate them in different ways. The mother takes them as potential suitors, as persons that a woman is to amuse and enchant. The daughter will discover sooner or later that men need attention and care, that only a woman can make them feel comfortable and at home even in their own house. Yet whenever she arrives at such an opinion of hers, the mother will be delighted. The mother does not particularly want to take care of men in those ways, although she will, if she has to. Well, her daughter is most welcome to it. Let her be the *mother* for her sons, whereas she herself continues to be unchallenged as her husband's beloved wife. If she has married optimally, i.e., the oldest brother of sister(s), her husband is likely to want just that. He may even resent a little the maternal virtues of his own daughter, especially when she tries to play them on him. Mother and daughter can even be friends of sorts, but are at their best on issues other than men. The mother has not much trouble acting the little girl, and her daughter eventually even less acting the big one.

If a *son* is the *youngest brother of brother(s)*, he and his mother do not find it easy to come to terms with each other. She is used to the loving care and courtship of senior boys and fathers. He is among the least prepared to understand a woman. He is so used to being guided by his brother(s) and older males in general and, at the same time, is often so much in protest against any guidance and so erratic in his ambitions and goals, that his mother cannot make heads or tails of him. She tries patiently and gracefully to treat him as she has treated the other males in the family, but with him it is of little or no avail. It seems he always does the unpredictable, the impossible, the tactless, the rude. He is making a fool of himself, especially before women. Oh, if only he could get an experienced woman, any experienced woman, to teach him the graces, beauties, and the wisdom of life. In her fading hope, the mother may even conspire to get him such a woman, but he might foul up that effort too. Only if his father—preferably an oldest brother of sister(s)—or possibly his own oldest brother would take him aside and devote time to his inner education, may he pick up some things about women. Yet to the extent that these men do reach and influence him, he may develop a strong relationship to them, or to men in general, and be off the track again.

If a *son* is the *youngest brother of sister(s)*, he and his mother may not have much in common either. However, he is in a more fortunate position than the youngest brother of brother(s). He has sisters to take care of him and to relate to. He does not depend entirely on his mother for his contact with females. And if need be he can always look for guidance and clues from his father. If his parents have been optimally matched, the father will be an oldest brother of sister(s). From such a father he may learn after all how to treat a submissive and very feminine woman—his mother. The father, on the other hand, may envy him a little for his good luck with the girls, in the family as well as outside. The son does not seem to exert himself at all, but is still getting their favors. And at that he does not seem enough of a male. As the first and only boy, he should have more determination, more pride, or something. On the whole, the parents and their children may form two groups, psychologically more separate from each other than parents and children are in other types of families. They can leave each other alone with greater ease. Hence, neither the daughters nor the son will have much difficulty making a good choice for marriage.

If a *son* is the *oldest brother of brother(s)*, he and the mother may get along quite well. He would be eager, from his early life on, to guide and control even mother, and to excel in a field of work, sometimes beyond his father. He may appear superior to his father because of his power over, and skill with, men. The father has not got too much of that, or at least he does not seem to care. Usually, the mother has not minded that trait of the father, but in periods of external crises, or simply as she and the father have grown older, she may have looked at her son with increasing pride, even for those (on her scale) less important aspects of men, such as leadership, professional competence, and indomitable determination. It will also suit her fine that her son is not the greatest in his conduct with women. This is all right with her. After all, she is not married to him, and besides he exercises a considerable amount of self-control in his contacts with her. As a matter of fact, she may consider it her very mission in life—aside from being a good and loving wife to her husband—to soften and refine her son's attitudes toward girls, to render him sensitive to the potential pleasures and delights contained in a woman, and to make him a little more of a ladies' man than he would ordinarily tend to be.

If a *son* is the *oldest brother of sister(s)*, he and his mother are usually quite happy and content with each other. After all, he is precisely what she has been used to from her own early life on, and what she has selected for a husband (in case of an optimal match). Her son knows how to take and spoil women. He has had plenty of practice with his sisters, and while they were not good enough for his full devotion, she herself apparently is. At any rate, he tends to adore her, and she loves his gentlemanly ways, his tact, his understanding. In fact, she sometimes wonders how he could develop such good manners when his own father, even if an oldest brother of sister(s) himself, is not perfect. Her age in relation to her son may be partly responsible. She permits him to treat her like a delicate young lady. But this is not the whole story. She has given birth to him. He was still very little, when she was already grown up and beautiful. And she *is* in love with father. All of which puts him at an initial disadvantage compared to his father for which, he feels, he has to make up. The men in the family can, of course, switch the females without much difficulty, but also without arousing any wrong ideas. They all know that father and mother are the ones that really belong together. That is why they, the children, can participate so fully in the family life. Such may be their interpretations. And when the children marry, it will be fine with the parents. The mother is generally graceful and pleasant about her daughter-in-law. She *can* let her son go to another woman. She knows that in some unobtrusive and quiet way he will remain hers as long as he lives. Everything he does for his own happiness is fine with her. Whatever she could do to influence him, she has done long ago.

## CHAPTER 23

## Parents—Additional Comments

The interaction of other parental sibling positions with the sibling positions of their children can be inferred by interpolation. Intermediary positions held by children may be emphasized in one direction or another by the parent's sibling position, and vice versa. In dealing with a particular child, or with all of them, parents of intermediary positions may find the portrait of one position more practical and useful than that of another. In fact, the picture that is wanted by the majority of children may thereby become the stronger one, provided it does not conflict with the spouse's wishes. Otherwise there will be a tug of war similar to those described for several of the patterns of parent-child interaction.

Single children whose same-sex parents grew up with brothers and/or sisters tend to adopt features of the sibling position of that parent. One might say that single children have no sibling position. Hence they can have no conflict with their same-sex parent's sibling position. Conversely, a parent who has been an only child—though in general he (or she) will not be too good with children—is in no immediate conflict with any of the children's sibling positions. Only if both the same-sex parent and the child are singletons may they have something like a conflict. Both of them would want to be the only one for the third member of the family.

Twins can be dealt with according to their positions among other siblings, if they have had any, and somewhat like siblings themselves, if they are non-identical. Their chief general conflict

165

with children of their own will be the children's apartness in time and growth, just as parents of other sibling configurations may have a little trouble wising up to the degree of togetherness prevailing among their twin children.

Some general trends prevailing throughout these patterns may also be noted. If same-sex parents and children are having a rank conflict, any conflict in which the parent is the senior, at least predominantly so, and the child the junior, will usually be more favorable in its outcome than the opposite. Parents with senior sibling positions are somewhat more desirable and impressive for children of the same sex than parents with junior sibling positions. Senior children can identify with their senior parents and divide their domains. They have the advantage of proximity (see also page 111). Junior children can be good and willing children. They can submit to their same-sex parents and receive guidance and protection. Parents, on the other hand, who have been junior siblings, are likely to leave their senior children somewhat short of a teacher to learn from and identify with, and their junior children somewhat short of leadership. In cases of optimal matches between the parents (which, by definition, require complementary ranks), these problems are likely to be small.

If opposite-sex parent and child have no rank conflict, they still tend to be somewhat better off with each other, if the male (i.e., either father or son) is a senior, and the female (mother or daughter) a junior. However, if they *do* have a rank conflict, the child's future relationship to the opposite sex may be affected adversely. If the parents are not optimally matched and have a rank conflict with each other, the child may be able to identify easily with the same-sex parent, but would learn from him, or her, only how to handle a conflict-ridden marriage. But even if the parents are optimally matched, there might be some difficulty. In that case the child would have a complementary rank relationship (i.e., no rank-conflict) with the same-sex parent. Hence the child is likely to get along somewhat better with that parent than with the opposite-sex parent. But precisely that may be the wrong preparation for later life and the selection of a spouse. The degree of concomitant sex-conflict prevailing among the parents will aggravate or mitigate all these possible troubles proportionally.

Generally it can be said that conflicts between the parents and conflicts between a child's sibling position and a parent tend to be mitigated somewhat by the implicit absence or reduction of conflict between that child and the other parent, or between another of the children and the first parent. Conflicts that are not too severe and prevail along with some no-conflict relationships in a given family may even make for a richer family life and a better preparation for the great big and highly variegated world.

Monosexual sibling configurations have only the parents to draw on as far as heterosexual relationships are concerned. There is no peer relationship to prepare them for marriage. To the extent, however, that a sibling configuration approximates an even balance of sexes, this emphasis will shift away from the parents. Conflict prevailing among the parents and losses suffered by them operate the other way. The more severe they are (conflict and loss, that is), the greater also the likelihood that children will inherit the parents' conflicts and losses no matter how favorable their own sibling configurations may be. The distance of a given child from the parents, i.e., the number of intervening, or older, siblings, will determine how much a person is affected by conflicts and losses prevailing among the parents as well as by conflicts resulting from discrepancies between the child's sibling position and those of his parents. The greater the number of older siblings, the smaller the direct influence of the parents upon a person.

The parents' relationship with each other tends to bear perhaps most significantly on a person's own choice of a partner for life. If the parents have been optimally matched, the person is likely to come closer to his optimal choice. Optimal matches of parents set ideal paradigms. A poor match of the parents, one in which sex and rank conflicts between them are pronounced, will put a person in a dilemma. On the one hand, he must try to get away from what his parents had and, if at all possible, choose differently. On the other hand, his parents' marriage is the oldest and strongest example for him to go by. So, how can he plan to choose differently, or even hope to be able to? Hence it comes as no great surprise that, in his choice of a partner, such a person often ends up precisely where his parents are, psychologically speaking, in spite of the hard try to get away from them (see also page 11). Of course, running away will seldom solve anything anywhere. Coming to terms with the parents, understanding what their trouble may have been, and only thereafter choosing a partner for good will improve a person's chances to do better than his parents did. If the person's own choice of a partner is better than his parents' only by a step rather than all the way, the gain is probably more trustworthy. Varying degrees of conflict between a person's own sibling configuration and that of the parents may heighten or lessen a person's chances in that respect.

## CHAPTER 24

## Children

There may be conflicts between a person's own sibling configuration and that of any of his or her children. These conflicts can be treated analogously to those existing between the sibling configuration of a person's parents and his own. Implicitly the preceding chapters (of Part III) contain all about children that is relevant in this context. Obviously, the same would hold for grandparents—they are the parents of a person's parents (and the parents are their children).

What should be mentioned, though, is the different appreciation that different sibling configurations generally receive. Some are apparently more desirable than others. A boy first, then a girl, and, if more children are coming, another boy and another girl, etc., would usually be considered ideal. Somewhat less attractive is a girl first, then a boy, etc. A number of boys first, followed by a number of girls would appear better than a number of girls first, followed by a number of boys, but both would be looked at as slightly worse than strict alternation of sexes. "Boys only" would be among the less favorable configurations, although boys tend to be valued higher than girls throughout the world. Hence parents often do not mind having boys only. They may console themselves with the hope that sooner or later the boys will bring the missing girls into the house. Once the boys have come that far, though, they tend to leave the parents' house and set up one of their own.

"Girls only" is often thought of as the worst of all configurations of children. Yet they are not without implicit promise. One day they will bring the boys along. Although, in Western lands,

the girls are the ones who really have the option, they will usually choose in the spirit of the parents (if the parents have cared for the girls). The parents' preferences tend to be their own. Hence through educating and grooming their girls, the parents are in a sense working toward sons, toward sons-in-law. What is more, the children that their daughters may bear their husbands will be *their* grandchildren. The young mother's parents seem to have more of a title to their grandchildren than the father's parents, although the latter contribute the name.

Having only one child is often not thought of as worse than any of the other configurations of children. Yet as far as the effects on a person's later life and crucial personal relationships are concerned, it may well be. One would wonder, too, why parents could make up their minds on one child only. Not that any particular parents should have had more children, under all circumstances. In some cases even one child is already too many.

It should also be mentioned that parents with lopsided, or altogether monosexual, configurations of children may be wise if they gang up with those of their relatives or neighbors whose configurations of children lean in the opposite direction. The more these contacts approximate sibling relationships in extent and intensity, the more "incestuous" will they come to appear to the children, and the smaller the likelihood that they will marry their playmates. Other, fresher, persons are needed for ultimate hetero-sexual relationships, just as with siblings.

Coeducation in kindergarten and grade school may also be of help. There the boys get their girls, and the girls their boys—all of about the same age, something that even the brothers of sisters and the sisters of brothers do not have at home (except in cases of twins). What holds for the parent-sponsored early friendships would hold here, too. The close and steady contact at grade school would render the situation somewhat incestuous in its psychological effects. The boys and girls rarely choose final partners for life from this situation, unless there have been some explicit and considerable interruptions of contact, so that any subsequent encounter would be one of strangers again. But even then the complete strangers, those never met before, have better chances of making a hit.

An untoward effect of coeducation, however, may be the blurring of sex identification by too early exposure to the opposite sex. Boys are with girls and girls with boys at a time when they have hardly any use for each other, and they may be hindered from becoming to any great extent what they are themselves. Thus, relatively too many young men and women, once married, do not quite know what to do with each other in a broader and deeper sense. They may propagate, to be sure, sometimes for lack of anything else to do, but then they have little to offer to their children.

## CHAPTER 25

## Losses

It has been pointed out before which events and experiences should be subsumed under psychological losses, and what general laws determine their significance (page 12). Losses have also been considered along with the major hands of the game, i.e., with the chief character portraits. This chapter adds a few more aspects.

The effects of parental losses can come down on the children, just as parental conflicts do. Both conflicts and losses may make trouble for the children while they grow up, and predispose them for poor matches—for partners with whom they are actually in conflict (as appraised by their sibling configurations) or, who have suffered losses themselves. The parents' conflicts may, in turn, have been the results of conflicts and losses prevalent among *their* parents.

The general effect of any loss is twofold. There is the inevitable, though often unconscious, interpretation of the loss as punishment, no matter how innocent the person lost or the loser actually was, and there is the diminished freedom of choice in matters of friendships, love relationships, and marriage. People who have suffered losses or inherited the effects of losses endured by their parents are more prone to choose partners rashly and anxiously, and thereby to hit upon people with whom they will be in conflict or who are the victims of losses themselves. The most massive way of passing on a loss to children is, in fact, to make a poor choice of a spouse oneself: to generate children from wrong premises to begin with. Anyway, it looks as if such an underprivileged person, i.e., the victim of direct or inherited losses, desires to set himself up for punishment. The loss, that's what he got from his dearest persons, or, at least, that's what a parent got from a dearest person of his (and the parent cannot help, even insists on, conveying the loss). So how can he expect anything different thereafter? In fact, since the loss is imminent, how can he but wish for it. Unconsciously he will choose people who are troubled, with whom he senses trouble, and who might eventually leave him, or her, anyway. Often they are people who have suffered losses themselves. If not worse, he might choose an incompatible person, someone he could not possibly get along with (nor without, as it happens), or someone who would stay only in order to make him suffer forever.

Loss of father

The most severe of all losses would be that of a parent during early childhood, surpassed only by the loss of both parents. So that the child survives at all, somebody will have to step in as a substitute parent. Much will depend on the details of this substitution. Close relatives (such as uncles and aunts, much older siblings, grandparents) with whom the child has been fairly familiar would be on the favorable end of the possible range, and a succession of orphans' homes with, say, an average of twenty children to an adult, on the other. Foster homes, i.e., regular homes, preferably of a couple who have already (had) children of their own, would be somewhere in between. If the child has siblings, losing them too would, of course, contribute to the severity of the loss of a parent.

Slightly less severe, although still pathogenic in various cases, are losses of a parent in late childhood and early adolescence, or losses of a sibling in early childhood. Neither one of these losses is likely to break up the home. If it should, as might happen with the loss of a parent, enough of the home is usually preserved, either in actuality—the house is retained, or (some of) the remaining family members stay together—or symbolically, e.g., by the possibility to visit the lost (divorced) person, or at least to recall him or her in conversations with the remaining family members, to look at his pictures and letters, to keep, or even develop, his property. (All of these possibilities could be looked at also as help and guidance in mourning.) Even if the youth should end up alone, he will, at this age, be no longer at the utter mercy of circumstances. He can make his preferences known, try for alternatives, protest, and fight, in order to improve his lot. This holds for girls as well, although they seem to be better protected by their parents, their fathers in particular, than boys. Fewer girls than boys end up abandoned.

The loss of siblings, even when occurring in early childhood, is still less likely to break up a home. It almost never does. An aspect that makes that loss more difficult to digest, though, is that the sibling has almost never been as indispensible as either of the parents was and is. In fact, like any sibling, the one lost may have been a nuisance much of the time, so that his or her exit is slightly welcome, especially when the lost sibling was of the same sex. Hence the loser will feel guilty. As outlined before (see page 114), older siblings losing a younger one may have more reason to feel guilty over the loss than younger ones losing an older, even though the younger ones may find it a little harder to handle whatever guilt they do have. All these considerations hold for losses of parents as well. In the child's eyes each is his rival for the other's affection. However, one of the worst mistakes one can make is to assume that, under normal conditions, a child would *really* want to rid himself of any rival parent for good, or that he could possibly be better off, if this happened. The intact family is still the best of all in which to grow up.

To the extent that the loss of a sibling (or of a parent) has been welcome—along with being painful—there will be guilt. The loser cannot help thinking that he has brought the loss about. It matters little that, in reality, this may often have been utterly impossible. Feeling guilty, however, means wishing for punishment (rather than not wishing it, but expecting it anyway, i.e., waiting to be hit by a retaliatory surprise attack). And choosing one's friends, dates, and spouse poorly may well serve to provide the punishment. In other words, although the loss of a sibling would generally tend to be easier to take than the loss of a parent—other things being equal—the greater ambivalence and guilt associated with the loss of a sibling may make up somewhat for the difference.

Still less severe losses would be those of a parent in adulthood, and the loss of a sibling at that time would be even lighter. Not that either kind may not be felt painfully and deeply, but by itself it almost never causes any psychopathology. It does so only in cases where the present loss is reviving previous, more severe losses, or in cases where the loser was still abnormally dependent upon the person lost. Losses of friends, dates, or even spouses, although often precipitating rather violent grief and demanding long mourning in order to be overcome, would still tend to be less severe and generally less pathogenic than the aforementioned losses. Substitution is usually easier. In many respects the person lost had been chosen as a sort of substitute for people who have been with a person from as far back as he can remember, such as parents and siblings.

Losses of one's own children—during their childhood—are usually still easier to overcome, although grief may be the strongest, most conscious and most demonstrative of all. Here, substitution is often under the control of the parents. They have created that child, and they could create another. While they are still young enough, they often do. Yet guilt over wishes to get rid of the child, no matter how sporadic and insignificant they were, may aggravate the loss. Parents have had to wish for a child in order to get one; even more, they have had to wish for everything that the child could possibly have wanted or needed. Otherwise they would not have known what that was, could not have fulfilled it, and the child would not have survived. So, if the child is lost, through an illness or an accident, the thought that they, the parents, caused the loss, perhaps merely by neglect, is almost inevitable even with the most loving of them.

From this it becomes plausible that some parents who really do not want their children, who feed, take care of, and play with, them only reluctantly, if at all—they may hire nurses instead—will be seriously bothered by a loss of such a child. They have made this happen. They have "killed" their child. And they have often trouble getting over this strong belief. Needless to say, the parents would tend to be troubled people anyhow. Why, otherwise, would they not want children and still have them? Why would they marry someone with whom they might not want to have them? Why would they make such a poor match? Well, conflicts prevailing among their parents, conflicts between them and their parents, losses suffered by themselves and/or by their parents, even conflicts and losses affecting the grandparents, or merely having been an unwanted child oneself, all this may have contributed to make the people troubled.

Among the drastic cases of indifference to, or hatred of, one's children, unwed mothers are perhaps the most frequent ones. Usually an unwed mother does not and cannot really want her child. Otherwise she would be married. Or she would at least have a man who would *want* her to have a baby and give it to him, so that the two of them could take care of it and enjoy it. As it is, an unwed mother cannot even be sure that the man ever wanted *her*. If circumstances force such a mother to keep her child, she will generally be in greatest conflict as a mother, and feel most guilty, if anything should happen to the child, even if she seems to deny it by her conduct.

Inversely, being the child of such an unwed mother is among the poorer predicaments of growing up. Usually the mother cannot hide very well her ambivalence toward the mere existence of her child, especially if it is a girl. In addition she may not be able to provide the true, or any other, father. Thus the child may grow up without a father, which is worse than having a father and losing him. One might argue that the child who has never had a father would not know what he or she is missing. Yet even the most painful loss has a positive side; it would leave a person with some idea, no matter how deeply buried, of what it was that he had once had, and he could try to find it again. To a person who has never had a father it would not even occur to look for one. The vacuum is worse than the loss.

The worst of all predicaments would be total abandonment at birth. If a child lives through this, it may be thanks to ever-changing, necessarily indifferent care by nurses, but there is no real parent, nor anybody who would consider the child his, hers, or theirs, with all that this implies. Even the most ambivalent parent would generally be better for the child than no parent at all. Such a parent may still cause a lot of trouble for the child, but as long as he is there, the child could make some sense of it, no matter how weird. That is not saying, though, that another person could not be a better parent figure for that child than the true parent.

# PART IV

## Examples of the Game

For those among the readers who do not yet find themselves engaged in games with hands taken from their own family, from friends and their friends, from colleagues or people they are dealing with professionally (as teachers, ministers, psychiatrists, social workers, officers, lawyers, businessmen, youth leaders, etc.), a few examples shall be given.

They are cases of persons that have been studied psychologically or in psychotherapy. However, a prediction of the type and severity of their psychological problems, conflicts, and disturbances will be given on the basis of *no more than* the crude and minimal data about their family constellation. These predictions will be implemented by brief case histories of the persons in question.

The examples will also give the reader an idea of a portion of the consultant work I have been doing in counselling centers and psychiatric institutes in Boston, Worcester, New Orleans, Topeka, and Vienna. To illustrate what knowledge of the "game" could do, I sometimes asked for the data on sibling positions of the persons concerned and of their parents as well as on losses suffered, *no more*. I then proceeded to portray the persons, their principal conflicts, and the approximate course of their psychological treatment. These blind diagnoses were generally accurate in four out of five cases, and were often said to furnish better and tighter explanations of the problems involved than the respective psychotherapists or counsellors had reached, in spite of their infinitely greater familiarity with their cases. With additional information on special circumstances such as prolonged illness, financial difficulties, migration, drastic unusual events, constitutional peculiarities and the like, or even merely on age gaps between siblings, spouses, parents and children, parents and their siblings, etc., the "fifth case" could always also be accounted for satisfactorily.

## CHAPTER 26

# A Boy in Psychological Treatment

Fred, nine years old, was the younger brother of a sister seven years his senior. His father was the older brother of a sister three years his junior, his mother the older sister of a brother three years her junior. The father's parents were the oldest brother of a brother, a sister and another brother, and the oldest sister of a sister and a brother. The father's mother had lost her father in her late childhood. The mother's parents were the youngest brother after three girls and the oldest sister of altogether three girls. This could be expressed symbolically in the following manner (see Part V for explanation of these notations):

$$b(b,g,b)/[\dot{f}/g(g,b)/m]//b(g_3)/(g_7)b/g(b_3)//(g,g,g)b/g(g,g)$$

father's parents     father   ↑ mother   mother's parents

Fred

## *Prediction*

In this constellation, Fred, because of the great age difference from his sister, would be a mixture of a younger brother of a sister and an only child. He will expect his sister to take care of him while he is following his interests and talents with some abandon, but he will also ignore his sister altogether or treat her somewhat like a servant or inferior member of the family.

From his parents he would inherit a conflict over authority. Both of them have been used to living with peers of the opposite sex, but either would like to be the master of the other, and

181

neither would willingly submit to the other, if it could be helped. Both want to be seniors.

This parental conflict is likely to affect Fred more than his sister. The sister finds a duplicate for her own sibling configuration in that of her mother who also has been the older sister of a brother. So the daugther can readily identify with her. Her relationship to her father involves conflict, because the father has been used to a *younger* peer of the opposite sex in his own childhood, but the conflict would not be any worse than the one the father has with the mother. Fred's sister can identify with her mother even in her relationship to her father.

Fred, on the other hand, does not find a duplicate of his sibling configuration in that of his father. He cannot easily identify with him, because the father was the *older* brother of a sister. The father would tend to boss and control a woman. He, Fred, would rather have her take care of his daily needs and submit to her wishes, as long as they do not interfere with his hobbies. To the extent that Fred does identify with his father, he will tend to maltreat his sister in odd ways, especially since the father would now be inclined to do so himself. Until the arrival of Fred, his daughter was just their (only) child. Now she has also become an older sister, exactly like his wife; both his wife and his daughter, he would feel, are contesting his authority.

Fred would also sense that he can be for his mother and even his sister what the father cannot be: a bit of a little boy, someone who can let the woman run the show at times. As a matter of fact, he may take advantage of it and become the spoiled star of the family. The father would not like that and grow jealous of Fred, but he may also discover that he can treat his son somewhat like a girl, as, a good while ago, he treated his sister. He may begin to spoil Fred, although his wife would, at that point, accuse him of making a girl of his son.

This is why Fred, more than his sister, would be at the mercy of the parents' conflicts. His sister has also been more involved in them, ever since Fred was born, but at least she has had seven years in which she was not, and that could have given her enough immunity to withstand present stresses.

Fred's parents have a rank conflict, but no sex conflict, and neither of them has suffered early losses. Their match is not too bad. Such parents should find relief from their rank conflict with the arrival of children. Apparently Fred's parents did not, or they would not have waited so long (seven years) to try for a second child. Hence the conflict of the parents may be more severe than their own sibling configurations alone would suggest. A glance at the grandparents may clarify that.

The father's father had been an oldest brother (of two brothers and a sister). So Fred's father has been strengthened in his position of an oldest sibling and, through identification, may have assumed features of the oldest brother of brothers himself, of a person, that is, who likes to lead men and be more of a tough guy with women. The father's mother had been an oldest sister (of a sister and a brother). So even the father's parents must have had a rank conflict which may have been mitigated by the fact that the father's mother lost her father in her late childhood. Her mother became a widow and she a fatherless girl. Through identification with her mother as well as through her own experience, the father's mother must have assumed, to an extent, the attitude of a forsaken woman herself. Such a woman may be unable to indulge in her own wishes or defend herself well against frustrations and aggressions from others. If ever she would stand her ground, the same thing could happen—she'd be left again. Thus the father's mother may have been meek, reticent, and submissive because of the loss she suffered, and the father's father may have had broader and stricter control over her than would ordinarily have to be expected. In other words, Fred's father was tacitly prepared to show his woman by action who was boss, if she would not believe him.

Fred's mother had a father who must have been used to having women take care of him and at the same time have been somewhat overwhelmed by the opposite sex (three older sisters) and reluctant to marry. The mother's mother (oldest of three girls) may have had to grab him almost by force, rather than attracting him by feminine charm, and she would tend to boss him a lot. Thus these grandparents prepared Fred's mother to expect extreme submission from the man in the family and to be more bossy and less motherly than she would have been on the basis of her sibling configuration alone.

For these reasons, the authority conflicts that Fred's parents had with each other may have been more severe than their sibling positions would suggest. Rather than catching on to the fact that children are the juniors they need, they stopped after one, at first, possibly because it was a girl. Mother had won, so to speak. When they had another child at last, mother's configuration had been duplicated. Then their trouble became obvious.

Fred's situation might be improved if some person, an aunt (say, father's sister), a greataunt, or a governess who has been the younger sister of a brother or perhaps even of a sister, were to participate in their family life. That way the father would have a junior female around and demonstrate a happier, though less important, relation to a woman than that to his wife and daughter. Fred could practice with that woman, too, and he could transfer skills so acquired to his mother and sister, and win his father's approval, although mother and sister themselves may not be too comfortable with the change.

In the light of all this and knowing that this was a case of psychotherapy, Fred's problems should be those of confusion over his own sex, over the authority he can hope to exercise, and over his notions of married life. He may act like a very spoiled girl, but also rant like a wild man, be unmanageable at home and unsuccessful with this behavior at school, hence possibly quite shy while there.

*Case history*

Fred had been brought to the guidance center because of his severe temper tantrums at home. He was said to have been quite moody and often listless, inconsiderate in the company of guests, and too fond of the maid of the house, an older woman who had also functioned as Fred's nurse and governess. Until not too long ago that woman would let him crawl into bed with her if he

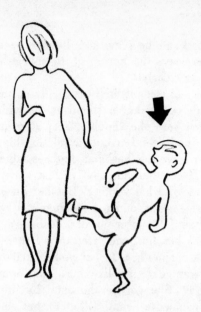

woke up at night and felt frightened in his own bedroom. His parents would not let him crawl into theirs. In school as well as among the neighbors he had no friends at all. He would not mingle, and he would get furious over attempts by his parents to bring children to the house or, as it happened, even to bribe them into playing with him. He would kick and abuse his sister Gloria, although much of the time he seemed to show a fair amount of affection for her. Academically he did quite well in school.

Fred's father was a rather successful real estate man who had taken the business over from his father, a self-made man who had built it all up himself. In the course of counselling with Fred's father he described his wife as too stern, principled, and always speaking her mind. Once he called her a thoroughbred and wondered whether he should not have married a cow, or at least someone as placid and easygoing as his sister. She had married a physician, borne him two boys and a girl and was very happy, he claimed. With respect to his son, he had been at a loss. He did not know too well how to communicate with him, and he spent far too little time with Fred, both he and his wife felt. He was not close to him. With Gloria this was different. She had always been very affectionate. Later he remarked, however, that he would just as soon have her leave the house, go to college anywhere in the country, and marry early.

Fred's mother, an elegant, highstrung person, busy with various women's clubs, described her husband as the wrong man for her. She had not been sure she should marry him until the day she did. After Gloria had been born, their relationship was so bad that she was ready to leave her husband, but her father persuaded her to stick it out. Her father had always had a tremendous respect for women, and so did her brother. But her husband was aggressive, inconsiderate, mean, and a hypochondriac, at least much of the time. She had felt closer to her husband's father while he was alive than to her husband. Her own father had never been firm enough with her mother. In her youth Fred's mother resolved that she never wanted to be like her. That woman was selfish, willful, unmotherly. She got her husband by proxy and through her letters. She can write beautiful letters, but she does not mean what she writes, Fred's mother claimed. To this day she is unable to do anything for her children or grandchildren except when everybody watches her and can see it. As a businessman, Fred's maternal grandfather was reasonably successful at first, then made changes twice, and is now barely getting by. This has also upset his wife who had always wanted to be a society woman. According to Fred's mother, her father's business partners have all been stinkers. Businessmen don't have morals, though, she says, this does not hold for her father or her brother. They have never uttered as much as a white lie, in contrast to her husband.

In the course of treatment, Fred slowly moved away from the role of a spoiled child to that of a boy who can and wishes to compete, can take moderate defeats and will risk making overtures to others without clamming up as soon as things do not quite go as expected. He became more boyish in his interests as well as in physical appearance, began to show pride in his achievements and shame over incidents of cowardice, both of which he had been strongly denying so far, found more pleasure with his parents (who were giving him more time and changing somewhat in their own behavior), his sister's friends, and his own classmates, and playmates of the neighborhood. He became rather outgoing, was mingling easily, accepting and extending invitations, participating in contests and games with increasing vigor. Treatment was discontinued, when he seemed to have become stable in his new outlook on life, and his parents appeared to have found a more compromising balance with each other and their life situation, including their maid who, incidentally, had been the youngest of three girls in her own family.

## CHAPTER 27

## A Wife Returning to Her Parents

Kathleen, a young mother, had left her husband after eight years of marriage and returned to her parents. She had been an only child of a father who was the youngest of altogether seven children, and of a mother who was the younger of two girls. Her father and his next older sister were the only children of his father's second marriage. His half-siblings of his father's first marriage were two brothers, then a sister, then a brother and a sister. Kathleen's husband had been the older of two boys and the son of a father who had been the oldest brother of two girls and a mother who had a younger sister and two still younger brothers. Her oldest brother had died soon after the mother had been born.

Kathleen and her husband had two children, a girl and a boy, who were four and two at the time Kathleen left her husband. She took her children along. Their family constellation could be represented symbolically like this (see Part V for explanation of notations):

$$b(g,g)/(b)g(g,b,b)//b(b)/g,b_2/g//(b_h,b_h,g_h,b_h,g_h,g)b/(g)g$$

| his father | his mother | husband | ↑ ↑ | her father | her mother |
|---|---|---|---|---|---|

children |

Kathleen

*Prediction*

As an only child Kathleen would ordinarily tend to believe that she was the only person that mattered, that she could always count

on the support of benevolent older people, and that she would not
be particularly keen on having children. Her mother has been a
younger sister of sisters. Therefore Kathleen will also show features
of her mother's character. She would tend to be capricious, competitive, and flirtatious, try to play men against each other at first,
and perhaps wish to settle only for the most special of all. Under
certain circumstances, though, a person like Kathleen could be
scared into taking the one next at hand for a husband.

Her parents are not too well matched. The mother must have
had some trouble getting used to living with a man, and both
father and mother would be much in need of guidance and leadership which they have failed to afford each other. As a younger
brother of a sister (the only true sibling he has) the father would
expect the woman to take care of his every little need, to buffer
him against hardships of the world, and to let him be the delightful,
charming, careless clown or, perhaps, the gentleman living by his
whims. His demands would be especially strong in view of the
conflict that he and his sister must have been engaged in with
their half-siblings. They were outnumbered and, depending on
the age gap separating the two sets of siblings, possibly at a
disadvantage, even if their father tried to give every one of his
children of his time, attention or property. What do those two
latecomers want? They have everything, above all, they have a
mother, whereas we, the original ones, have lost ours. (This is
assuming that the father remarried after his first wife had *died*.)
In the light of all this, there must have been a lot of overt conflict between Kathleen's parents. They may often have been on
the verge of separating.

Such trends would make Kathleen somewhat wary of marriage.
What complicates matters is the parents' tendency to make their
child into some sort of guide or leader as early in her life as possible.
Kathleen, on the other hand, could hardly learn from either parent
how to be that leader. The parents' adventure or accident of
parenthood (so that they might get something like a parent rather
than a baby) failed. They had no more children. Kathleen could
have succeeded to some extent only in her late childhood or in
adolescence, i.e., after having been exposed sufficiently to extra-

familial guides, such as teachers, scout leaders or even figures of literature. Relatives, such as the father's sister or the mother's sister, or (preferably maternal) grandparents, if around, could also teach her something, but they are likely to be occupied too exclusively by Kathleen's parents. Kathleen, possibly, had been newly tempted to believe that she could get a true parent after all, but—after failing to wrest these relatives from her parents or persuade them to stay—she will be even more disappointed. Extrafamilial idols would be less prone to let her down. Following them, she could become an authority in a field of knowledge or skill. However, long before Kathleen could fulfill her parents' wish for guidance to some small and peripheral degree, she must have sensed the parents' wish and somehow also her own inability to oblige. This could have made her feel unwanted and possibly guilt-ridden, especially since the father would be more likely to blame her mother for anything that went wrong than vice versa.

Kathleen's own choice of a husband was not the best one either, although one may wonder whether there is a best one for a person coming from parents who have been in clear conflict with each other. If she would choose someone like her father, she would be familiar with the problems involved in marriage, but inherit those very problems. If she chose someone very different in terms of his family constellation, say, an oldest brother of sisters, she would have to be taught all anew how to breathe those engaging airs and often remain too scared to ever get used to them.

As an older brother of a brother, Kathleen's husband would probably be tough with women and more in love with himself, other men, or work than with his wife. He may have married her for certain boyish qualities he recognized in her or for some resemblances she had to him. His tendency to boss or mastermind other people and to expect unconditional surrender for little in return (i.e., to expect secret but maximal mothering) would be aggravated by the authority conflict that prevailed between his parents. Kathleen's husband could have learned from his father how to be a ladies' man, and treat women in ways they like, if that man had been married to a younger sister of brothers. His mother, however, would not let his father treat her like a woman in their own family. She herself had presided over a girl and two little boys, after she had gotten rid of her older brother quickly. If she suffered from any guilt over this, it would be accompanied and countered by a sense of her own power, and this second aspect would become dominant altogether once her little brothers had arrived. She may feel that through her mere presence she had given her father two sons that lived.

Anyway, Kathleen's husband's mother would be inclined to treat her two sons like her younger brothers. Hence, Kathleen's husband would be a little like a younger brother of sisters through the treatment he has got from mother, something of an older brother of sisters through his identification with father, and a witness to a struggling and strife-torn marriage, possibly with father doing the giving in. Under those conditions he may have concentrated more heavily than other oldest brothers of brothers on his sibling and on relationships to junior men in order to avoid all the other apparent contradictions. Underneath the surface, he may have been a better match for Kathleen than a quick glance would lead one to believe, but on the surface he was probably very hard on her, and she, in response to this, quite unable to play along, yield, or give a faint appearance of a motherly person. Her husband would get along poorly with her father, and better with her mother. She would get along all right with his father, but be quite ambivalent about his mother. Their children duplicate Kathleen's father's sibling position, and that may be an additional source of contention among the parents. This duplication gave Kathleen's father a first opportunity to recognize himself and to be a little more of a father than he had ever been with his own daughter, and gave Kathleen a chance to show him how good a mother she could be (and might have been even for him, her father, if he had only let her or had waited). Kathleen's husband, on the other hand, although getting a son, may have found it increasingly difficult as time went by to identify with his son. He was being spoiled, would not obey, would never become a man, would not accomplish what he had outlined for him, and would surely grow up to be like his father-in-law.

The aggravations caused by the son probably brought the ailing marriage to the point of separation, but it is conceivable that the break could be mended. The separation may teach them that they had not fared too badly with each other after all. His father and her mother (who may have found themselves quite fond of each other) may persuade Kathleen to return to him. And Kathleen, who would be quite fond of her father-in-law and lean a lot on her own mother—partly because as a child she must never have felt quite able to do so—Kathleen might return to her husband. If he could get some help, psychologically or otherwise, he may discover features of the younger brother of a sister and the older brother of a sister in himself, and become kinder to his wife and more accepting of his son. Even his own daughter might teach him a little in that respect.

## Case history

Kathleen had been a somewhat nervous child and a poor eater, but showed artistic talent early in her life. In school, however, this seemed to have become an asset only in her upper teens and at the Academy of Arts which she went to after high school. There she met and eventually married Frank, a teacher at the Academy and her senior by nine years. She had admired and adored three other teachers before—two of them older women, the third a man some forty years older than she—and tried to follow their leads, impress them by her work, and do them shy but sensitive favors., One of the first things Frank did in their relationship was to break up her ties to all three of them, implying that he would not even consider seeing her otherwise. He also discouraged her in her artistic work to some extent, wished that she would, for a year or two, knock her fingers off as a typist, and accused her that she had always had it too good. But he appreciated her artistic taste and criticism. They married in a surprise move, emphasized the insignificance of the ceremony, and had their first child not until four years after they had been married. He often went out with the boys, schoolmates and veterans he had been in the war with. He sometimes did ask her to come along, especially when a few others brought their wives, but she never went. First he got quite angry at that, but eventually resigned himself to it. He was of little, if any, help to her after the children had arrived, but Kathleen's mother and mother-in-law were only too willing to step in, the mother-in-law quite obviously with the intention of taking over the show.

Kathleen's mother was still a pretty woman and a tireless worker, but very much under her husband's domination. He was fourteen years older than she, a heavy smoker and eater, bragging from time to time about certain women of top families whom he could have married instead of her. He had a good position in a large building firm, but wasted money and showed little foresight on family matters. Some hobbies of his, however, such as gardening and electronics, happened to come in quite handy in the difficult times during and after the war. Kathleen's mother kept the money and the household together, and provided even an apartment through the financial help of her father. She won a manifest hold on her husband only after he had begun suffering from stomach ulcers. She could, from then on, control his eating and help him abstain from smoking, coffee, and liquor. He had shown little interest in his daughter until she won a prize in high school for the best painting in a large exhibition.

Frank's father had died in a train crash a little before he and Kathleen got to know each other. Kathleen had never met him, but he was described to her by Frank as a quiet and thoughtful man, retiring in manner and speech, but warm and kind. Frank had felt more affectionate toward him than he had toward his mother. The latter was a very energetic and strong, but crude person whom Kathleen found utterly overwhelming. His mother had taken a job in a large bakery, after his father had died, and had soon advanced to a leading position in the firm. She had always been trying to boss her sons (both of whom, incidentally, had moved to another city) and also her siblings. Her sister lived in another country, but came faithfully to their family reunion every Christmas, either with or without her husband. The older of her two brothers held a position that he owed to her, and the younger brother was practically living off her.

Kathleen claimed that the relation with her husband got really intolerable when their second child arrived. Maybe one was already more than they could take, she expressed. Though they had gotten used to the daughter, they should not have had the boy. It really got to be too much for them. Frank would stay out nights, come home drunk, and be very hostile and abusive to her when he was at home. He resented particularly that Kathleen could not relate any better to his mother. And he refused to see her father. On rare occasions, he could still be quite nice and affectionate. His own brother usually succeeded in loosening him up, when he and his wife came for a visit. His brother's wife had also been helpful in this and other respects. She was an older sister of a brother. Colleagues and others considered Frank an outstanding artist and a good teacher, but a difficult person to be with.

Frank's sister-in-law and Frank's aunt (his father's youngest sister) were instrumental in bringing about Frank's and Kathleen's reunion after six months of separation. Until then he had had only occasional contacts with the children and a few telephone conversations concerning them. Now their marriage is still far from happy, but somehow they seem to have struck a balance. At any rate, both children are thriving, getting along with each other, apparently unaffected by their parents' conflicts.

## CHAPTER 28

## A Criminal Prisoner

Archie, 39 years old, a prisoner of seven months, was the younger brother of a sister six years his senior, and the son of a father who had had an older sister and an older brother, a younger sister and two younger brothers, and of a mother who had been the youngest sibling of an oldest boy and altogether three girls. The father had lost his mother in his late childhood, his older brother in his early childhood, and the older of his two younger brothers in his late childhood, not long before the mother died. The mother herself had lost her mother in her early childhood.

Archie was married to a wife some four years his junior and had had two children, both girls, five years apart in age. His wife was the youngest of three girls, the only child of her father's second marriage and a late-comer at that (twelve years younger than her next-older half-sister). The father's first wife had died. Archie's wife's father had been the third oldest of altogether seven children. He had had an older brother and an older sister, two younger brothers and, following them, two younger sisters. Her mother had had an older brother and an older sister. This could be expressed symbolically in the following way (see Part V for explanation of notations):

$$[f/\overset{\cdot}{m}//(g,\overset{\cdot}{b})b(g,\overset{\cdot}{b},b)/(g_6)b/(b,g,g)g//f/\overset{\cdot}{m}]/g,g_5/$$

| ↑ | his father | ↑ his mother | ↑ children |
|---|---|---|---|
| his father's parents | | Archie | his mother's parents |

$$[(b,g)b(b,b,g,g)/(g_h,g_h;)g/(b,g)g]$$

| her father | ↑ her |
|---|---|
| Archie's wife | mother |

## Prediction

Archie would have grown up to be a girls' boy, expecting his sister and others to take care of his affairs, if his sister had not lived as an only child for six years. She could not have been too willing to look after him. At least she could not learn much about it from their mother. The mother is likely to have been a somewhat seductive woman, though also competitive as well as too dependent. The loss of her mother would have been buffered by her siblings. At that time she may have been the one whom her father, her brother, and one of her sisters wanted to relieve of, or even spare, the pains of mourning. But the other sister was probably quite jealous of her and made it difficult for her to enjoy these favors. On all those grounds, Archie's mother may not have been too ready to nurse her son and take care of his daily needs so that he could pursue wholeheartedly his hobbies and interests.

This is aggravated by Archie's father. He not only lost his mother in his late childhood, something that may have made him tend toward depression and some steady, though seemingly inexplicable, longing, but he also lost two brothers. The death of the older one during his early childhood must have created confusion and guilt in him, and the death of the younger one (whom he must have experienced much more consciously as a rival) could have made things worse, in fact, intolerable, if he did not turn around altogether and take the death as proof of his own power. He disposed of his enemies, and reinstated, at last, a good balance of sexes in his family. However, punishment followed immediately. He now lost his mother. If he did not want to go out of his mind with grief, he must have concluded that somehow this was his doing too, that somehow he had triggered this loss or had even wanted it. She may have died because she loved the other two sons so much and hated him for wishing them out of his way. She may have died because she loved the father more than anybody else. Archie's father buried his abominable wish, firmly resolving neither to wish nor do more harm to anybody, man or woman. After his mother's death Archie's father may have seen his older sister turn more to his youngest brother and even play a so-so wife to his father, something he did not like, but would do nothing about from there on. In fact, he himself probably found some bitter consolation with his youngest sister. Later he married a person who may have been feminine, attractive, and capricious, though somewhat subdued, but definitely unable to give him, her husband, what his oldest sister used to bestow on him until the mother died. He had to bear even that lest he—or fate—run rampant altogether.

This describes the kind of father with whom Archie must have identified. Although Archie had not suffered any immediate losses himself, the father's losses and the father's reactions to them were passed on to him. These losses are also the most conspicuous and relatively unusual aspects of his family background. The mother's losses were smaller.

Archie's sister must have found her father reticent, unresponsive, even gruff. Thus she was probably forced to identify with him rather than relate to him, and that too made it difficult for her to accept, and feel warmly toward, her brother. What Archie would have picked up about the marriage of his parents would be something like this: Father is too tough. He does not even talk. Mother is too soft and tender. He is poor company for her. She should have married someone else. Marriage is no happy affair.

Archie's wife probably had been the pampered baby in her family, with features of an only child and some of those of a younger sister, this because of her identification with the mother and because of her own position. Her older half-sisters must have resented her a lot. They had lost their mother, were cheated by their father, and perhaps tried to leave home as early as they could. Her mother would have been a feminine and submissive person, although also somewhat of a tease, if she could get away with it. The fact that she married a widower (possibly considerably older than herself) may indicate that she had not got away with much. After they married, her husband (who had not suffered any early losses in his life) would probably let her breathe freely. With his daughter he might have been a doting fool. Hence, Archie's wife would want to follow her feelings and wishes as she pleased and show no inhibitions about men. She may have done so before the two were married and/or she may still be a big flirt with their present male friends.

Archie would not like that. He must have felt his father's rage in himself, believing unconsciously that he could hurt very badly and kill if he let loose. But like his father, Archie must also have kept feeling a strong force against doing harm to anybody, especially one's wife. His mother, who had also suffered a loss, was readier than his wife to subordinate herself to a man, anyway. Archie's wife confronted him with a much more difficult task in that respect.

Since Archie has been in a penitentiary for the past seven months—the only information about his crime that we have—let us try to derive, on the basis of all previous considerations, what he may have done. Theft, robbery, embezzlement? No more likely than with any jailed person picked at random. Slander, tax evasion, conspiracy against the government, etc.? Not too likely either. Assault, manslaughter, murder? More likely. Whom could he have assaulted? Probably a family member. It was in the family where Archie's father had been successful with *losses* as well as deadly frightened because of this success. People other than family members must have been less of a temptation to his father. If there was a conflict, he could simply avoid these outsiders. By psychological inheritance this would hold for Archie too. So who might have been the victim of Archie's assault? His father? No. He was too stern, powerful and at the same time reticent, to be anything but awesome. His mother? No. She was too submissive, too subdued, and sweet. She did not challenge father or anybody very much. Archie's sister? A more likely target. She was an older sister, and it was with his own older sister that Archie's father may have had a real gripe. He may also have made clear to his daughter in no uncertain ways that she should take good care of Archie, a matter in which she was not likely to oblige. If Archie's father ever showed rage and fury, no matter how quickly he stopped himself, it was probably with his daughter. She in turn would be tempted to retaliate, at least in her thoughts.

But Archie had left the home, was married, and had his own

family. Those in the family are more likely to have challenged him into a real attack. His wife? She could have. She might have aroused his jealousy. On the other hand, he may have known what he was getting into with her ever since he started dating her. And she was a youngest sibling, the pampered one, the cutie. How could he lay hands on her, either then or now? Did his father ever raise as little as his voice against Archie's mother? Probably not.

His older daughter perhaps? Well, assuming average circumstances to prevail, she may be about fourteen years now, and her little sister nine. At the time when Archie committed his offense, she may have been a little over thirteen, an age at which girls can make a bit of a nuisance of themselves to their parents. They get more seriously interested in possible dates, clothes, movies, cars and the like, but above all in boys. If she has not been interested or fond of her little sister, this would become very obvious now. If her father, Archie, had been an oldest brother, he might have forced her into an obedient affection for her sister, but Archie was not. He probably began to hate her, just as his father could have hated his own older sister and his own daughter, Archie's older sister. Archie, the same way, must have hated his older sister, but the only older sister whose antagonism and selfishness he could combat at the time of the crime was his own daughter. As a matter of fact, as her father he had every right to hate these traits of hers. If Archie did commit assault or murder, she is the most probable candidate.

Could his younger daughter have been the victim? Not likely. For one thing, her mother, Archie's wife, can easily identify with her, and also serve her well as an object of identification. The older daughter cannot identify with her mother. The only female in the family with whom she could readily identify would be Archie's sister. But Archie's wife is prone to be in conflict with that woman, too, and would dislike her daughter for such unfaithfulness even more. By contrast, the little one would be even more of a darling to both parents.

In summary, then, we could say that Archie has taken over from his father a severe and unresolved conflict about the treatment of people, in particular close females. Upon sufficient provocation he may break out from the old stalemate between devastating attack and extreme guilt over the consequences. He could do something that he would be sorry for ever after. Concretely, he could have assaulted and murdered his older daughter or possibly, though less likely, his wife.

## Case history

Archie was a clerk with an adequate salary, a car, and a little house in the countryside from where he commuted to work, before he was committed to the penitentiary. He had been known by friends and colleagues as an industrious and conscientious, but obstinate, person with a bitter humor. He looked happily married, to them, although his wife revealed later that their marriage was far from happy. Their characters did not agree at all. Recently, i.e., a few months before he committed the offense, their relationship had improved a little.

They had met toward the end of World War II when men were scarce and he had had a medical discharge from the army. His knee had been battered by a shell; and his leg had remained stiff. She had been engaged twice and dated several men before, but somehow they had all seemed to lose interest after a while. She had not been particularly attracted to Archie, but he seemed the only one left, she felt. Besides, he was a member of the gang from which most of her dates and both fiancées had come from. They all had gone to the same school, lived in the same general neighborhood, and were still in contact with each other. In fact, if some of those friends and her own parents had not comforted and consoled her off and on, she would have divorced Archie long ago. Archie, she claimed, had the same tough and potentially vicious mind as Jeanne, his sister. That girl had not married to this day because she was smarter than any man she met. Now she is going to be an old maid. Perhaps Archie was not quite as vicious as she. He had beaten her occasionally during the early part of their marriage, mostly because of his suspicions of other men, but he had never really hurt her, and in a way she had not even minded his very firm hand with her and in family matters in general. But emotionally she had felt gypped all along.

Archie had adopted a kind of humorous attitude toward his wife, one that was not even sarcastic: "She wants fun, and to be the center of the boys' attention. She loves to drink and spend money once in a while. She has actually been a good wife, on the whole, not really extravagant, and faithful to me ever since our marriage, but needs to be watched and kept in check." The only thing that had originally irked Archie was that some of his friends had possessed his wife before their marriage, and although the one most beloved to her had been killed in the war, there was another one of whom she was still uncomfortably fond. She had been a good mother to their children, although a little hard on Liz, the older one. Liz had always struck them as a very intelligent girl who matured rapidly both mentally and physically. The little one was more of an average child, neither as beautiful nor as smart as Liz, but very cute and cuddly.

Archie's offense was a violent assault on Liz when she had disregarded his orders, been out with boys, and come home three

hours later than promised. He had hit her with an iron bar and broken her spine, so that she had been paralyzed in her legs. But she was improving and had begun to walk again. He had not meant to hit her that hard. He was very sorry. He did not believe now that his daughter had really betrayed his good faith in her, but he was outraged at the time, especially since she had expressed so many fancies and illusions all along. She had plans to become a movie star, a model, marry a count, get a Jaguar. His sentence was two years, but he hoped to be out before that. He lost his job. Well, he could find another one. And there was the hardware store which his father would leave him as soon as he got out of jail. The father wanted to retire anyway. He had been very nice about the whole thing. It almost seemed as if he, the father, had had the bad conscience. Archie actually did not know what had overcome him at the time. He had been intent on slapping Liz, he remembered, but then this iron bar had been there, and the next thing he knew was Liz lying on the floor, unable to get up. Even so he deserved the sentence. In court Liz had claimed that he had threatened several times to kill her if she would not obey him to the letter. He may have said it, but he could never truly have meant it.

Liz appeared relatively unaffected, at least now that her gait was almost back to normal. Even her little sister's expressed hatred for her—because she had brought their father to jail—did not seem to make much of an impression on her. She would not be afraid to live in the house after the father had returned home. She knew that he had not wanted to hit her as hard as he had, and he would not dare to raise a hand against her now. Maybe she had overdone it with her spite of her father. But she had no reason to change now, to forego any fun that was coming to her. If she did not have enough sense to know where to stop, it was too bad for father. But she thought she did.

## CHAPTER 29

## A Mental Patient

Sheila is a 27 year old girl who has been in mental hospitals for the past ten years. She has a sister, one year older than herself, who is now married and has two children, a girl and a boy. Her father, now sixty-five years old, has had an older brother and two older sisters—five, three, and two years his senior. He has also had two younger siblings, a girl eleven years, and a boy thirteen years his junior. His father was separated from the rest of the family while he himself grew from five to ten years of age. The old man had emigrated to the United States, and it took him five years until he was able to pay the fare for the rest of the family. Less than three years after they had all arrived he died. Sheila's mother had an older brother, a younger sister, and a still younger brother. They all married before she did, and all of them had children. Her parents had lived until three and two years ago. She herself had died of cancer about four years ago at the age of 58. About two years later Sheila's father remarried a widow who had been the oldest sister of two younger brothers and a still younger sister, and who had two grown sons from her first marriage who were no longer living with her. Symbolically, Sheila's family constellation would look like this (see Part V for explanation of notations):

$$\overset{\textstyle .}{f}/m//(b_5,g_3,g_2)b(g_{11},b_{13})/(g_1)g/(b)g(g,b)$$

father's parents     father     Sheila     mother

*Prediction*

Sheila's father had been witness to a separation of his parents. By age, he would have been the one most vulnerable to the loss of his father, but it was buffered for him by his older siblings and his mother's presumable conviction that they would be reunited in the not too distant future. By the time the reunion occurred, however, he must have pretty much forgotten life with father. He had hardly got used to him again when his father had given his mother another two children, and then died himself. Hence the older children had to look after the family or at least after themselves. The oldest brother, the most logical successor to the father, must have been about eighteen by that time and capable of earning a living, but probably also interested in getting married. His parents' temporary separation had hit him when he was already ten years old. He had been witness to adequate and plausible relationships between his parents throughout his formative years. Sheila's father, on the other hand, learned early that a marriage can break up. So why marry? Why reach out for too much, if you can have everything you want right here at home? At any rate, he is the more likely of the two brothers to stick it out at home, even if the burden of providing should creep up on him in the process. The two older girls would also have felt called upon to chip in, but with a temporary loss of the father in their early lives, with the final loss in their adolescence, they may have tried to find a safer haven than their own family with almost any man who would come along. There may also have been a feeling among the three older siblings something like: "We have taken care of you (Sheila's father) long enough. Why don't you take over now?"

It is likely that Sheila's father was the one who ended up as the head of household soon after his father's death. He got the mother at last, and he had two little children of hers to take care of. Such a course of events is also indicated by the late date of arrival of his own children, which probably also meant a late marriage. He was 37 when his first daughter was born, and his wife 34, which is rather late for a woman, too. His wife came from a family with no apparent complications (no losses of parents or siblings; her parents presumably matched well enough to let all of her siblings get married without too much difficulty and make a go of it, as evidenced by their having children) so she must have been either not very attractive to other men or not too anxious for inner reasons to get married. One thing sometimes goes with the other. She might have felt too sensitive, shy, and ambivalent about people in general and about men in particular. Considering the lack of evidence of any losses suffered or severe conflicts prevailing in her original family, this facet of her character could be hereditary. She may have been one of those people who find life difficult or even unbearable, without being the victims of any trauma to speak of.

If that were so, however, she would be more accepting of a man who is somewhat older, has taken care of a family and little children before, and also has had the comforts of his own mother all along. Sheila's mother would probably sense the father's unconscious dependence on the support of a motherly person, but also that somehow he must have managed to get the support, and would not depend for it too heavily on her. If he got it, she would too, may have been her implicit (and probably mistaken) reasoning. Even so, they did not really make a poor choice with each other. Both duplicate for their spouse at least one of the sibling positions they have held in their original families, and they have come from relatively similar configurations anyway.

If Sheila's mother had indeed been a vulnerable person, she would be likely to create trouble for her first daughter rather than her second. However, the first one is married and has children, whereas the second one started having very manifest troubles at seventeen or probably sooner. Which means that Sheila, in addition to having had a somewhat dependent father and a nervous mother, may have been affected hereditarily, and was thus ill equipped to cope, especially with her sister. The struggle among the siblings must have been quite inarticulate and confusing to her because of the small age gap, possibly aggravated by the father's ambivalence toward his own much younger siblings, his children, and the sex

of his second child. And if she resolved her problems for the time
being, she would have done so chiefly by denying that there was
a struggle. She may have got all she wanted while acting like a
capricious and whiny baby, or she may have been an exceptionally
quiet and good child instead.

It would not be too surprising if there had been some case of
mental illness among her ancestors.


*Case history*

Sheila had been a very pretty and angelic child who gave her
parents no trouble whatsoever. However, at twelve, shortly after
she had started menstruating, she was sent to a summer camp,
and became intolerable to the camp within a few days. A month
later she was committed to a mental hospital and sent home after
six months. She was then put in a private boarding school from
which she had to be recommitted to mental hospitals several
times. For the past ten years she has never been out of mental
hospitals, except for weekends or a few days in a row.

Her father had married so late because the burden of caring
for the two late-comers in his family—after immigration to the
United States—had rested with him. His older siblings had moved
out of the house almost as soon as their father had died. He had
resented their doing this ever since. He would not talk to them
if he met them, he said, but had lost touch with all of them anyway.
One died a few years ago. Both his younger siblings were un-
happily married, the childless brother for the second time. His
sister worked very hard to support her ailing and drinking husband
and two boys, one of whom had lost a leg in an accident.

Sheila's mother had been a beautiful woman, but quite shy
and a little nervous, the husband explained. She worried a lot,
and when Sheila got ill, she thought day and night about her. She
felt it had been her fault. She had had one miscarriage before
having the two girls. She was quite upset about that and received
psychotherapy in order to get over the shock. Later she had begun
to be excessively concerned about her and other people's health,

and had actually been ailing for a few years before her death. Her older brother had been in a mental hospital for two years with a psychotic depression.

The father's new wife was a big motherly person who liked to live and eat well, but also knew how to take care of him and his health in ways he found very comfortable. He even said: "I have never had it so good." Eventually she persuaded him to retire. They had enough money, and they were going to take regular long vacations in the South. And he insisted that his older daughter could take care of Sheila while they were away. She could visit Sheila in the hospital or take her home for weekends, just as they themselves used to do throughout the year. According to the step-mother, Sheila's visits at home had been quite strenuous on Sheila's father. But the stepmother could apparently take good care of the patient, too. Sheila had been very hostile when she met her for the first time after they were married, but had since taken to her relatively well. The stepmother's own sons were both married and visited them occasionally. Sheila's father did not particularly care for those visits either, but seemed to be much less upset than when Sheila visited.

## CHAPTER 30

# A Young Man Bereaved by Many Losses

Carl, a young man of twenty-four who works in a factory, is the youngest of three children. His mother had brought an illegitimate girl into her marriage. The second girl, however, was his true sister. His mother had had an older brother, an older sister, and two younger brothers, both of whom perished in a fire when she was about eight or nine years old. Her mother died of tuberculosis when she was thirteen. Carl's father had been an orphan since birth, and had grown up in an orphanage until he was adopted by a cousin of his mother and her husband, at about the time he started school. Carl's mother and her father died in a car accident while his mother was driving. Carl was four years old at the time. His father put the older girl in an orphan's home, the younger with a family, and Carl with the same relatives who had brought *him* up. The father then took up with a woman who drank, began to drink himself, and lost contact with all of his children. Carl's foster-grandmother had been the oldest sister of four other girls and her husband the youngest and only son after three girls. They had no children of their own. This could also be expressed symbolically in the following manner (see Part V for explanation of notations):

$$\overset{:\ :\ :}{f/b/m}//\overset{:\ :}{(g_h,g)b}//\overset{:\ \cdot\cdot\ \cdot}{f/(b,g)g(b,b)/m} \rightarrow (g,g,g)b_s/b/g_s(g,g,g,g)$$

$$\underset{\underset{\text{father}}{\uparrow}}{} \quad \underset{\underset{\text{Carl}}{\uparrow}}{} \quad \underset{\underset{\text{mother}}{\uparrow}}{} \qquad \underset{\text{foster-father} \uparrow \text{foster-mother}}{} \atop \text{Carl}$$

## Prediction

This is an overwhelming history of losses. Carl would be a ladies' boy, a person to whom the girls flock, and who would expect them to cater to him and look after his daily needs. He would merely follow his inclinations, interests, and talents. But these attitudes got badly shaken, when he lost not only his mother but, psychologically speaking, also his two sisters and father.

Even before that he must have sensed the losses that mother and father had suffered. His mother must have felt quite guilty over the loss of her younger brothers, or at least over the loss of one of them. If she loved the other one (presumably the younger) dearly, she may have thought of his loss as the punishment she deserved. The loss of her mother would have been an additional blow, possibly construed by her as the true retaliation for some bad wishes she had had for her younger brothers. Probably it did not help much to have had that trauma buffered by her older siblings.

How do we know? For one thing, she went on punishing herself. She got herself an illegitimate child, which means that the man from whom she had it did not really want her. And she had probably known all along that this was what she should expect of him. Then she got herself an orphan for a husband, a person who had not been wanted by either his father or his mother. True, he had foster parents, but he started having them quite late —when he was about six years old. Furthermore his foster parents had been childless themselves. It is likely that his foster mother, as an oldest sister of sisters, bossed and controlled his foster father, and if they could not have children of their own even though they wanted them (why else would they have adopted Carl's father and been willing to take Carl too), it was probably considered his fault. His foster father, on the other hand, must have been somewhat wary of the other sex. He had had too much exposure to it in his original family. If anything, he wanted to be left alone by women or maybe discreetly cared for by them, but not really bothered or involved in their chitchat.

In attempting to identify with his foster father, Carl's father would assume those features himself. He also would not learn about marriage as a happy experience. His foster mother must have appeared too uninviting, too unfeminine in her character even to him. Yet, had the foster parents been perfectly matched with each other, he would still have the drawn out shock of his experience in the orphanage, and hardly be able to trust the happiness of his present family life.

For all those reasons, Carl's father is likely to have been an unstable, insecure person, looking for some mysterious, inexhaustible supply of favors, gratifications, and affection that he had never quite had in his early life. Hence his marriage to a girl who had slipped and was already a mother; she could take him on not only as a husband but also as a child. Hence, further, the complete breakup of the home after his wife's death and his recourse to a drunkard girl and drinking.

Fate hit Carl (and his father and his mother) so hard that, even with a strong psychological constitution, Carl must have become a disturbed person, tending, already under minor stresses, to revert to early and primitive forms of interpersonal relationships and gratifications. He is in danger of taking to drinking, of depressive psychotic episodes, of at least mild schizophrenic reactions, or of developing a rather schizoid character. He would have trouble marrying or even venturing any serious steps in that direction. Relatively his best stronghold may be work, provided he had sufficient talents and they were recognized and fostered early enough. He may cling to work vehemently in order not to have to long hopelessly for an all-powerful unconditional provider, nor to get entangled with girls and become dependent upon them. What could they possibly do but let him down.

## Case history

Carl had been a potentially brilliant student in school, but he tended forever to flop in the final phases of his studies. Even so he graduated from high school at seventeen, from college cum laude at twenty, only to start working in a rather inferior and futureless position of laboratory assistant in the research center of a large chemical firm. He was described by colleagues as quiet and withdrawn, reliable in his work, but slow, fussy, odd, and distrustful in his social contacts.

His foster mother had consulted with a psychiatric agency in worry about Carl's seclusion in an awful little apartment of his own, although he could have continued to live in their comfortable house. When she had tried to have him back home after he graduated from college, he had called her a monster, the only time she had ever heard him use a curse word. But he still felt that way about her, she claimed. Yet she had thought that she had done everything she could for him. Her husband had been against adopting a child, but she had gone ahead anyway and won him over with adopting Carl's father. When it came to adopting Carl her husband's consent was much less of a problem.

Now Carl came to visit them about once a month, but he chiefly visited her husband, she explained. Carl hardly talked to her, but he did talk to him, and when he left, her husband would usually see him to the station. Carl's foster mother implied that her husband had never been too much of a man, that he did not have a will of his own, and that Carl had taken after him a lot, although not altogether. For how could he, otherwise, have taken such a stubborn stand on the job he chose—no position for a boy with his brains—and on his move to the apartment. He could live much more cheaply and comfortably with them.

Upon inquiry, Carl's foster mother revealed that Carl had had very little contact with girls. He had always been a reticent and shy boy who almost loathed affection. Only once did he seem in love, with a student when he was in college. But she probably did not even know he existed, let alone how he felt about her. The foster mother learned about it from a letter that he had meant to write to the girl, but had torn up. (She had pieced it together.) Earlier, in his last year of high school, he must have had a crush on a girl although nobody found out who she was. Even in the mental hospital where he spent six weeks for observation that summer, after graduation, he would not tell anything about the girl. He had developed a peculiar kind of spell. He hardly slept, and did just about nothing but brood. They were quite concerned and eventually took him to the hospital. He recovered after a while. The whole experience had never been mentioned since.

He had no boyfriend either, his foster mother said. He had never been on very good terms with any of his classmates, but now he had literally nobody. He could have shared an apartment with somebody, but he refused to. The only person with whom he did have occasional contact was a crazy painter, a man some ten years older than he who ran around in corduroy suits and sneakers, and lived with a very young and utterly gone girl who wrote poems. One poem a year.

"Oh, he has occasionally asked for his sisters. He sort of cherished the older of the two, his half-sister, but she was no good. Eventually she went West and became a show girl at some crummy place. She is lost. She does not even have an address. His other sister is all right, but we never cared much for the family she lived with. She became a salesgirl. She is married now and has a little boy."

The agency advised Carl's foster mother that he would need psychiatric help, but warned her that it might be difficult to persuade him to seek it. Her husband could perhaps talk to him about it at an opportune moment. However, nothing was heard from her or Carl thereafter.

## CHAPTER 31

## A Young Architect

Otto, a man of twenty-seven, had a sister two years his senior and a brother three years his junior. Otto had graduated from an engineering school in his home city where he had studied architecture, and entered a well known architect's firm as an assistant. His father had been the youngest brother of an older sister, of an older half-brother whom his mother had brought into her marriage as an illegitimate child, and of an older half-sister whom his father had brought into the marriage from a premarital relationship of his own. Otto's mother had been the oldest sister of two brothers. Two of Otto's grandparents were still living, the other two had died only in the last few years. This could be stated symbolically by the following expression (see Part V for explanation of notations):

$$(b_h, g_h, g)b/(g_2)b(b_3)/g(b,b)$$

father $\qquad\qquad\uparrow\qquad$ mother

Otto

The particular question asked in this context was how Otto would fare at his job and what kind of girl he might go out with and eventually marry.

*Prediction*

Otto would show features of a younger brother of a sister, i.e., tendencies to attract girls willing to mother him and look after

him, and he would have been comfortable in this role, had it not
been for his younger brother. His arrival jeopardized Otto's position. He must have seen his sister cater to his younger brother
with more abandon and grace than he could remember her showing
him. He would be jealous of her and the brother. His sister should
not spend so much time with this young brother, and he in turn
should not only look up to his sister and dote on her, but also
should try harder to make a play for him, Otto. At least he should
emulate him. After all, he was his older brother. He should obey
him. But that fellow did not. Otto would be somewhat torn between
his two roles, not quite at ease in either, and hence a bit of a
problem even in his extrafamilial social contacts. Not a serious
problem, though.

In his relationship with his father he has another complication.
His father had been the youngest brother of a brother and two
sisters, i.e., the youngest of four, and the youngest of the two in
the family that were born in wedlock and were probably the
privileged. In either respect, Otto could not identify with his father
as easily as could his younger brother. His father, in turn, would
recognize his own position in his youngest son and shortchange
Otto a trifle. What is more, he would not be too fatherly a father
in the first place, leaving the tasks of parenthood more or less to
his wife, an older sister used to taking care of younger men.

In his relationship to his mother, Otto should find more comfort. The first of her younger brothers is likely to have put up a
similar fight as Otto did for his older sister and for, as well as
against, his younger brother. But she understood what this first
brother was up against—something similar to what she had been
up against when he arrived. She could take her second brother in
stride and probably help her first brother to get used to him too.
She must have been even better prepared to sympathize with Otto
and help him get accustomed to his younger brother than she had
been with her own brothers.

At any rate, Otto would probably be quite fond of his mother,
and his family background as a whole, though burdened with
some conflicts, cannot have been a truly unhappy one. He may
have been, and may continue to be, somewhat of a troublemaker

for his family as well as for his friends, acquaintances, teachers or employers, but the troubles would not be too serious and could usually be mended without much effort. He would tend to be quite whimsical and dictatorial at times, but also competitive whenever challenged. When the latter is the case, his superiors could easily call him to order about his whims, whereas at other times they may have more of a problem.

With girls he may also put up fights of sorts. He would tend to find himself an older sister of brothers. She would know how to take him. But because of his younger brother he may also have a strong wish, at times at least, to get away from older sisters and go on a binge, say, with a youngest sister of sisters. Unconsciously, he would want something super-feminine, a willful and capricious person, a star perhaps, but he would soon lose his patience and return to older sisters again, even to his own sister. Ultimately he would be best matched with an older sister of two brothers. Full duplication of a person's sibling configuration is, relatively, the most likely to succeed in family backgrounds like Otto's where the parents have been happily matched, and no losses have been suffered either by them or by the person in question. If he married such an oldest sister of two brothers, he may even permit the younger of her two brothers to live with them or be around the house a lot. As a matter of fact, they may become good friends. He may be able to tolerate him much better than his own brother, and develop the feelings of friendship and affection that he could never wholeheartedly indulge in with his brother.

It is worth considering briefly what his sister and his younger brother might do with *their* work situations and friends of the opposite sex. This could accentuate Otto's portrait further.

His sister will show the features of an oldest sister of brothers in a rather pure form. Not only does she have two younger brothers to take charge of, she also has a mother who was precisely in that position herself. She should have no trouble identifying with her wherever her own experience and ingenuity does not suffice. And she has a father who had been the younger brother of a sister (or, if you like, the youngest brother of two sisters and a brother), was well-matched with his wife, and was inviting her, his daughter, to cater to him and take care of his various earthly needs. However, she would also be the one to sense whatever trouble there might have been between the parents more clearly than either of her brothers. There was no immediate trouble, but her father's father and mother had apparently had some difficulties. They had had illegitimate children. That meant that at one time the father's mother had been a bad woman, and that the father must have realized that somehow. What is more, the father's father also brought an illegitimate child into the marriage. Why did that child, the father's half-sister, not stay with her mother? That's where illegitimate children are more likely to end up. Who forced him to keep his child? What woman could pull that one over on him? Was he a weak man? Or was it just that he could not abandon a little girl? Anyway, would his only legitimate son, Otto's father, not sense all that and be somewhat ashamed of it?

Otto's sister must have concluded that, if everything was fine in her parents' marriage, it certainly was not with her paternal grandparents, at least when they started out with their marriage. Even to this day that half-uncle and half-aunt are the dark side of the family with which one had better avoid contact. "Love relationships have their dangers," Otto's sister must have felt, "and my father knows it. Even though he won't tell me, I know it, in fact, from him."

Otto's sister may find it just a little bit harder than other oldest sisters of brothers would to settle down for a marriage of her own. She is an ever so slight candidate for slipping, possibly picking up a man who has slipped, or perhaps entering a relationship in which the man is slipping. That is, he may be married to another woman and not really willing to divorce his wife. Hence Otto's sister may also stay more attached to her work than other girls, preferably as a chief secretary for several men, as a social worker or nurse, as a teacher or physician.

Otto's younger brother, on the other hand, has not only less conflict about his role as the youngest brother of a sister—he *is* the youngest, can let his mother and his sister give him all kinds of treats, and can identify fully with his father—but he is also the one best protected against the only problem we know of in the parents' marriage. This younger brother is less likely than Otto to be puzzled by what his sister has picked up about their father. The younger brother can follow the call of his talents with greater abandon and less conflict. He can really choose what he would like to do, whereas Otto, the frustrated leader of (younger) men, is prone to have been influenced also by some wishes for power, grandeur or becoming a genius at all costs.

## Case history

Otto nearly flunked a course necessary for his graduation as an architect, because he insisted on his version of a special architectural assignment. His colleagues had advised him against it. He also fell into disfavor with another professor for calling him at odd times about trifles. And once, in a clumsy maneuver at a department party, he poured wine over that same professor's pants. Similar things were said to have happened in high school.

At work he was considered very competent and gifted, but willful and somewhat unpredictable. He would have no trouble holding his own, but sometimes he made himself a pain in the neck for the others. In one of their firm's projects he behaved very stubbornly, attempting to push a poor point through. But good men have their moods, was the boss' conclusion.

While studying architecture, Otto had dated a girl and been as good as engaged to her, but when celebrating his graduation,

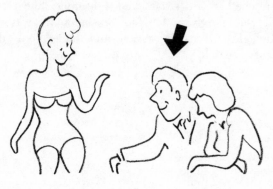

they had gone to a nightclub, and he had hopelessly fallen in love with a strip teaser. He persuaded that girl to quit the night club, paid for her private acting lessons—after he had urged her to try for admission to the city's drama school and she had failed— and lavished every penny on her. A year later she had become the mistress of a banker's son and returned to night club life. Otto had a hard time getting over it. Eventually there was a rapprochement with his fiancée (an only child and daughter of a mother who had been the older sister of a brother), helped along by Otto's mother and sister. At that time he was quite instrumental in winning his firm a sizeable contract. His fee enabled them to marry and set up their own household. There were no children yet (three years later).

The night club girl, incidentally, had been the sixth and youngest child of her father's first marriage, and had left the father's farm in a village some hundred miles south to try her luck in the big city. Her mother had died when she was three years old. Her father had remarried and had four more children.

Otto's sister, head social worker in a general hospital, was engaged to a man eight years older than she who had lived separated from his wife and was waiting for his divorce. He had no children. Before meeting him, Otto's sister had been going with two men in a row, one her age, a younger brother of a sister, and another some three years her junior, a singleton. The two men were physicians. Her present fiancé was a lawyer in public service.

Otto's brother, a biologist, was getting ready to marry the oldest sister of altogether two sisters and a brother. She came from a fairly well-to-do family in the food business. He was working in an ornithological research station and hoped one day to do independent research.

# PART V

## Some Theoretical Considerations

Those among the readers who like more formal reasoning to go along with the game may find the following considerations useful and suggestive. It should be said, though, that they contain nothing that has not been said or implied elsewhere in this book. Hence it can be skipped by readers who dislike symbolic designations and mathematical formulas.

The number of possible types of "homosexual" and "heterosexual" matches is legion, even if only rank and sex of the partners' siblings and of their parents' siblings are varied (see page 6). Therefore any comprehensive list or matrix (permitting understanding of a particular match by classifying it—putting it in the appropriate box) would be unmanageably large, at least without data processing machines. Since the vast majority of players in the game of family constellation is without such a machine, two avenues are suggested that seem practical. One is a kind of algebra with which family constellations can be written and handled more easily than in words. The other is a set of mathematical formulas with which the conflicts inherent in a given match can be expressed.

## CHAPTER 32

## Algebra of Family Constellation

Let us call the older brother of a girl b(g), the younger brother of a boy (b)b, the middle sister of an older brother and a younger sister (b)g(g). Let us symbolize a lasting interpersonal relationship, such as a marriage, by a slash. *Example 1:* (g)b/(g)g(b), which means that the younger brother of a sister has married the middle sister of an older sister and a younger brother. *Example 2:* b(g,g)/(g,g)g(g), which means that the older brother of two girls is married to the second-youngest of altogether four girls. *Example 3:* (b,g)b(g)/(b)g(b,g), which means that the husband has had an older brother, an older sister, and a younger sister, while the wife has had an older brother, a younger brother, and a younger sister.

In example 1 the marriage duplicates completely for the husband what he had at home, whereas it does so only in part for the wife. She would tend to have a partial sex and rank conflict. In example 2 the husband gets almost what he had at home. Only polygamy, i.e., two wives, could improve his lot. The wife, on the other hand, would have a full sex conflict and a small rank conflict. Example 3 represents an optimal match, although a more complex one than its simplest paradigms: b(g)/(b)g and (g)b/g(b).

An algebraic test of fit of a heterosexual match can be made on the basis of the assumption that complete complementarity of sex and rank between the spouses would be ideal. Therefore, conversion of all sexes and all ranks in one of the spouses' sibling configurations should yield two identical expressions in cases of optimal fit, and only partial identity, or none at all, in all other cases. Thus $b(g)/(b)g$ will change to $b(g)/g(b)$ after conversion of rank order, and to $b(g)/b(g)$ after conversion of sexes (in the wife's sibling configuration). Similarly $b(b,g)/(b,g)g$ will change to $b(b,g)/g(g,b)$ and to $b(b,g)/b(b,g)$, and example 3, $(b,g)b$ $(g)/(b)g(b,g)$ to $(b,g)b(g)/(g,b)g(b)$ and to $(b,g)b(g)/(b,g)b$ $(g)$. In all three cases "subtraction" after the two transformations would yield zero on both sides.

Example 1, on the other hand, will be transformed from $(g)$ $b/(g)g(b)$ to $(g)b/(b)g(g)$ and to $(g)b/(g)b(b)$, and subtraction would leave a remainder; $b(b)$, or to be precise: $0/0,b(b)$. This relationship, translated back to $(g)g$, would be the one in the wife's sibling configuration that is not duplicated in her marriage. If the husband had a younger sister in addition, and the wife an older brother, $(g)b(g)/(b,g)g(b)$ would change after two transformations to $(g)b(g)/(g)b(b,g)$. Subtraction would also leave $b(b)$ or, retranslated, $(g)g$ as remainder. Compared to example 1, however, "dilution" is smaller. Of three (in general: n-1) sibling relationships that the wife has had, two are perfect matches for the sibling relationships of the partner, whereas only one of the two sibling relationships that the wife has had in example 1 is matched by her partner; or of altogether five sibling relationships that the spouses have brought into their marriage, only one found no duplicate, whereas in example 1, one of three such relationships found no duplicate.

Example 2, $b(g,g)/(g,g)g(g)$ changes to $b(g,g)/(b)b(b,b)$ after two transformations, and subtraction will make no difference. The remainder, after retranslation, will be the original expression. None of the altogether five sibling relationships that the spouses brought into their marriage found a duplicate there. Yet with the same numbers of siblings, things could even be worse. If example 2 would change to $b(b,b)/g(g,g,g)$, two transformations will yield $b(b,b)/(b,b,b)b$ before retranslation, which symbolizes a complete rank and sex conflict. If the example would change to $b(g,g)$ $/g(b,b,b)$, two transformations will yield $b(g,g)/(g,g,g)b$, which would indicate a rank conflict, but no sex conflict. And if it would change to $b(g,g)/(b,g)g(g)$, transformation to $b(g,g)/(b)b(b,g)$

indicates a partly optimal match, the remainder being $b(g)/(b)b$ (b), or rather $b(g)/(g)g(g)$ after retranslation.

It may often be found desirable to include the parents. Algebraically this could be done by writing the husband's parents' match on one side and that of the wife's parents on the other side of the "equation" that represents the couple in question. Hence $b(g)/g(b)//b(g)/(b)g//b(g)/(g)g$ would mean that the husband's father was the older brother of a sister and had been married to the older sister of a brother, whereas the wife's parents had been the older brother of a sister and the younger sister of a sister.

The conflicts prevailing among each parental couple can be treated as indicated. Rank and sex are transformed, correspondingly, for one side of each marriage of the expression. Our example would yield $b(g)/(g)b//b(g)/b(g)//b(g)/b(b)$, and after subtraction, but before retranslation: $b(g)/(g)b//0/0//b(g)/b(b)$. This would show that the couple in question has been optimally matched, but has "inherited" conflicts from the parents. Another example, $b(g)/(b)g(g)//b(b)/g(b,g)//(g)b/g(b)$, would yield $b(g)/(b)b(g)//b(b)/(b,g)b//(g)b/(g)b$, and $0/(b)b,0//b(b)/(b,g)b//0/0$, and demonstrate a kind of opposite constellation: the parents are well matched, but the couple in question has conflicts over rank and sex.

In order to trace conflicts prevailing between the partners in question *and* their parental identification figures, configurations on corresponding sides of each equation can be subtracted for two adjacent marriages at a time. The first example would yield $0/g$ $(b)//0/(b)g$ and $0/(b)g//0/(g)g$ for remainders, and the second example $b(g)/(b)g,0//b(b)/g(b)$ 0 and $b(b)/0,g(g)//(g)b/0$. In the first case the husband would have no identification conflict with his father, but his wife would with his mother. He would also have no identification conflict with his father-in-law, but his wife would with her own mother. In the second example the husband would be in an identification conflict with his father and father-in-law, whereas his wife would be in partial conflict with her mother-in-law and her own mother.

In order to establish conflicts prevailing between the partners in question *and* their opposite-sex parents or parents-in-law, configurations on corresponding sides of each equation must be transformed in rank and sex for two adjacent pairs at a time. Besides, the order of partners must be reversed for one of the two pairs. For the example 1 this yields $b(g)/(g)b//b(g)/b(g)$ and $b(g)/b(g)//b(b)/b(g)$. After subtraction, the remainders are $0/(g)b//0/b(g)$ and $b(g)/0//b(b)/0$. This means that the wife has no conflict with her father-in-law or with her father, whereas the husband does have conflicts with his mother-in-law and his mother. The second example would yield $b(g)/(b)b(g)//(b,g)b/b(b)$ and $b(b)/(b,g)b//(g)b/(g)b$, and after subtraction $b(g)/(b)b(g)//(b,g)b/b(b)$ and $b(b)/(b)b,0//(g)b/0$, respectively. This means that the wife has no conflict with her own father, but does with her father-in-law, and that the husband is neither on good terms with his mother nor his mother-in-law.

In all cases the relative number of zeros indicates the harmony or disharmony within the relationship in question.

For obvious reasons, inclusion of the parents will be imperative with persons who happen to be only children. Such a person's marriage may be represented, e.g., by $[b(g)/(b)g]/(b)g$ which, incidentally, would represent an optimal match among the person's parents as well as an optimal match between him and his wife. If the sex of the person in question should also be designated the above expression could be written like this: $[b(g)/b/(b)g]/(b)g$. Among the worst matches possible would be the following: $[(b)b/b/(g)g]/(g)g$, or even $[(b)b/b/(g)g]/[(b)b/g/(g)g]$. In other words, the match between an only child of a younger brother of a brother married to the younger sister of a sister, and the younger sister of a sister, or even the same only child married to another only child in precisely the same predicament. In cases of optimal matches among an only child's parents it might be found sufficient to designate his own (missing) sibling configuration by that of his same-sex parent, since that parent is the one whom he will tend to grow after the most. Thus $[b(g)/(b)g]/(b)g$ could also be written as $[b(g)]//(b)g$.

It may often be desirable to include also the children that a couple happens to have. Their configuration may duplicate that of one, or both, parents, or it may fall short of it by all degrees and thereby precipitate conflicts in additon to those already prevailing. We might designate $b(g)/b,g/(b)g$ to be the marriage between an older brother of a sister and the younger sister of a brother who have had two children, a boy and a (younger) girl. Subtracting the children's configuration will leave $0/b,g/0$, which means that the children create no conflicts for their parents. With $b(g)/b,g/g$ (b), subtraction will yield $0/b,g/g(b)$, which means that the mother will have a rank conflict not only with her husband, but also with her children. She would wish for her son to become a younger brother, and for her daughter to become an older sister. Family $(g)b/b,g/g(b)$ will permit no subtraction even though the parents are optimally matched. Both of them would have rank conflicts with their children. In family $b(b)/g,b/g(g)$ there will be sex conflicts in addition. Neither parent is prepared for the heterosexual sibling relationship of their children. Family $b(g,b,b)$ $/g,b,b/(b)g(b)$, after subtraction, would be $b(g,b)/g,b,b/(b)g$, indicating that both father and mother find one of their sibling relationships duplicated with their children. Obviously, the number of (dual) sibling relationships that parents find duplicated with their children, expressed in proportion to the number of (dual) sibling relationships that they brought into their marriage, will be a measure of the amount of conflict which the configuration of their children will create for them.

Age distances in a sibling configuration can be represented by indices. Thus $(b_9,b_2,g_1)b(g_7,g_9)$ would mean that the person has brothers nine and two years older than himself, a sister one year older, and two sisters seven and nine years younger than himself. Often it ·may be sufficient to designate only the age distances between any direct neighbors in a sibling configuration that are, say, greater than six years. A semicolon could do that. Hence the sibling configuration above could also be written in the following manner: $(b;b,g)b(;g,g)$.

Step- and half-siblings could also be indexed as such. Sibling configuration $(b_s,g)g(b,b_h)$ would mean that a girl has an older stepbrother, an older sister, a younger brother and a still younger half-brother. One of her parents brought her stepbrother into their marriage, and later one of her parents remarried, presumably because of loss of the other parent, and had another son.

Finally, *losses* of persons constituting one's family constellation could be designated by dots put on top of the lost person, i.e., of his algebraic representation. One dot could indicate that the loss occurred during one's late childhood and adolescence, and two that it occurred even sooner. Thus $b(b,\dot{g})/(g)g//(g)b(g)/g,g,b/(\dot{b}, b)g//(b)b/[\dot{b}/(b)g(\dot{g})]$ would mean that the middle brother of two sisters, the son of an oldest brother of a brother and a sister (the latter of whom died in his late childhood) and the younger sister of a sister, married the youngest sister of two brothers (the older of whom died in her early childhood), the daughter of the younger brother of a brother and an only-child mother (who happened to be the daughter of an only-child father who died in her late childhood, and a mother who had a senior brother and a junior sister, the latter of whom died in the mother's late childhood); and they have three children, two girls and a boy. With respect to losses, however, the notation suggested may prove insufficient except as a preliminary shorthand method of designation. The number of losses relative to the number of (dual) relationships that constitute a family constellation will be a measure of the degree to which they come to bear on the person in question.

If the sibling configuration of a person's parents were not known, f and m could designate father and mother respectively. In practice these symbols will mostly be used for a person's grandparents if at all. In case any of the grandparents have died or been lost otherwise during a parent's early or late childhood, this should always be recorded. Thus $[\dot{f}/b(g)/\dot{m}]/g,b/(g,b)g$ represents a family configuration in which the husband has lost his father in his early childhood and his mother in his late childhood. The wife has suffered no early losses. They have two children, a girl and a younger boy. This could also be written in the following way: $\dot{f}/\dot{m}//b(g)/g,b/(g,b)g$.

Friendships between persons of the same sex could be written and handled in similar ways, although transformation of ranks only will be enough for a test of fit. Thus $b(b,b)/(b,b)b$ would yield b(b,b)/b(b,b) or 0/0, which would be an optimal match. Identical positions such as b(b,b)/b(b,b) or (g)g/(g)g would make for strong conflicts of rank, represented also by transformations to b(b,b)/(b,b)b or (g)g/g(g), respectively. Heterosexual sibling relationships, on the other hand, should create conflicts over the (same) sex of the friend regardless of rank complementarity. Thus b(g)/(g)b, although yielding b(g)/b(g) after rank transformation, will not be an optimal fit because of the girls. Each friend would tend to transform the other into a girl, or rather not to become friends to begin with. They might become friends with each other's sisters instead. Friendship b(b,g)/(b,g)b, however, would indicate a partly optimal fit, and so would b(b,g)/(g,b)b. In fact, the latter might even be better.

Trios, quartets, etc., could also be handled in these ways. Relationship [b(b)/(b)b/(g,b)b] would designate the friendship between the older brother of a brother, the younger brother of a brother, and the younger brother of a sister and a brother. The fit would have to be evaluated by matching every member against every other like this: b(b)/(b)b, (b)b/(g,b)b, and b(b)/(g,b)b. Transforming the ranks for the same side of each match yields 0/0, (b)b/b(b,g), and 0/0,b(g) before retranslation. The number of zeros relative to the number of relationships would indicate how good a trio, quartet, etc., it is, and the remainders would spell out the conflicts that continue to prevail.

It is feasible, of course, to treat any of the equations representing heterosexual or homosexual relationships in terms of ranks only, regardless of sex, and in terms of sex only, regardless of rank. This is actually how the remainders of the examples above have been interpreted implicitly as to the kinds of conflicts that they represent.

## CHAPTER 33

## Formulas of Family Constellation

Sometimes it may be found necessary to express the conflicts involved in interpersonal relationships more precisely than the algebra of family constellation would permit by itself, although the latter will probably continue to be useful as a system of designation.

The degree of sex conflict prevailing in a marriage can be expressed for each spouse by $d_s$, the coefficient of sex distribution, as a function of the number of his same-sex siblings ($n_s$) over the number of his siblings:

$$d_s = \frac{n_s}{n-1} \tag{1}$$

In formula (1), n is the number of children that constitute a spouse's own sibling configuration. Hence in $b(g,b)/(b)g$ the husband's sex conflict would be 0.50, whereas in $b(b,b)/(b)g$ it would be 1, i.e., maximum, and in $b(g,g)/(b)g$ it would be zero. In $b(b,b,g)/(b)g$ his sex conflict would be 0.67, and the same would hold of $b(g,b,b)/(b)g$, although proximity of the sister is ignored thereby. In all of these examples the wife's sex (and rank) conflict is zero.

The degree of overall sex conflict ($d_{s_m}$) prevailing in a marriage could be expressed by

$$d_{s_m} = d_{s_b} + d_{s_g} \tag{2}$$

whereby $d_{s_b}$ is the husband's sex-distribution coefficient, and $d_{s_g}$ the wife's. The maximum value of $d_{s_m}$ is 2.

228

Similar considerations would hold for rank conflicts. If there is one at all, it would have to be multiplied by $d_r$, the coefficient of rank distribution, expressed by the difference between the number of junior and the number of senior siblings over the number of siblings of the person in question:

$$d_r = \frac{n_{jun} - n_{sen}}{n-1} \tag{3}$$

In formula (3), $n_{jun}$ is the number of siblings that are juniors to the person in question, and $n_{sen}$ the number of siblings that are senior. If $d_r$ is positive, we are dealing with a person who is more of a senior himself. If $d_r$ is negative, he is more of a junior. The absolute value of $d_r$ indicates how much. Thus (b)b(g,b) would have a value of $d_r = 0.33$, and (b,g)g a value of $d_r = -1$. The man would be somewhat of a senior, and the woman a complete junior.

In analogy to formula (2) the overall rank conflict that would prevail if those two, or any two for that matter, got married, would be expressed by

$$d_{r_m} = d_{r_b} + d_{r_g} \tag{4}$$

Therefore (b)b(g,b)/(b,g)g would have an overall rank conflict of $0.33 - 1 = -0.67$, i.e., a certain degree of juniority conflict. The couple would remain somewhat in need of a senior. Similarly b(g,b,g)/g(b,g) would have an overall rank conflict of 2, i.e., the maximum of a seniority conflict in which both will seek (or try to transform the other into) a junior, whereas, e.g., (g)b/(b)g would have $-2$, the maximum of a juniority conflict; b(g)/(b)g would be zero in rank conflict, and so would be (b,g)b(g)/(g)g(b,b).

Formulas (3) and (4) could also be taken to refer merely to siblings of the opposite sex. Rank relationships to these would tend to matter more in a marriage than rank relationships to same-sex siblings. Such treatment would at least be feasible, if $d_s$ and $d_{s_m}$ are considered concomitantly.

Another kind of conflict will result from the fact that marriage, at least in most parts of the civilized world, is a relationship between no more than two people, whereas sibling configurations may, within reason, be composed of any number of persons (n). Hence marriage will, for many people, differ in number from peer relationships they had at home. The discrepancy coefficient ($d_n$) expresses the relationship

$$d_n = \frac{n-2}{n} \qquad (5)$$

In this formula the numerator should actually be $n-n_m$, where $n_m$ would be the number of people that constitute a marriage. But as long as neither polygamy, polyandry, nor a combination of the two, are customary, formula (5) is sufficient. Single children will, of course, show negative values. They get literally more in marriage than they had at home. With spouses having one sibling only, $d_n$ will be zero. The larger n, the closer will $d_n$ approximate 1.

For a marriage as a whole overall discrepancy in number would be expressed by $d_{n_m}$, the discrepancy coefficient of husband and wife together:

$$d_{n_m} = \left| d_{n_b} \right| + \left| d_{n_g} \right| \qquad (6)$$

Thus with 2 being the asymptotic maximum of $d_{n_m}$, a match such as b(b)/(g)g will represent a discrepancy of zero, b(g,g,g,g)/(b)g one of 0.60, b(g,g)/(b,b)g one of 0.67, and b(g,g,g,g)/(b,b,g)g one of 1.10, whereas b/(b,b)g would be equal to 1.33. Note that only absolute values are added in formula (6).

Formulas (5) and (6) could also be taken to refer merely to siblings of the opposite sex. In that case n would be equal to the number of opposite-sex siblings plus one.

Still another kind of conflict concerns the degree to which the configuration of children duplicates their parents' sibling configurations. This could be expressed:

$$d_{ch} = 1 - \frac{n_d}{n-1} \qquad (7)$$

In formula (7) $d_{ch}$ is the coefficient of conflict between a person's sibling configuration and the configuration of his children; $n_d$ would be the number of (dual) sibling relationships of a parent that have found (one or more) duplicates in his children, and n would be the number of children that constitute the parent's own sibling configuration. With $b(g,b,b)/g,b,b/(b)g(b)$ the husband would have two relationships, $b(b)$ and $b(b)$, repeated with his children. Hence $d_{ch_b} = 0.33$. The wife would find only one relationship repeated, namely, $g(b)$. Therefore $d_{ch_g} = 0.50$.

As an alternative to formula (7), the following formula may be used:

$$d_{ch} = 1 - \frac{2n_d'}{n(n-1)} \qquad (8)$$

In this formula, $\frac{n(n-1)}{2}$ would be the number of all dual relationships that prevail among n children constituting a parent's sibling configuration, including those of which the parent is not an immediate partner; $n_d'$ would be the number of all those of their dual relationships that find duplication in any of the relationships prevailing among their children. With formula (8) the example used above would yield $d_{ch_b} = 0.17$ and $d_{ch_g} = 0.33$. Yet formula (7) is not only simpler, but probably just as meaningful.

Note that the number of children that the parents have is not reflected directly in either formula. If parents $b(g)$ and $(b)g$ should have five children, say $b,g,b,b,g$, their $d_{ch}$ values would be the same as if they had just two children, say $b,g$. If their children are to be included explicitly, formula (7) would have to be rewritten to read as follows:

$$d_{ch} = 1 - \sqrt{\frac{n_d}{n-1}} \sqrt{\frac{2n_d'}{n'(n'-1)}} \qquad (9)$$

In this formula $n'$ would be the number of children that the parents have, and $n_d'$ the number of all dual relationships prevailing among their children for which the given parent has (one or more) duplicates in his own sibling configuration. Hence example $b(g,b,b)/g,b,b/(b)g(b)$ would yield $d_{ch_b} = 0.18$ and $d_{ch_g} = 0.29$.

Example $b(g)/b,g,b,b,g/(b)g$, however, would yield values of 0.37 for both parents, whereas with $b(g)/b,g/(b)g$, $d_{ch}$ would be zero for both of them.

In most cases, especially where the number of siblings that constitute each parent's sibling configuration and the number of children they have themselves are not too grossly different, formula (7) will be sufficient. After all, the chances of duplication of the parents' own sibling relationships will tend to be greater, the larger the number of their own children. Hence the latter is at least indirectly taken into account anyway. Besides, parents may continue having children regardless of whether they have already got the constellations of children they wanted or not. In the first case they are trying again because all went so well; in the second, they keep trying.

For a marriage as a whole the degree to which the configuration of children duplicates their parents' sibling configurations is expressed by:

$$d_{ch_m} = d_{ch_b} + d_{ch_g} \qquad (10)$$

Thus $d_{ch_m}$ of $b(g,b,b)/g,b,b/(b)g(b)$ would be 0.47, of $b(g)/b,g,b,b,g/(b)g$, 0.74, and of $b(g)/b,g/(b)g$, zero.

A compound rank and sex estimate of conflict prevailing in a particular match is expressed by

$$d_{s_m , r_m} = \frac{d_{s_m} + \left| d_{r_m} \right|}{2} \qquad (11)$$

If discrepancy in number $(d_n)$ and conflict with the configuration of children are also to be included, the estimate of all conflict $(d_t)$ existent in a given marriage is expressed by:

$$d_t = d_{s_m, r_m, n_m, ch_m} = \frac{d_{s_m} + \left| d_{r_m} \right| + d_{n_m} + d_{ch_m}}{4} \qquad (12)$$

The maximum values of both $d_{s_m, r_m}$ and $d_t$ are equal to 2, although $d_t$ will approach it only asymptotically. The minimum values are zero. An example of $d_t = 0$ would be $b(g)/b,g/(b)g$.

Relationships between people of the same sex, i.e., homosexual friendships, can be treated analogously. As a matter of fact, formulas for $d_r$ and $d_n$ (formulas 3, 4, and 5, 6, respectively) would remain the same, except that they might, as an alternative, be computed from the same-sex siblings only, rather than from all siblings. In formulas (1) and (2), however, $n_s$ should be the number of opposite-sex siblings rather than same-sex siblings, whereas formulas (7-10) would not apply at all. Therefore $d_t$ would read like this:

$$d_t = \frac{d_{s_m} + \left| d_{r_m} \right| + d_{n_m}}{3} \qquad (13)$$

In formulas (11, 12, 13) the denominator is obviously equal to the number of coefficients that are being pooled.

There is one more all-important characteristic that must be included in these considerations: final *losses* occurring among the people that constitute a person's family constellation. Not that there would not be all kinds of other losses, too. Temporary separations, illness, surgery, physical attacks, seductions, etc., all tend to have specific traumatic effects on the victim, but generally these are small compared to final losses. So powerful are final losses that even if only the parents have been afflicted by them, they may still come down to the person in question. A significant aspect of what he experiences and thinks of such a loss is how the parents or even his own siblings have taken it.

The following formulas attempt to capture the rules by which these final losses abide:

$$l = \sum_{i=1}^{n_l} l_i \tag{14}$$

$$l_i = \frac{1}{\log \frac{1}{k}} = \frac{1}{-\log k} \tag{15}$$

$$k = \frac{a_l\, t}{a_o\, a\sqrt{a}(\bar{n}-1)} \tag{16}$$

In these formulas, $l$ stands for the overall cumulative loss a person has suffered; $l_i$ stands for any of $n_l$ individual losses suffered; $k$ is the measure of each individual loss. As for the determinants of $k$, $a_l$ is the age of the person lost, $a_o$ the age of the oldest person in the immediate family. The ratio $a_l/a_o$ could be called the age coefficient. The length of time that the lost person has lived with the person in question is represented by $t$; $a$ is the person's own age. All of the determinants of $k$ can be measured in years for the time at which the loss occurred. The number of persons that constitute the family (including parents, siblings, and the person in question) is represented by $\bar{n}$.

In order to take into account what a given loss has done to the balance of sexes in the family, $l_i$ should be multiplied by the reciprocal of $c$, where $c$ is the change of sex balance coefficient:

$$c = 1 - (s_b - s_a) \tag{17}$$

$$s = \frac{n_{s_l}}{\bar{n}} \tag{18}$$

In formula (17), $s_a$ stands for $s$ after occurrence of the loss, and $s_b$ for $s$ before the loss. In formula (18), $s$ is the sex balance coefficient, $n_{s_l}$ the number of persons in the entire family that are of the lost person's sex, and $\bar{n}$ the number of persons that constitute the family. Perfect balance will yield $s = 0.50$. The larger the $c$ (which, of course, will scatter around 1 in its empirical values), the smaller the effect of the loss in question. Hence formula (14) should actually read like this:

$$l = \sum_{i=1}^{n_l} \frac{l_i}{c_i} \qquad (19)$$

An example shall illustrate this briefly. Suppose the older sister of a sister has lost her mother at the age of 4 years. The mother was 30, the father 33, her sister 2 years old at that time. Hence $k = \dfrac{(30)\,(4)}{(33)\,4\sqrt{4}(3)} = 0.15$. Therefore $\dfrac{1}{k} = 6.6$, $\log \dfrac{1}{k} = 0.82$, and $l_i = 1.22$. The change of sex balance coefficient c would be $c = 1 - (\dfrac{3}{4} - \dfrac{2}{3}) = 0.92$. Hence $l_i$ as computed by formula (19) would be $l_i = 1.33$. Had father been lost instead, c would have been equal to $c = 1 - (\dfrac{1}{4} - \dfrac{0}{3})$, and $l_i$ accordingly larger ($l_i = 1.64$, if we ignore the changes that this situation would also create in k).

If that girl should also lose her sister, say, five years later and after her father had remarried a woman his junior and turned 38, her sister 7, and she herself 9, and another child, a boy, had been born to them 3 years ago, the following values would result: $k = \dfrac{(7)\,(7)}{(38)\,9\,\sqrt{9}\,(4)} = \dfrac{1}{82}$. Therefore $\dfrac{1}{k} = 82$, $\log \dfrac{1}{k} = 1.91$, and $l_i = 0.52$. Now c would be $c = 1 - (\dfrac{3}{5} - \dfrac{2}{4}) = 0.90$. Therefore $l_i$ would be 0.58 according to formula (19). And the overall loss $l$ that this girl has suffered would be $l = 1.33 + 0.52 = 1.85$.

One might argue that in these formulas substitution of another person for the lost one has not been accounted for. This is not quite true, though. If no new person is recruited to take the lost person's place, the remaining ones will, of necessity, substitute for that person. Only if a family should consist of no more than two persons in all, mother and child, would the loss of the mother leave nobody to substitute for her. In that case, however, the child would have small chances of survival. In terms of our formulas, a 4 year old's predicament of this kind would yield $k = \frac{1}{2}$, $\log \frac{1}{k} = 0.30$, and $l_i = 3.33$. Since $c = 1 - (\frac{2}{2} - \frac{1}{1}) = 1$, $l_i$ would be the same also by formula (19). This is plausible in the sense that the loss of the mother will not change anything in the balance of sexes. There was no male to begin with, and there is none now. If that child were only one year old instead, the following

values would result: $k = 1$, $\log \frac{1}{k} = 0$, and $l_i = \infty$.

If a new person takes the lost person's place for good, any subsequent loss will reflect this fact as it did in our example. If new persons substitute only temporarily, such as in the case of hired personnel, nurses, maids, tutors, and the like, each change will, in a sense, be an additional, though small, loss and appear as such in our computations. It may be desirable, however, to include the present age of the person in question. After all, the effectiveness of losses does seem to fade as time goes by. Hence formula (19) should perhaps be rewritten to read:

$$l = \frac{1}{\log a_p} \sum_{i=1}^{n_l} \frac{l_i}{c_i} \tag{20}$$

In this formula, $a_p$ would be the present age (in years) of the person in question.

The amount of loss prevailing in a marriage (or, *mutatis mutandis*, in any interpersonal relationship) would be equal to the sum of losses suffered by its partners:

$$l_m = l_b + l_g \tag{21}$$

In formula (21) $l_b$ is the loss suffered by the husband, and $l_g$ the loss suffered by the wife.

At this point an overall formulation shall be ventured in which the conflicts over rank, sex, number of siblings, and configurations of children as well as losses suffered are included:

$$P_m = (d_t)^{1+l_m} = \left[ \frac{d_{s_m} + \left| d_{r_m} \right| + d_{n_m} + d_{ch_m}}{4} \right]^{1+l_m} \qquad (22)$$

In formula (22) $P_m$ expresses the overall prognosis for a match. All other symbols have already been explained. $P_m$ will vary between zero and infinity, but the vast majority of cases will be between values of 0.1 and 100, and a large bulk of them between 0.5 and 20. The smaller $P_m$, the better the prognosis.

Losses that a person's parents have suffered could, of course, be included, too. In fact, the same would hold for all conflicts that they may have had over rank, sex, number of siblings, and configurations of children. Hence rather than compute the parents' influence in each of the component measures of $P_m$, the values of $P_m$ could be computed for the parents, the grandparents, the great-grandparents, etc., and added to $P_m$ of a given couple. Formula (23) describes the relationship:

$$P_{m_t} = P_m + \frac{\sum P_{m_1}}{4} + \frac{\sum P_{m_2}}{16} + \frac{\sum P_{m_3}}{256} + \text{etc.} \qquad (23)$$

Here $P_{m_t}$ would express the overall prognosis of a match when the matches of ancestors are considered, too. $P_{m_1}$ would be the sum of values of $P_m$ computed for the husband's and the wife's parents, $P_{m_2}$ the sum of values of $P_m$ computed for all four grandparental marriages, $P_{m_3}$ the sum of values of $P_m$ computed for all eight great-grandparental marriages, etc. In practice it will be found, though, that the third summand is usually quite small, and the fourth one already negligible. As a matter of fact, it will probably suffice to use formula (22), at least as long as $l_{m_t}$ is substituted for $l_m$, and to compute $l_{m_t}$ in analogy to $P_{m_t}$.

As for losses affecting relationships between persons of the same sex, formulas (14-21) would be applicable as well, although $l_i$ in formulas (19) and (20) would have to be multiplied by c rather than by the reciprocal of c. On the other hand, formula (14) may be considered sufficient by itself. In formula (22) $d_t$ would have to be computed from formula (13) rather than from formula (12).

It may also be of interest to compare the amount of conflict prevailing in a present match with the amounts inherent in the matches of each spouse's parents. If $\dfrac{\Sigma P_m^{\ 1}}{2}$ is larger than $P_m$, the spouses would be on the road to relatively greater happiness, and vice versa. Their $P_m$ values need not be small per se. It is not easy for a person to free himself of his family constellation under all circumstances, even if his parents have been quite poorly matched for each other. The farther he tries to break away, the closer may he ultimately find himself to the original situation (see also page 167). His home may have been an unhappy one, but it was still the only one he had. Therefore, a moderate improvement of his own match over that of his (poorly matched) parents will often be more reliable than a radical change resulting in values of $P_m$ close to zero. Other circumstances could be so much at odds, that they might upset the relationship. Besides, the person is not used to smooth relationships, and will tend to rough any up. He will try to create the conflicts that are not there at first.

Concluding this chapter, I want to advise caution, particularly in the use of the formulas. They are only approximations, no more. Some of the relationships postulated, such as the summation theorem implicit in many of the formulas, could be questioned, although all empirical checks made by the author seemed to be compatible with it. The best use that can be made of these formulas will not be with individual cases, but with groups of people, however small. The formulas may permit comparisons and psychological evaluations of a kind not inherent in other devices.

# EPILOGUE

If by now the reader has become an enthusiast of this game, I would like to warn him. What the game reveals can be passed out to others—friends, relatives, especially parents—only with tact and careful consideration. Even then the reader will find that he may have to pay penalties. He has conveyed something relevant, perhaps something eminently meaningful, he thinks, and yet they know him no thanks. In fact, they may sometimes get outright angry and refuse to play the game. Try not to get as far as that, but if you have, turn off the "heat" as soon as you realize it. Give them time. Let them think it over. Don't bring up the subject when you meet them the next time. Wait until they begin to ask questions. Give them this book to read, if they want to.

If, on the other hand, the reader should be appalled, scared, or annoyed by the prospects advanced, I advise him to put the book aside and let the matter rest for a while. (Maybe someone else would want to look at the book in the meantime.) Let me assure you, though, that you will not have to get a divorce, break off your friendships, file law suits for or against parents, change your profession, your philosophy, even your children, or go back to an early love of yours, just because the book seems to imply that. Remember that you have been playing this game before you ever read this book. You need not now apply its rules and principles to your own affairs. *You have already done so.* The book has merely made you more conscious of them, and unless you have learned to understand clearly what kinds of "hands" and games you have played in the past—and what kinds your parents have played—you are in no better position to manipulate your future than a person who has never heard of this game. And let me assure you further that there is no hand whatsoever that could not, in principle, be good for some kind of workable game, and no game in progress that could not be continued and possibly improved.

Does this book affect individual freedom and dignity? I believe it does: it *increases* both. All knowledge does, no matter how shattering it may appear to the ignorant and superstitious.

239

As for the empirical evidence which is (as indicated on pages 20 and 128) based on clinical and diagnostic contacts with some four hundred cases, I would be among the first to claim that the investigation must go on. I have only presented the general structure of the theory and those details that have come most validly to my notice. I am also aware that the forces and patterns of family constellation interact with hereditary givens, such as vitality, intelligence, or special talents, and also with the broader environment, as represented by socio-economic, educational, ethnic or even political determinants on one hand and a person's anatomy, physiology, accidental pathology, etc., on the other. These interactions will also have to be studied more elaborately, although in my experience the forces and patterns of family constellation come through quite strong in every one of these interactions.

It should also be mentioned that a number of specific experiments have been conducted to test some derivative assumptions.

One assumption was that patients seeking and receiving psychotherapy should, on the whole, come from parents who have been matched more poorly, by the duplication criterion (see page 6), than would be expected by chance. Experiences of loss should also prevail among them or their parents to a greater than average degree. This was found to be true with three samples: one of 40 adult patients, one of 20 children frequenting a counselling center, and one of 93 children taken from three psychological guidance centers (Toman 1959b, c, Toman and Gray 1961).

Another assumption was that same-sex friendships should tend to duplicate the friends' sibling relationships in cases of monosexual sibling configurations, and that they should tend not to form in the first place in cases of heterosexual sibling configurations on both sides or in cases of identical sibling positions. This was borne out with a sample of friendships formed in a high school class of 35 boys (Toman 1959b) and to an extent with a sample of 102 friendships formed among female college students (Gray 1960).

Still another assumption was that good and poor marriages, as defined solely by the degree to which the partners duplicate or fail to duplicate sibling positions for one another, should differ as to time of formation and overall success. The poor marriages (that nevertheless lasted) should be entered at a later age of the partners, the partners should be less successful professionally, and they should have fewer children. This was confirmed with a sample of 8 good and 7 poor matches (Toman 1960a).

Still another assumption was that divorced couples should tend to fail to duplicate for one another sibling positions they held at home. This tendency should be less marked with couples who stayed married for longer periods of time and had children. Losses —generally among the reasons for poorer choices of friends, partners, or spouses—were expected to exceed chance at least in those cases where failure of couples to duplicate sibling positions for one another was less pronounced. All of this turned out to be so with a sample of 16 divorces (Toman 1961).

Finally, an unusual choice of profession (i.e., unmarried foster-mother for a group of some nine children all coming from broken homes who lives with the children in Children's Villages, a Central European institution) was expected to show among the persons concerned (the foster-mothers): large numbers of siblings, a predominance in number of females over males among them, and, most important, losses suffered that would have had to be severe enough to make them wish to do something for orphans, but not so severe as to render them unable to. This was found to be true with a sample of 14 women, as compared to a control group of women working in Children's Villages in other capacities. However, those in the control group, who had wanted to become foster-mothers but never made the grade, had suffered the severest losses (loss of both parents in early childhood). (Toman 1959b.)

Although life data—things accomplished, interpersonal relationships formed, losses suffered, etc.—have been treated throughout this book as something better than test data, it was assumed that self-rating or projective personality tests would reflect characteristics of sibling positions that have been outlined, provided the tests have been tuned to issues such as relations to work, peers, authority, the opposite sex, the same sex, children, loss, etc., and provided also that enough care is exercised in selecting the subjects. Their parents as well as losses suffered by them or the subjects themselves will have to be given consideration too, even if merely in order to establish that the selection has been random.

This assumption—traceability of characteristics of sibling position through personality tests—was confirmed with 36 subjects in a projective test allowing objective evaluation (picture arrangement). Subjects in senior positions with respect to their siblings behaved significantly different from those in junior positions (Gray 1960).

It is evident, on the other hand, that the data of family constellation could be considered test data themselves. What is more, they merely have to be asked for, are usually given freely and take a few minutes to establish. If evaluated with the help of the theory advanced in this book, they might well be more powerful and predictive than any known psychological test taking the same amount of time or even much longer to administer.

Other studies bearing on problems of family constellation (e.g., Berman 1933, Damrin 1949, Fischer 1952, Goodenough and Leahy 1927, Guilford and Worcester 1930, Hooker 1931, Helen L. Koch 1955a,b, 1956a,b,c, 1958, Krout 1939, Lasko 1954, Levy 1931, Martensen-Larsen 1956, 1957, Meltzer 1941, Patterson and Zeigler 1941, Rosenow 1930, Sears 1950, Shield and Grigg 1944, Stagner and Katzoff 1936, Wile and Jones 1937), all conducted before the present theory had been available publicly, have not infrequently been inconclusive, occasionally contradictory and, at any rate, too limited in theoretical and methodological scope. As a matter of fact, a few of them can be called paradigms of how to ask isolated questions haphazardly and work out some uninspired gimmick of a method to get *no* answer. These criticisms do not hold for studies that explored on a broader basis either some aspects of the basic constituents of family constellations, say, losses, (Bowlby 1951, Anna Freud and Dorothy T. Burlingham 1943), or many aspects beyond the basic constituents, even if the studies neglected the latter (e.g., Bossard 1956, Hollingshead 1950, Landis and Landis 1948, Locke 1951, Parsons 1951, Terman 1937, Winch and McGinnis 1953). Almost any study taking an articulate system-approach seems to be more likely to turn up with worthwhile results in this infinitely complex field than any hundred little hit-or-miss studies with which the professional psychological literature abounds. Well, the author of this book took a system-approach. Whether the result has been worthwhile is for the reader to decide. That it is only a beginning, the author has resolved himself.

## Securing Data on Family Constellations

For all research purposes the guide printed here should be followed as closely as possible. After a number of data collections, however, the instructions will probably have been assimilated by the record-taker who can then do without them.

If an item or question of the guide does not quite apply to a person, the most meaningful approximation should be attempted. If, e.g., somebody is not legally married but is living with as well as providing for the family, consider him married. If he is not formally separated, yet neither living with nor even providing for the family, consider him separated. If somebody is not dead, but missing, consider him dead. If a person has foster parents, all of their data should be secured in analogy to those of the person's parents.

If a person does not recall certain data precisely, he should estimate them to the best of his knowledge. If he can give only some data, but not others, say only the death of a person but not his birth year, he should give whatever he can. If there is an opportunity to check doubtful data with relatives or people who might know, he should do so. In that case it may be practical to write up the questions for him that he should try to answer and have him contact the record-taker again by phone or mail.

If a person is, or has ever been, married, be sure to secure data about his or her spouse's family constellation too. If the spouse is unavailable, have the person provide the information as best as he can.

## Guide for Securing Data

1. State person's name (and maiden name), sex, date and place of birth, present address, home address, present profession, date of marriage, (maiden) name of spouse, date and place of birth of spouse.

2. Ask person for his/her siblings (including those who have died, also step- and half-siblings): their first names, sex, age (e.g., 3 years older, 5 years younger than person), whether step- or half-siblings, whether dead, age at death, year of death, whether married, year of marriage(s) and of termination of marriage(s) through death of spouse, divorce, separation, etc. (*note* if through death). State for each sibling separately number of their children (exclusive of stepchildren, but including their own children from all of their marriages, also those children who have died), number of sons, number of deaths.

3. Ask person for his/her father's name, date and place of birth, present address, present or last profession, year of marriage to person's mother and year of termination of marriage (e.g., 1928-55, or 1935-now), years of father's previous and/or subsequent marriages, year of father's death. Ask for person's father's siblings in analogy to (2).

4. Ask person for his/her mother's (maiden) name, date and place of birth, present address, present or last profession, years of her previous and/or subsequent marriages and terminations, year of her death. Ask for person's mother's siblings in analogy to (2).

5a. Ask person for his/her paternal grandfather's name, year and place of birth, his chief residence, his chief profession(s), year of marriage to paternal grandmother and of its termination, year of his previous and/or subsequent marriages and terminations, year of his death, and inquire whether he had one or more older brothers, older sisters, younger brothers, younger sisters, and how many siblings in all.

5b. Ask person for his/her paternal grandmother's (maiden) name, year and place of birth, her chief residence, etc., in analogy to (5a).

5c. Ask person for his/her maternal grandfather's name, etc., in analogy to (5a).

5d. Ask person for his/her maternal grandmother's (maiden) name, year and place of birth, her chief residence, etc., in analogy to (5b) and (5a).

6. Ask person for his/her children (including those who have died as well as stepchildren who live in his/her household): their first names, sex, and birth years, whether stepchildren, whether dead, age at death, year of death, whether married, years of marriage(s) and termination(s) through death of spouse, divorce, separation, etc. (note if through death). State for each child separately: number of their children (exclusive of stepchildren, but including their own children from all of their marriages, also those children who have died), number of sons, number of deaths.

7. State date and place at which this record was taken; also name and address of record-taker.

# Bibliography

Adler, A., *The practice and theory of individual psychology (1920).* Harcourt, Brace, New York 1929.

Adler, A., *Understanding human nature (1927).* Greenberg, New York 1946.

Adler, A., *Social interest (1933).* Putnam, New York 1939.

Ansbacher, H. L., and Ansbacher, Rowena R., *The individual psychology of Alfred Adler.* Basic Books, New York 1956.

Berman, H. H., Order of birth in manic-depressive reactions. *Psychiat. Quart.,* 1933, 7, 430-435.

Bossard, J. H. S., *The large family system: An original study in the sociology of family behavior.* University of Pennsylvania Press, Philadelphia 1956.

Bowlby, J., *Maternal care and mental health.* World Health Organization, London 1951.

Burgess, E. W., and Wallin, P., Predicting adjustment in marriage from adjustment in engagement. *Amer. J. Sociol.,* 1944, 49, 524-530.

Damrin, Dora E., Family size and sibling age, sex, and position as related to certain aspects of adjustment. *J. Soc. Psychol.,* 1949, 29, 93-109.

Fischer, A. E., Sibling relationships with special reference to the problems of the second child. *J. Pediat.,* 1952, 40, 254-259.

Freud, Anna, and Burlingham, Dorothy T., *War and children.* Medical War Books, New York 1943.

Freud, S., *A general introduction to psychoanalysis (1916-17).* The Standard Edition of the Complete Psychological Works of Sigmund Freud, Hogarth Press, London 1953, etc., vols. 15, 16.

Freud, S., *Beyond the pleasure principle (1920).* Stand. Ed., vol. 18.

Freud, S., *The ego and the id (1923).* Stand. Ed., vol. 19.

Freud, S., *The problem of anxiety (1926).* Stand. Ed., vol. 20.

Freud, S., *New introductory lectures on psychoanalysis (1933).* Stand. Ed., vol. 22.

Freud, S., *An outline of psychoanalysis (1938).* Stand. Ed., vol. 23.

Goodenough, F. C., and Leahy, A. M., The effect of certain family relationships upon the development of personality. *Ped. Sem.,* 1927, 34, 45-71.

245

Gray, B., *An investigation of the family constellation as a basic personality determinant of personality development.* Unpubl. dissertation, Brandeis University 1960.

Guilford, R. B., and Worcester, D. A., A comparative study of the only and non-only child. *J. Genet. Psychol.*, 1930, *38*, 411-426.

Hollingshead, A. B., Cultural factors in the selection of marriage mates. *Amer. Sociol. Rev.*, 1950, *15*, 619-627.

Hooker, H. F., The study of the only child at school. *J. Genet. Psychol.*, 1931, *39*, 122-236.

Jung, C. G., *The psychology of the unconscious.* Moffat, Yard, New York 1916.

Jung, C. G., *Psychological types.* Harcourt, Brace, New York 1923.

Jung, C. G., *The integration of personality.* Farrar and Rinehart, New York 1939.

Koch, Helen L., Some personality correlates of sex, sibling position and sex of sibling among five- and six-year old children. *Genet. Psychol. Monogr.*, 1955a, *52*, 3-50.

Koch, Helen L., The relation of certain family constellation characteristics and the attitudes of children toward adults. *Child Developm.*, 1955b, *26*, 13-40.

Koch, Helen L., Children's work attitudes and sibling characteristics. *Child. Developm.*, 1956a, *27*, 289-310.

Koch, Helen L., Children's attitudes toward their peers as related to certain characteristics of their siblings. *Psychol. Monogr.*, 1956b, 70(19), No. 426.

Koch, Helen L., Some emotional attitudes of the young child in relation to characteristics of his siblings. *Child Developm.* 1956c, *27*, 393-426.

Koch, Helen L., Der Einfluss der Geschwister auf die Persönlichkeitsentwicklung jüngerer Knaben. *Jb. Psychol. Psychother.*, 1958, *5*, 211-225.

Krout, M. H., Typical behavior patterns in 26 ordinal positions. *J. Genet. Psychol.*, 1939, *55*, 3-30.

Landis, J. T., and Landis, M. G., *Building a successful marriage.* Prentice Hall, New York 1948.

Lasko, J. K., Parent behavior toward first and second children. *Genet. Psychol. Monogr.*, 1954, *49*, 97-137.

Levy, J., A quantitative study of behavior problems in relation to family constellation. *Amer. J. Psychiat.*, 1931, *10*, 637-654.

Locke, H. J., *Predicting adjustment in marriage: A comparison of a divorced and a happily married group.* Henry Holt, New York 1951.

Martensen-Larsen, O., Family constellation analysis and male alcoholism. *Acta Psychiatrica et Neurologica Scandinav.*, 1956, Suppl. 106, 241-247.

Martensen-Larsen, O., The family constellation analysis and alcoholism. *Acta Genetica et Statistica Medica*, 1957, 7, 441-446.

Meltzer, H., Sex differences in parental preference patterns. *Character and Personal.*, 1941, *10*, 114-128.

Parsons, T., *The social system.* The Free Press, Glencoe, Ill. 1951.

Patterson, R. M., and Zeigler, T. W., Ordinal position and schizophrenia. *J. Psychiat.*, 1941, *98*, 455-458.

Rosenow, C., The incidence of first-born among problem children. *J. Genet. Psychol.*, 1930, *37*, 145-151.

Sears, R. R., Ordinal position in the family as a psychological variable. *Amer. Sociol. Rev.*, 1950, *15*, 397-401.

Shield, J. A., and Grigg, A. E., Extreme ordinal position and criminal behavior. *J. Crim. Law and Criminol.*, 1944, *35*, 169-173.

Stagner, R., and Katzoff, E. T., Personality as related to birth-order and family size. *J. Appl. Psychol.*, 1936, *20*, 340-346.

Terman, L. M., *Psychological factors in marital happiness.* McGraw-Hill, New York 1938.

Toman, W., Repetition and repetition compulsion. *Int. J. Psychoanalysis*, 1956, *37*, 347-350.

Toman, W., A general formula for the quantitative treatment of human motivation. *J. Abn. Psychol.*, 1959a, *58*, 91-99.

Toman, W., Die Familienkonstellation und ihre psychologische Bedeutung. *Psychol. Rundschau*, 1959b, *10*, 1-15.

Toman, W., Family constellation as a basic personality determinant. *J. Indiv. Psychol.*, 1959c, *15*, 199-211.

Toman, W., Family constellation as a character and marriage determinant. *Int. J. Psychoanalysis*, 1959d, *40*, 316-319.

Toman, W., On the periodicity of motivation. Nebraska Symposium on Motivation (Ed.: Jones, M. R.), University of Nebraska Press, 1960a, 80-95.

Toman, W., Haupttypen der Familienkonstellation. *Psychol. Rundschau*, 1960b, *11*, 273-284.

Toman, W., *Introduction to psychoanalytic theory of motivation.* Pergamon Press, London, New York 1960c.

Toman, W., Family constellations of divorced and "happily married" couples. *J. Indiv. Psychol.*, 1961 (in print).

Toman, W., and Gray, B., Family constellations of "normal" and "disturbed" marriages: An empirical study. *J. Indiv. Psychol.*, 1961, *17*, 93-95.

Wile, I. S., and Jones, A. B., Ordinal position and the behavior disorders of young children. *J. Genet. Psychol.*, 1937, *51*, 61-93.

Winch, R. F., and McGinnis, R. (Eds.), *Marriage and the family.* Henry Holt, New York 1953.